Richard Ruxton grew up i   ley emigrated to England wh   ful career in industrial engine   He and his wife now live in rural France, where .... .on for writing and other activities, such as sampling the local wines, which are designed to distract from any real work. A life-long fan of pirate radio, classic rock music and obscure cultural references, he has drawn on his long-forgotten duties at a water treatment plant for the title of this memoir. *River Clarified Filtered Soft* is his first book.

AN IRISH TALE OF DURATION,
DIVILMENT AND GRAND CRAIC

RIVER CLARIFIED FILTERED SOFT

RICHARD RUXTON

MOSAÏQUEPRESS

Published by
MOSAÏQUE PRESS
Registered office:
70 Priory Road
Kenilworth, Warwickshire CV8 1LQ
www.mosaïquepress.co.uk

ISBN 978-1-906852-60-3

In the good times will we still write stories?
Yes in the good times we will also write stories,
About the good times.

(With apologies to Brecht and others)

Contents

Introduction

If it's true that life can be like a colourful fruit-bearing tree, giving sustenance and beauty to all in its vicinity, then surely memories are its roots. Memories are like pressed flowers, and remain with you as do photographs, report cards, scraps of paper and things you've preserved for reasons that now escape you. They're like pages from your life's book hidden away in some seldom-opened drawer.

Memories warm you over the years. They bring a smile to your face in quiet contemplative times. They prepare you for everything, and in subsequent dark and lonely nights you will have this Milky Way of memories to help you see out the dawn.

When you are young, memories can waltz away from you before you get in step. As you get older, they slow down a bit. They become a collage of truths, half truths, suspicions and aspirations. And so you can tweak that quote, strengthen that punch line, adjust that ending. And why not? Should we wear the past like a shroud of shame or celebrate our version of it? Inevitably we all strive to become good memories, so that loved ones may smile when they think of us while we're here, and when we're gone.

It has become obvious to me that memoirs are notoriously and famously unreliable, but that they are also the best thing to help you through life. Embellish if needed, add humour certainly, but look after them, cultivate them, and they will look after you.

These are some of my dearest memories, as I remember them – more or less.

1

'Once upon a time in the Fishery'

I was four, the day was bright and breezy as late summer can be on that part of the coast, and I remember it as if it were yesterday. Mam kissed and hugged me out the door at exactly eight o'clock. I know this because our cuckoo clock, the pottery factory horn and a church bell in the distance confirmed it more or less together.

Hugs lasted a long time in those days. I seemed to live in hugs. Nevertheless this one was a bit hurried, a bit unreal, as though I was being shoved out the door to cope with whatever followed.

Down the garden path I walked, looking the bee's knees in my new white shirt, khaki shorts and Clarks sandals, my school bag – as yet untainted by the lingering smells of onions, apples, oranges and spilt milk – across my young shoulders. I could see Mam watching me through the kitchen window. I heard a faint 'Bye bye, see you later.' Then I was off.

That first day at school was always going to be different. It was the first day for my cousin Sally too. We were both quite young, maybe a little too young for the experience ahead. Someone said we made up the numbers to keep school viable in the diocese; so off we were sent. I think we both felt a bit put upon, to tell the truth. When you start school it truly is the end of fairy tales for you.

Our destination that sunny morning, and many thereafter, was Carysfort National School. Sally's brother John and her sisters Algy and Betty were already at this school. On the weekend my Auntie Connie had said, 'They'll meet you at the corner' – "they" meaning my cousins – 'and you can all go up to school together.' So I rushed off to meet them.

The Corner was near where I lived, one of those familiar places whose names were embedded in our everyday language, the lexicon of our lives. Names such as the Big Belly, the Blocks, the Brow, Janey's, the Links, the Hanging Stone, the Back Guts, the Back Field, the Sconce and many more that to us were names in capital letters marked the perimeter and boundaries of where we lived and played.

When I reached the top of the back lane, the Harbour Road lay in front of me. To my left was the road down to the river and dock. A custard-coloured dog, asleep in the middle of the road, suddenly raised its head and gave me the eye. He seemed mystified by my direction, but he quickly lost interest and resumed his dreams. All these other boys were heading to a small squat building barely visible behind a high wall. Directly in front of me stood the Catholic Boys National School; but this school was not my destination.

To the right I could already see my cousins slowly crossing the wide road and shouting for me to hurry up. I shuffled – trotted – past Mr Reilly's shop. I was not usually out and about this early, and was surprised to see him hard at work filling up shelves, whistling quietly as he did to a tune coming from somewhere within his house.

His home and shop was in a brand new building. My journey took me past many different types of houses; some were dilapidated, in near ruins, and had no roofs or windows. At night they were like squat comical ghosts with big vacant eyes staring at passers-by. Others were pretty cottages with roofs of thatch hanging over the windows like quizzical eyebrows. Whitewashed with pride, speckless with their scrubbed doorsteps, they were dazzling in the summer but turned a dull grey in the winterlude. Occasionally one was demolished to make way for a new house. With it came new people and sometimes new kids. Some houses had cold corrugated rusty roofs, like sheds. A constantly dripping and constantly used water fountain ahead, hinted that some houses had not yet got running water.

Across the road, next door to Mrs Condren's house, I saw a couple of firemen busying themselves in and around the Fire Brigade shed. Several fire hoses were stretched along the road and the fire crew was rewinding them neatly into circles. Gruffly and silently they went about their work, seemingly indifferent to their circle of admirers. One of the firemen sitting in a chair polished a copper bell. It was as if they were preparing for an inspection or a parade. The copper and red of the fire engine brightened this shadowed side of the road.

I hurried past Mr Kearns' house. As usual he was leaning over the garden wall and exchanging pleasantries with the passing traffic, a mug of tea in his hand.

'Off to school?' he said to me quietly as I passed.

'Yes Mr Kearns, it's my first day.'

'Have a good time,' he replied, 'and don't get any slaps.'

I heard this phrase several times during the week. It began to concern me. I began to fear for my wellbeing.

I could see my cousins waiting in the near distance – unhurried, unstressed. We were early for the journey ahead with time to take in the morning sights and visit a sweet shop on our way.

Behind the houses on the left was open pastureland, a damp reed-filled home to about twenty milk cows. We just missed their early morning run to the milk parlour. Along the road the cows left a pungent mixture of scutter and urine, which was already slowly disappearing down the drains along the road. Everyone did their best not to get splashed, picking our way through on tippy toes. Avoiding this mess became our daily nightmare.

Several sweet shops were destined to tempt us along our way. We decided to visit the first one we came to. Mrs Myler's was a tiny shop. It sold all sorts of temptations. Mrs Myler was very generous. She always included a couple of sweets 'for the cat' when she counted out your selection. She wore her hair plaited, framing her shiny ruddy cherubic face. She always wore a lap-over apron that was all the fashion with women then. There was just a hint of widow black in her appearance.

As she served the others, I noticed the door behind her was ajar. Looking in I saw a huge room full of neatly made bunk beds. Mrs Myler, it seemed, as well as selling sweets to school children, offered accommodation to workers in the Avoca Mines. The beds were arranged in neat rows, as you might see in a prison movie.

Back outside, we argued about which route to take. I knew we could go up the main street or up the ditch, a shorter way behind the street... Both had their attractions. John silently decided, at least for today, that we travelled up the main street to school. We followed behind him, guzzling our sweets and toffees.

We were a slow-moving, freewheeling band, sometimes getting in the way of people rushing to mass or to do early shopping. We passed the men's barber shop with its wonderful revolving red striped pole and its fading black-and-white photographs of improbable men's hairstyles.

Sally had bought aniseed balls and continually pursed her lips to emphasise the pleasure of the flavour. Her lips were now a bright blood red. That'll look pretty when we get into school, I thought.

I was quite familiar with the Main Street, but somehow our early morning start brought new experiences with it. The smells of the fish stalls, the seasoning from the butchers and the musky aroma of Hessian sacks outside the seed merchant suddenly seemed a little alien in the soft autumn air. The colours and sweetness of confectionery being loaded into Brennans' delivery vans was a delight, the drivers and helpers shouting and joking with people passing by.

There were very few cars about. Owning one was still a genuine rarity. However at the bank corner a car did pass us, with well-scrubbed and well-dressed kids looking at us through the back window, perhaps wishing they could walk to school like us and buy sweets and taffies. On other cold and blowy days it might be a different story...

Ahead of us stood the Catholic church, and that bright morning it seemed a hive of activity. Townsfolk with self-conscious haste were busily running up and down the front steps that led to its imposing doors. Others hung about in groups at the railings, Old men in caps and overcoats smoked. Women with shopping bags at the ready talked and gossiped.

The Catholic church building was square and grey and squat with high metal railings separating it from the street, a stern spinster staring down disapprovingly at the people scurrying past, frowning at those who dared to smile and those who were going about their innocent business.. It had a faintly ominous and courthouse-like appearance.

No plant or shrubs adorned the area about it; its murmuring chants, its flickering candles and its low lights always seemed foreboding to me. There were rumours that they buried priests under the floor inside. I always rushed past without looking in. I hated its monotonous bell that seemed to emulate those final steps to the graveside.

We headed up St Mary's Road, with the Chapel on our left and a terrace of well-maintained houses opposite. To me this road seemed the centre of all school activity in the town; there were several school entrances to choose from. Children were arriving by foot, on bicycles, in cars, on buses. There was an abundance of mothers urging their charges to behave.

Some children were walking hand in hand, some were alone. Others moved along in noisy gangs and groups... They ran madly hither and dither, delirious with excitement and heady freedom. They seemed not to care a jot that their liberty was to be short-lived. Some began to realise what direction they ought to be aiming for and began to peel off, shouting goodbye to family or friends. I noticed groups of girls skipping down the road leading to the Catholic Girls Primary School. Others played tag and ran blindly towards their destination. Around the entrance to the Technical School, groups of older kids smoked, some looked like they were clicking their fingers and singing. It was all a bit strange and grown-up.

Boys of all ages kicked balls to each other; pushing each other and then pretending to trip. Others punched each other violently on the arms; it was if school was the last thing on their minds. I was exhilarated and looked forward – with some trepidation, I must admit – to similar deviations at my destination. If this was regular school, I felt I was going to have a wonderful time.

2

'The school around the corner'

Directly in front of me a large iron gate opened menacingly. Inside I could see a desolate gravelled area. Several groups of children stood about close to the walls. Some were sucking their thumbs and others holding hands. They seemed lost, not knowing where to go, or what to do; waiting to be gathered in. It seemed we had collectively stumbled into a life that was both mysterious and frightening

As I gazed at this foreboding scene, John banged the gate shut behind us. Everyone who had been looking nervously towards the school buildings now looked back towards the gate with a sense of dread. I had a feeling that this was the end of something and perhaps the beginning of something else but I wasn't quite sure what. There were so many things I was unsure of.

Outside on the road there was pandemonium. If I expected something similar on this desolate side of the wall, it wasn't to be. I heard a serenade that haunted me for years. As the throngs of children walked by, they enthusiastically sang 'Proddy, Proddy on the wall, half a loaf will do them all' in an ever-increasing crescendo. This was all new to me but I discovered later that older children had suffered it for years. Ever helpful in these matters, John told us of a similar song we could sing in reply, but with a smile added that if we were caught repeating it, Mr Smythe, the headmaster, would give us six of the best, a euphemism as inappropriate as the punishment it stood for.

Leaving us to ponder the repercussions of such actions, John quickly disappeared into the Senior school. Algy walked us like lambs around the corner to the Junior classroom.

Another big girl ushered us into the newish building that was the Junior school. This girl sweet-talked us into a large room that was to be our world for the next few years and told us to sit in some vacant benches at the back of the room.

I looked around. It was a single room, bright and airy. On the left were high windows that almost reached the roof, on the right several waist-high windows were open to the late summer air. A large skylight was already letting in the strong morning sun and catching the clouds of chalk dust that we lived with constantly.

At the top of the room, behind a modern styled desk, and slightly hunched over, sat Mrs Jacobs. We frequently saw her with her husband and daughter at church and around the town. We knew a little about her. We knew her students referred to her as 'Mrs Jacobs with the hiccups' which mystified me a little.

Several older girls were busy helping Mrs Jacobs control the activities. They had the air of circus ringmasters, we being the temperamental animals. A general din emanated everywhere in the room but this came to an abrupt end when one of these girls, after checking the clock, loudly clapped her hands and shouted 'Roll call!' This girl called out names, promptly receiving the reply of 'Anseo' from the name's owner, as loud as possible it seemed. Children nearby coaxed us new starters to answer similarly. Shyly and sheepishly we complied.

When the roll call ritual was finished Mrs Jacobs stood up. She was a small woman. Her horsey outdoor type of clothes seemed to compliment her healthy ruddy complexion. She seemed dressed to blend in with what was in the room and sported a multi-coloured knitted scarf. Despite the colourful clothes, I'm sure many of the new starters considered her to be a witch, warily watching her every move.

She went to the blackboard and wrote down her name. This was surprising as most of the new students couldn't read. As an afterthought she reminded us that the headmaster was Mr Smythe and that he would come to see us sometime that day. This had a big effect on the older children, with many uttering audible 'Sirs' and holding their hands to faces in dismay. Subsequently we awaited his visit with some trepidation.

Throughout the day at intervals, Mrs Jacobs' daughter or her husband brought her cups of coffee. Invariably she left it standing until skin formed on the top. She had a little black metal thing on her desk which we found out was a tuning fork. She used it like a regular fork to remove the skin from her milky coffee and place it on the accompanying saucer. This was possibly the most disgusting thing that I had ever witnessed in my young life and it put me off drinking coffee for many years.

I soon noticed that in our Infants school singing was recurrent, even on our first day. It was an easy way to keep everyone occupied and attentive. We sang all sorts of songs, but mainly hymns. *All Creatures Great and Small* and *Away in a Manger* were particularly popular among the older kids. After several false starts the class got into a kind of rhythm. Mrs Jacobs tried continuously to get the whole room in tune. The big girls continually coaxed and urged us to blend in with the others. It seemed that not everyone understood the concept of 'in tune.' New kids confused volume with being in tune, inevitably resulting in laughter and giggles from the older kids. This derision certainly put us in our place. We were down the pecking order and we certainly knew it.

It was obvious to Mrs Jacobs, and to us, that work was needed on our singing. She did her best to control our endeavours with the tuning fork. This handy little instrument had multiple uses. As well as sounding a note and lifting the skin off the coffee, it was also used to chastise us for misdemeanours. A bong on the head or a rap on the knuckles usually followed some minor infringement of rules or behaviour. We were soon all at war with this little black fork.

We learned very early that six of the best was the ultimate sanction. Mr Smythe, we were told, usually administered this, requiring the poor reprobate to cross from one building to another and politely ask the head master for the punishment.

After what seemed an eternity, Mrs Jacobs picked up a bell from her desk, rang it and declared a Toilet Break. To this day I'm not sure if Mrs Jacobs realised how welcome this break was. Nobody had bothered to mention to the new starters the process of putting your hand up and asking permission to go to the toilet. The older children in the front rows filed out in a very orderly way, while we in the back waited until they had all exited through the single door before we moved.

Once outside, this choreographed order broke down. Children spilled down the steps into the playground like a lorry load of racing pigeons newly given their freedom. They ran hither and thither, to and fro, until they realised what direction they ought to be going. Eventually the boys veered to the left and the girls to the right, towards their respective toilet.

I noticed some kids had come out with sandwiches or some other items to eat. I suddenly felt the pangs of hunger myself, but getting past the bigger boys into the crowded toilet was more pertinent...

It seemed that quite suddenly one of the big girls began ringing that bell summoning us back inside. Going back inside was noticeably slower and required much cajoling from the bigger girls.

When we got inside and shyly took up our seats, the activities were much the same as before. We resumed our group fidgeting and communal nose-picking with a diffident ease. We were each given a chalkboard and asked to draw something. While we got on with our activities, the real business of the school unfolded before us. Older kids were given work to do at their desk while we self-consciously scribbled on our slates, checking what others were up to and mimicking those who seemed to know what they were doing.

The new calmness in activities gave me an opportunity to take stock of my new surroundings. Around the room were quotes from the bible, written with coloured pens on coloured paper which made them difficult to read. These gems of wisdom encouraged us to be good and Christian-like. The bible quotes, these uplifting messages in fading ink, were destined to be a familiar sight. .

Some of the posters were new; others looked older, judging by the way they pulled away from their sellotape supports. In fact quite a lot of objects hanging on the walls looked old. There were displays of knitting, pieces of cloth that had ornate button holes in them and many, many pictures and drawings.

At that moment, I think I was disappointed by my experience. We were ignored more or less for the next hour or two; gradually breaking ranks, getting out of our seats, moving around and trying out the newfound freedom of going to the toilet every ten minutes.

The bell rang again, surprising us. This time everyone was slower getting out into the playground. People were rummaging in their satchels, pulling out lunchboxes, bottles and flasks. Going down the steps, groups of kids were peeling off toward corners and shaded spots to eat their lunches. Some almost immediately started marking out hopscotch games in the dusty gravel that was our playground. Others began to skip with long ropes while eating their sandwiches. Sally and I were feeling a bit lost at this stage, but Algy rescued us.

She took us on a tour of the school. First of all she led us into Mr Smythe's school, the Senior school. He wasn't there; every day he went next door to his house for his dinner. We learned that frequently he came back early to read the newspaper. He struck me as the type of person who might occasionally write to their letters page complaining about some issue or other and comically ending with the line 'I also heard the cuckoo.'

Just inside the door we were shown where we could get hot water for our Bovril or Cocoa. A big girl who I had never seen before was in charge of hot drinks. It was her job. She promised to give us hot water whenever we needed it. The floorboards had a well-scrubbed and ancient look, with pencil-gobbling gaps here and there. If floorboards could speak, these ugly items would likely tell a tale or two. Dad could do a good job of work on these, I thought.

Looking around this room, it was everything I expected as a school. In all honesty I think I had been looking forward to school all summer. The excitement when Mam showed me my new satchel was unbearable. The whole idea of going to school appealed to me more than I cared to admit.

In the centre of the room was a large pot-bellied stove which, I was to learn, was the only heater in the room. It was similar to the one in Mrs Jacobs's classroom but looked older. Around the walls hung maps of the world, a pink world that would change colour before we eventually left this place. A huge map of Ireland depicting all the counties dominated the room. I found this map vaguely resembled a teddy bear, and on subsequent brief visits to Mr Smythe's school, it seemed this teddy bear figure stared at me menacingly... On the map of the world, a piece hung off at Sydney, Australia. I became obsessed with this bit of the map and wanted to pick it off and take it home.

Time had squeezed all colours from this room. Around the walls and between the head-high windows was an array of dark wood cupboards and bookcases that looked like they were never opened or the books ever moved. The dado and picture rails around the walls, the peeling paint and cracking plaster, chalk dust everywhere, satchels lying expectantly beneath the desks were all what I expected from Senior school.

Mr Smythe had a big old-looking desk. It had an untidy appearance with several opened books here and there as if at the ready for some hurried consultation. Behind the desk was the master's chair, a big and heavy piece of furniture that he often referred to as his 'lifetime chair.'

In one dark corner, and on an old wooden peg, hung two canes. Canes were familiar items to children in Arklow; you could buy them in shops around the town. They found their way into many homes. Algy pointed them out to us with almost salacious delight. In the early afternoon breeze, through an open window these canes moved almost threateningly; pendulum-like as if to assure us that they were always watching and aware.

We went outside with Algy to see all the places of interest. The playground was covered in dusty gravel that I was to learn was the bane of all mothers. Children sent off to school in pristine outfits were unlikely ever to return home in the same condition.

Beside the boys' toilet there was the firewood and coal shed. In the other corner beside the girls' toilet was the bicycle shed, which didn't have any bicycles. Next door to the bicycle shed was a locked garage which I found out later contained Mr Smythe's car, a bottle green Morris Minor. A pleasure I was soon to experience revolved about this shed and the car inside.

Due to Mr Smythe's love of country walking, the car remained in this snug garage for most of the week, cocooned from the ravages of the Irish weather. When it occasionally emerged for affairs of state, it took the efforts of both the Master and his wife to navigate out of the confines of the garage. Mrs Smythe guided the driver and simultaneously kept children safe from the reversing vehicle. When all seemed safe, Mrs Smythe daintily joined her husband, somehow always looking too small for her seat while her husband always looked too large for his.

In one secluded corner stood a big metal water tank with a flat top about the size of a kitchen table. Several of the older boys had already climbed up on top, and seemed keen not to let others up. This surely was the prime position for boys during break. I suspected it would be quite a few years before I was allowed on the tank.

It was evident from the rising din in the air that the other schools nearby also had their breaks at this time. Betty joined us and we sat down on a small wall facing the Tech which seemed to be a favourite place for Algy, and scoffed our sandwiches. I knew that Betty was often called Beatrix, especially if she was in trouble, which was frequently, but Algy was always called Algy no matter what. It took me by surprise then when I heard a big boy called Claude referring to her as Alice, occasionally calling her Miss Alice. Algy always seemed unimpressed.

A lot of older kids already began to play tag and other running-around games. The school playground gradually became a hustle bustle cauldron of activity. Strange games were being played here that were unknown to me and probably many other bystanders. In the playground children concentrated like they were studying for an exam. Some held their heads to one side; some their tongues sticking out. They looked so angelic. Perhaps it was because they were country kids and not familiar with gang type games.

The games being played here seemed very aggressive. Boys knees were soiled and copiously scabbed. The participants squared up to each other like some sort of sumo wrestlers, hands outstretched or stuck in their belts as if to confuse their opponents. Often a participant looked nervously into Mr Smythe's garden to see if they were being observed.

The games started sluggishly, as if somehow surprised the opponents might have the gumption to attack them. My size dictated that for the first few days at least, I hovered around the edges of this cockfight, learning the rules, observing the games warily, and when the push and shove came my way laughing at the vanquished and cheering the victors. There were times however that I was a little scared of theses activities, but there was always the certain knowledge that I had big cousins lurking.

The combatants knew each other and reminded each other of past infractions of obscure rules; individuals were heckled and jeered over new allegiances. There was a great amount of finger pointing and drawing lines in the gravel. This agitated gravel generated a fine dust and hung about the noisy throng.

In dry times the school yard was a desolate dusty spot devoid of tree or plant. In the Garden of Ireland the irony was noticeable and evident. My khaki shorts and white socks were destined to regularly lose their brilliance in this dusty arena.

Abruptly the bell rang again and heralded a cessation of hostilities. We all learned to hate this bell. Boys and girls turned heels and plodded wearily but in good humour back to their respective schools. Enemies arm in arm preparing to deal with the common foe. Everyone seemed to sense a long day yawned ahead of us.

Afternoon activities continued more or less as the morning session. We were introduced to a new blackboard with an alphabet etched perfectly into it and several lines below where pupils could enter and practice their endeavours. Panic set in that when it came to my turn. I thought I might not be able to reach these lines, but Mrs Jacobs's helper conveniently rolled it down to suit me. It was easy to become engrossed in these activities. We got encouragement from other new starters and from those who had obviously grown out of this particular exercise.

As I concentrated on the job at hand, tongue sticking out, I became aware of a rise in the noise about me. Mr Smythe had been spotted passing the window on his way to visit us. A general scattering of kids tried to get back to their seats. Although I didn't really know what was going on, I slowly made my way back to my place, watching the furious antics about me.

Mr Smythe breezed into a room which in a very short time indeed had gone quite silent. He was met with the sight of about thirty turned heads, most of whom said 'Good afternoon Sir.' Replying 'Good afternoon children,' he walked directly to the front of the class, nodding at Mrs Jacobs. A cane hung casually from the top pocket of his jacket. I was surprised that on the first day of school he had daubs of chalk here and there on his suit.

Mr Smythe was a big brutish man, but probably no more than anyone else to us small people. He wore peculiar half-lens glasses and peered over them while speaking or listening to you. These half glasses contrived to make him look intelligent and doddery simultaneously. From conversations during the summer with my cousins, I was quite aware that Mr Smythe, the headmaster, the master, was always addressed as Sir. He was a glossy ruddy man and was often seen walking about the country roads with his tiny wife. He was invariably a stride ahead of her; she constantly seemed to be having difficulty keeping up. Over his jacket, he occasionally wore a plastic mackintosh which billowed out behind him, like angels wings. He had big well-fed cheeks. Mrs Smythe gave the impression that her ultimate reason in life was to feed this lumbering man.

There was something else in that face. In large families, a visitor is treated with equal amounts of interest and indifference. People come and go without making much of a lasting impression. If you are an only child however, a visitor is examined, scrutinised, forensically, warily until all aspects, mannerisms, traits are exposed. I became a good watcher.

I stared at length at Mr Smythe, in my usual way, but I couldn't put my finger on exactly on what was amiss with the headmaster. He had a ponderous languid style of speaking, examining his clasped hands continually as he spoke at length. I had seen him crossing the school yard a few times that morning. He seemed an intense man who always seemed to be about to do something, some performance, some act. As he strode across the yard it seemed as if he was about to hoist a flag, or vault a gate. His stride was purposeful and deliberate.

He addressed the class and asked questions about what adventures we'd had in the summer holidays. The numerous shouts of 'Sir, Sir' seemed to eternally please him as the older kids vied to tell him how great their summer was. He eventually got around to talking to the new comers. Polishing his spectacles with his spotless handkerchief, he let it be known that he expected us all to behave and follow Mrs Jacobs's instructions. Naughtiness and misbehaving was not tolerated. Punishment was the solution to naughtiness and misbehaving. He introduced us to his cane, which he called the 'bata'.

To emphasise and authenticate this declaration he swept the cane sideways into the ample folds of his trousers. If his intention was to terrify us, it certainly succeeded. The silence of children in the room was telling. I learned eventually 'bata' was Gaelic for cane. It is interesting that the first word I learned in our language was to do with chastisement and pain. I wonder how many kids like me experienced this introduction. Little did I know that pain and chastisement were to be habitual in relation to the teaching and learning of the Irish language.

Mr Smythe turned and pointed to Mrs Jacobs. 'I want you all,' he said loudly 'to heed what Mrs Jacobs tells you. You should all try to be completely in tune with what she is trying to do to further your education. This will make your duration here Happy and Pleasant.' Sally looked across at me. Whatever could he mean by 'in tune'?

He also mentioned that Mr Poyntz would visit us in class and that we would soon begin studying for the Annual Scripture Exam, and if we were successful we'd win a prize. This cheered everyone immensely. A spontaneous show of delight enlivened the class.

It seemed no time at all after Mr Smythe left, the bell was rung. Suddenly the day was over... A mad rush for the door ensued. Children grabbed their bags and ran to freedom, some to catch the school van and some to meet their parents at the school gate. Outside children streamed onto the road, running off in every direction, screaming, no one holding back their happiness. A road full of children, both Protestant and Catholic, momentarily, fleetingly, united in joy. The scene truly emphasised the unfathomable mystery of dotty kids.

I remember rushing down the Main Street, eager to get home and report on the day's activities. Mam was interested in other children who started with me and with a frowned expression wondered how

I got so dirty in such a short time. Dad arrived back from work at six o'clock and immediately asked me if I got any slaps. I had other things on my mind though. 'What does duration mean?' I asked him.

Looking over his paper, his face partially hidden beneath a cloud of cigarette smoke, he replied, 'What do you mean, duration?'

'Well Mr Smythe mentioned our duration.'

'Oh right. What he probably meant was how long you might be in Carysfort.'

'Is that what duration means? And how long will it be?'

'Well it's seven or eight years in Primary school, and then you'll go to Secondary school. So maybe fifteen years altogether,' he concluded. I think I detected a hint of a smile.

As he reached for his cigarette he said: 'Don't worry son, it comes with being born.'

During my first few days at school, John constantly provided me with rules and regulations that needed to be remembered and adhered to. In some ways I was lucky to have John but he could dampen the spirits a bit. His casual references to being kept back a year gave me nightmares and added to the estimation of my duration.

That first night in my pyjamas, I readied myself to say my prayers. Kneeling down with hands clasped in front of my face, I thought about the day's adventures. Mam or Dad usually had to remind me to say my prayers, but tonight I needed no encouragement. As well as a brief mention of my parents, I concentrated wholly on the issues of slaps and 'Please please God, do not let me be kept back a year.' I began to worry from that day on.

3

'Where have all the good times gone?'

As soon as I started school I realised that my cousins and I were somehow different. I'm not sure if it was going to school, or whether our life in general pointed to this difference but it certainly contributed to my predicament. Grownups obviously knew we were a little different to others, but to our pals in the neighbourhood, that we now attended different school at the other end of town was bound to have some consequences. They also found it hard to grasp that we attended a boys and girls school. Mixed schools were a new thing to them.

Before going to school, nobody ever treated me differently. After staring school, I was occasionally asked if I believed in God. I had no answer to this mystery. I was quizzed about making Holy Communion and laughed at when I admitted I couldn't recite the Hail Mary. These were strange questions that I hadn't encountered before. Where this inquisitiveness came from I am unsure, but I felt that it must have originated in school. I was suddenly someone different. We were part of the community and apart from it at the same time. There was a sort of 'inbetweeness' to our lives. When I started school and joined parish activities, everything I did there, every heightened involvement, made this separateness more obvious and profound.

I lived in an area that was predominantly Catholic. My father and mother married when they were quite old. Marriage between the two religions was frowned on, and I think that this is part of the reason my parents married so late in life; it was difficult to meet other Protestants with so few about.

I was born a little more than nine months after they were married. I checked this out on my birth certificate when I was having doubts that maybe I was adopted. I was an only child. My parents were Protestants or Church of Ireland, as they preferred to call themselves.

Our house was in the old part of Arklow; the area was known as the Fishery. It got this name because it was where Arklow's fishermen lived. Originally houses were arranged around the Dock area and the river exit to the sea. In a gradual and random way the Fishery and town expanded upwards and outwards from the banks of the river and its two extensive and quite beautiful beaches.

The town became well known for these beaches. It swelled with beach-loving tourists during the summer, and was then quickly abandoned at the end of August

The river that cut the beaches down the middle was sluggish and smelly, and littered with old wooden boats in various states of disrepair. At low tides the town's inadequate sewage disposal was plainly evident. The River Avoca oozed to sea between two brutish breakwaters known as the North and South piers. To their left and right, the bend of the bay and its beautiful beaches swerved towards Porter's Rocks to the north and Arklow Rock to the south.

In what seemed to me a random manner, maritime tides gushed through these piers with an intense ferocity. This 'riverrun' was checked by the installation of an additional breakwater. Named the Graveyard, it was a place of anger in tidal moments, with crashing breakers and huge columns of sea spray. In quieter times it became a veritable Garden of Eden of colourful seaweed and sea life.

Our house was one of four in a new scheme, situated on the quay and facing out onto the River Avoca. To the right and about a hundred yards away was Arklow Dock, where numerous modern fishing boats were moored. Ours was a modern house with a toilet and bathroom upstairs. Mam told me that Auntie Connie and Granny thought that she was mad when she and Dad put their names down for the house. 'You'll starve yourself paying for that house,' Granny had said, but that didn't deter Mam. I suspect she may not have married until she had a decent house to move into. Dad sometimes used his bicycle to travel the hundred yards to his work, slowly edging his way while having that last cigarette, before reaching the workshop which of course was a 'no smoking' area.

In the Fishery there were about seven other Protestant families. We were related to most of them in some way. Mam's only sister, Connie, lived across Harbour Road in Tinahask, almost mid-way between Granny's house and Aunt Moll's. She had five kids: three girls and two boys. I spent a lot of time in the company of Connie and my cousins. Connie was the only active aunt I had during my childhood, almost becoming a second mother. We shared what we had and what illnesses we contrived to pick up. Mumps and measles became a mutual experience. They say cousins are friends that will love you forever. If you were lucky enough to have cousins, life was grand. My cousins were a part of my childhood that I never lost or forgot .The first thing that I can remember I did in their company. It dawned on me eventually that in fact I was their only cousin, while I had cousins nearby, in Gorey in Howth and further afield in Cork. I soon realised that as well as being an only child, I was sadly an only cousin.

Connie was married to Jack who was a deep-sea sailor. He was away from home a lot. He could be gone for up to eighteen months or more; an eternity to a small boy. He was away so much that I just about forgot that he existed, and then he'd turn up out of the blue, or so it seemed to me.

Fathers returning after lengthy absences were a common occurrence in the Fishery. Many men left the town to get work; as sailors, or to North American docks. These men suddenly appeared and then just as suddenly disappeared. They created much excitement when they went on view. The clothes they wore defined everything about them. Judgment of their prosperity or lack of it was determined by their appearance. If they had been prosperous they were dressed like the film stars we saw in the cinema, talking up how wonderful life was in the States, and generously offering Cuban cigars to old acquaintances. I was particularly fond of the aluminium tubes these cigars arrived in.

These men seemed to like snazzy straw hats which compounded the film star look. Their children also were seen with sloppy-joes and denim jeans, rounded off with black and white sneakers. I craved those stripy T-shirts.

Overnight, these kids suddenly became identical to the kids we saw in advertisements in Dell comics. These kids added insult to injury by offering all and sundry one of their newly arrived American sweets. One such kid earned the nickname 'Spangles.' We experienced the delights of Wrigley's chewing gum, and similarly we became obsessed with bubble gum.

Jack, Connie's husband, was a typical Arklow sailor. He dressed in dark clothes with a dark cap and navy blue woollen gansey underneath a dark coat. When he came home, he did all his own washing and darning. He carried on like he was still away at sea. I think he preferred being away. He could live his life at his own pace. He could be his own man. At home he had five kids that he barely knew, all growing up fast around him and challenging his right to be there...

Jack was completely bald. Dad said it was a result of contracting malaria in some foreign country. During the Second World War he'd served in the Merchant Navy and lost a couple of fingers in an accident. They said he received good disability pay from the navy on account of the injury.

Jack was one for the drink. When he came home, he spent a lot of time in the pub showing off how much money he earned. Connie went with him to try and keep him under control and hopefully retain some of this money. You learn the words 'stocious' and 'langers' at an early stage in those circumstances. When we found out that he was due home, my cousins, especially Sally, John and Bobby, were excited. I saw very little of them when Jack arrived home.

In his travels, he got to visit many distant countries, where he picked up nice gifts for everyone. Mam and I usually got a present from him as well. One time I got a battery operated police car. Mam got a Chinese dinner set and a cuckoo clock. I think Jack used to give Mam good presents because he had suspicions that she helped Connie make ends meet while he was away.

Jack could be fun when he was sober, but with drink in him he was annoying and a bit evil. At dinner time his favourite joke was to offer me piece of meat from his dinner plate, thinking I didn't notice he'd plastered the underside with mustard. You get caught by that sort of thing only once but Jack tried it on every day. His mother's maiden name was Spencer. He told everyone that he was related to the Royal family which possibly wasn't the most sensible thing to admit in the Republic.

One time he returned he brought home a canary – from the Canary Islands I suppose. He called it Joey. It seemed an odd name for a canary. I always thought of it as a budgie's name. He constantly threatened to bring a little monkey home, but it never did materialize.

Connie loved her memorabilia, her Royal family stuff. She owned a Coronation cup and saucer, plates with pictures of Charles and Anne with lots more on display in her kitchen. Mam had owned a few pieces herself but eventually gave them to a jumble sale. She said: 'It's not proper here in the South, you never know what people might do or say.' Connie's interest in the Royal family was profound, and might be put down to the time she spent working in Kent after the war. They all moved there when Jack got a job in Chatham Docks. Connie worked as a seamstress; she was very good at the sewing.

I expect that Connie and my cousins got postcards from Jack regularly. They must have missed him all the time. Every so often Connie told Mam that she'd 'fix up with her' because her 'allotment' had arrived from the shipping company. After this happened Connie seemed happy and Mam relieved.

Connie smoked. Mam didn't. My cousins all smoked as soon as they could. Cigarettes were always noticeable around their house. They say small comforts are a good substitute for greater ones. I never did learn to smoke.

Connie always seemed to have one in the corner of her mouth and with one eye permanently closed by the smoke. She seemed to subsist on cigarettes and tea. Her tongue was chisel-sharp but all this hid her good heart. She was a favourite of mine for there is no charm equal to tenderness of heart. Amid the shouting and arguing in her kitchen, she always spoke gently to me and included me in the general madness that was her house and children.

I knew from an early age that Connie was someone I could love.

She was a small woman with short hair and the long crooked nose that plagued the genes of our family. Often I'd sit with her as she swirled and peered into the dregs of her tea cup. I frequently was given tea with a drop of whisky in it, to ward off the cold. This came accompanied by a lefthander from her secret biscuit tin. Being in her company was so restful; it was like medicine making you better, your heart filled up like a balloon. Algy and Betty were taking after her. You could depend on them to stick up for you.

She used to make apple tart which she called 'Apple Daddy.' Mam didn't make it the same as Connie and if truth be known, I preferred Connie's version. Mam was a bit miffed about this. Connie's pastry was nicer and she used to add cloves which gave it a bit of a zing. Whenever Connie made Apple Daddy she'd keep some for me, or send Bobby or Sally over with some.

The two families somehow evened out just dandy. My cousins' travelling father was never present, but they had each other to compensate for his absence. My father was home all the time and I had my cousins to compensate for being an only child. The mothers were of course the real parents, the real heroes. Always ready to help, always providing, always finding the money.

A couple of doors to the left of Connie's house lived my grandmother on my mother's side. She was a strict old bat and kept a sprig of holly over the fireplace to beat us if we were naughty. When the holly began to disappear, she took to beating us across the backs of the legs with the flex of the electric kettle. Oh yes, a very nice old woman. Granny's maiden name was De'Ath. People in the neighbourhood pronounced it 'Death.' It didn't take us long to christen her Granny Death.

Granny's house was a thatched cottage without its thatch: sometime in the past it had been replaced with a corrugated iron roof. I remember it being painted an odd colour of red. Like most of the cottages in the Fishery, it had an outside toilet.

Granny owned a big black dog called Nugget. It was really old and cantankerous. One sunny afternoon the two families had been on the beach. On the way home, we called in to Granny's house to see how she was. I was first in the house and saw the chair opposite Granny was available. I raced across the room before anyone and threw myself backwards onto the chair. Unfortunately in the darkness of the room I didn't notice Nugget asleep. The dog reacted predictably to a five-year-old child landing on him. He growled from somewhere deep in is scrawny body and bit me enthusiastically on the leg. His jaws were clasped around my thigh for what seemed an eternity. When he finally released me, he slinked off as if knowing he was in big trouble. I was rushed up to the doctor and received the obligatory tetanus injection with accompanying stitches. After a few days I was right as rain.

The next week Bobby was running down Granny's yard and Nugget jumped at him and bit him on the head. I think he was beginning to like boy-blood. The police came and put the dog down. Biting one grandchild was obviously unfortunate, biting another was just stupid. I loathed black dogs from that day forward. Such incidents must have been hell on my mother's nerves, but thankfully for her well-being I survived the litany of other ordinary family mishaps.

Mam had four brothers. So with Connie, there was very little room in the small house for everyone when they were all growing up. The older brothers, Jack and Dick, joined the Merchant Navy during the war and eventually settled in Cardiff. Billy worked locally while Ronnie became a sailor.

Billy and Ronnie were the only ones living with Granny before she died. I think Mam thought Billy was incapable of looking after himself. I heard her say that she promised Granny she would look after them both. I don't think Dad was too happy with this death-bed promise when Billy moved in with us as a lodger.

Billy worked in the pottery, in the clay end. Mam used to work there as well before she married. Dad told me that she had a good job in the pottery, and was Uncle Billy's supervisor. Billy could have been Mam's twin in appearance: the same black hair, the same ruddy complexion and blue eyes. They both somehow avoided the dreaded Tyrrell nose. There however the similarity stopped. In temperament and generosity, they were definitely chalk and cheese.

Billy led a life that revolved around the pubs all week, Gaelic football on Sunday and in between, an awful lot of golf. As far as I know he was the only grownup in our family who played any games. He was supposed to be very good at golf and some said he could have been the club pro in Arklow Links.

A few years before Granny died, Billy was friendly with a girl from the Fishery. They were walking out and seeing each other for years. She was a Catholic. When Billy announced that he might marry the girl, Granny talked him out of it, saying she wouldn't leave him her house in her will if he turned. The priest did his bit as well with the girl. Billy realised he'd have to turn his religion if he wanted to marry. Granny and the rest of the family wouldn't let him do that. The girl's family insisted that she get married in the Catholic church. The two of them broke off the relationship under these sad and tragic circumstances. They were never spotted walking out or going with anyone else. At that time, changing one's religion was like enrolling on the devil's team.

As it transpired, Billy didn't inherit the house. It was left unexpectedly to Mam. I heard Dad say that if Billy really wanted to marry the girl he should have gone ahead and run off to England. Billy was a sad man. In the space of a few years, he'd lost a house and a girl friend. Dad inevitably came up with one of his sayings to describe the situation. 'Women and fish, it all boils down to the one that got away.' To me it was just another example of an unlived life.

Uncle Ronnie was the youngest of my aunts and uncles. He had a Cliff Richard hairstyle and he wore drainpipe jeans and suede shoes. He was the new generation. You couldn't help but like him. He had an easy charm. He and his friends dressed as close to Teddy Boys as anyone in the town. Most of them were sailors as well and were away at sea for months, if not years, on end. We usually saw him about every twelve months. Some of his friends had a band, which they called the Swinging Sailors. Some went away as Teddy Boys and came back looking like James Dean. They were a very popular gang with the girls when they were at home. When they went back to sea, the girls returned to the stay-at-homes. Being young, they rarely arrived back in Arklow with little more than new tattoos or the latest fashions.

Both Billy and Ronnie lived with us on and off. Family rows and arguments resulted in them often having to take digs around the town, but somehow they always made up and returned to our house on the South Quay.

Between Granny's and Connie's houses lived Mr and Mrs Kinch with their relative Harry. We weren't related to the Kinches. Their house was similar in size to Granny's. At the back however was a stable with a horse, hayshed with hay, a chicken run with chickens and a resulting dung heap. In the middle of all these small houses, this was a most interesting place for kids. The Kinches had none of their own but were eternally welcoming to children from the surrounding area. It was a great attraction and was the nearest us townie kids might get to a real farm.

To the right of Connie's house and few doors up, Mam's Aunt Moll lived on her own. Her house was one of the few thatched houses remaining in the Fishery. The walls were distempered white and the door painted bright red.

Mam made her dinner every Sunday and it was my job, rain or hail, to carry it across to Moll's. I hated it. Every Sunday I dreaded the call from Mam. 'Moll's dinner is all ready,' she'd say, pointing to the plates wrapped in a couple of tea towels. 'Bring that over to Moll, and your dinner will be on the table when you get back... And don't forget last week's plates.' Everyone in the house knew I didn't like this job, but there was no way out of it.

I set off up the lane. At this time on a Sunday the streets were deserted, not a sinner to be seen. The whole country was sitting down for their dinner except me. I think it was more the deserted and lonely streets that made me dislike this job than having to go to Moll's. By the time I got to her door, there'd be a little spillage and leakage on the towels and my arms. Her door was always locked and I had to knock. Through the window I'd see her struggling out of the chair, leaning on her walking stick; it was painful waiting for her to get to the door. By this point, I'd be hopping up and down with impatience. She must have had about four thousand locks and bolts on the door considering how long it took her to open it.

Finally when the door opened, I'd get the usual 'Oh it's you.' With that she'd turn around and lead me into the living room. Occasionally she turned her back on me and hummed a soft tune. Maybe she did look forward to my visit in some way. She usually had set the little table for dinner in anticipation of my arrival. I unwrapped the plates and put them on the table. 'Last week's are there,' she said, nodding towards the plates on the sideboard. Her hands were bent inwards and gnarled from rheumatism but they seemed a perfect fit for the walking stick she had with her at all times.

Often she started a conversation. 'Where are you off to now?' she'd say, without even looking in my direction. Sometimes she gave me money, but for all that it could be weeks before she gave me anything again. The door was shut behind me and I'd hear all the bolts and latches being put back into place.

She was a peculiar woman and stuck in a time unknown to me. She spoke the vocabulary of the past, referring to 'Ellis Island' and 'Yella buck corn.' Everyone she disliked was a 'Black and Tan' or a 'gurrier.' She didn't have electricity or a radio in her house.

Moll was widely regarded by the smaller children in the neighbouring houses as a witch. The grey hair and black clothes certainly added to this impression. She also had a scary black cat named rather confusingly Molly B and sometimes she wore a peculiar hat that almost swallowed her head. But Moll wasn't unique. Every street in the Fishery had its quota of little old ladies dressed in black, sitting outside front doors, knitting, snoring, watching.

My cousin Freddy lived in St Michael's Terrace past the Fur Factory, a mysterious and permanently locked building. His mam and dad were my Uncle Fred and Auntie Eileen. Mam didn't get on with Auntie Eileen. Over the years we had such little contact with her that I used to call her Mrs Cutland. Dad didn't like that. Uncle Fred worked in the coal yard, for another Protestant employer. He was a great character and fun to be with. Over time, things thawed out a little between Eileen and Mam and we were all on sort of speaking terms. Freddy always got on well with Dad though and often came to our house looking for help in something he was building or putting together.

I first met my Grandfather Ruxton in Cutland's house. He was interested in photography; he took a photograph of me standing on a large cement structure located directly in front of Auntie Eileen's house that had something to do with the town water system. This photograph of me, accompanied by a toy stagecoach on a string, had pride of place among the other family photographs that adorned our sitting room furniture.

Granddad Ruxton was a difficult man and his lack of popularity resulted in him being farmed out on a sort of rota to each of his sons and daughters. I remember him vaguely looking like a character from Dickens, with a dark suit and stovepipe hat. His period staying with us on South Quay ended abruptly when Mam, standing in the kitchen with a packed case by her side and putting on her coat and hat, gave Dad the ultimatum: 'It's him or me, make up your mind.' That's the last I saw of Granddad Ruxton.

My father's other brothers and sisters lived away from Arklow. It was a peculiar family in many respects. It was funny that my Uncle Jack and Aunt Rose were Catholics, while we were Church of Ireland. This strange affair came about when my grandfather's first wife died and he remarried, to a Catholic woman. He had two sons, George and Tom, by his first wife, and they were Protestant. When he had children with his second wife, the confusion set in.

As was common in the town, Granddad frequently worked away. If he was at home when a baby was born, he arranged a Church of Ireland christening. If however the baby was born while he was working away, his wife had the honours done in the Catholic church.

This randomness meant Eileen and my father were Protestant; Florrie in Gorey, Jack in Howth and Bill in Cork were all Catholic. I eventually began to realise I was a Protestant purely by chance, which didn't exactly nurture any deep sense of loyalty to either religion.

Adding to my confusion over our religious status in the community Dad began a lengthy working relationship with the nuns who ran the local secondary school for girls, which irritated the local Catholic carpenters.

They were livid when, on the back of his experience with stage production in the Marlborough Hall, the nuns asked Dad to help out in the set construction for St Mary's School annual opera. These operas were grand affairs, often produced by someone from the theatre or television world. The lead singer in the production was always a past pupil who had become famous in opera circles. One year they employed a local artist called Paul Funge for set design. Mr Funge was a well-known artist nationally and a college lecturer in the College of Art. Dad was assigned to him for set construction. He was very proud of his involvement in these productions, getting recognition on the programme alongside these great names. I think Dad found working with the artist a little difficult and they had many differences of opinion. Arriving home after one such challenging episode, he declared, 'Tonight, my son, I almost committed Fungicide.'

These nuns became frequent visitors to our house, seemingly quite content to arrive early in the afternoon and wait until Dad appeared from work. They always travelled in groups of two or three. They had an insatiable appetite for tea and cake, occasionally bringing convent-produced tarts and cakes. After the initial awkwardness on both sides, these nuns became good friends to Mam and Dad. They spent long afternoons chatting, gossiping and giggling with Mam, coming more frequently when she was unwell. I remember one of them telling me gushingly, 'Your father is a saint, Richard.'

That seemed highly unlikely to me, but he should have qualified for something with his commemorative crosses. It started as a request from the grieving relatives of a young man who had been killed on the road near the Kilbride Hall. Dad took it seriously. He made a cross about two feet tall using wood from a secret stash of mahogany. It had a small plaque at the Jesus position with the name and details of the deceased and was placed in a plinth of concrete near the site of the accident.

After that first cross, Dad's 'fame', as it were, grew and he was asked to make several other crosses, all for other tragic accidents.

Once I asked him how much he charged for a cross. He looked sharply at me and said, 'How could you charge anyone for such a thing?' If our nuns had known, Dad surely would have been elevated further in the Catholic hierarchy of good guys.

4

'He fell through the door'

If it is true that photographs are about nothing but the past, then the pictures in our house certainly confirmed this. The past was all around us. Dotted around the rooms were photographs of Mam and Dad's wedding day. Black and white pictures that somehow through age, damp or constant exposure to fire or cigarette smoke had acquired a quaint sepia hue. These photographs depicted two toothy, gaunt, self-conscious individuals, dressed in post war fashions. The impression of two people smiling for their particular friends but not for each other was hard to dispel. The wedding had taken place in St Saviour's Church. I recognised many of the people in the photographs because they occasionally called at our house.

In the passing years, both Mam and Dad had changed a great deal. Gone were the gawky slimness and the effects of Irish 1940's austerity. Whether by an improvement in diet, or contentment from marital life, they both had become plumper, rounder and healthier. Mam was taller than Dad, but I never heard that mentioned.

When I went to school, I expect Mam felt the loneliness; filling up the hours of my absence with long hours of radio, preparing meals, knitting and reading. She occasionally mentioned that peculiar feeling of 'no one to talk to'.

She had a ruddy face which was enhanced with small broken veins on her cheeks. People who came to the house said I had my mother's eyes which were steely blue. Others said, 'You're very like your mother' but meaning I had a similar temperament. She was generous in the extreme; relatives often took advantage of her. A recurring stream of

39

sob stories made their way to her kitchen; relatives out of work, no money, no food. All with their hands outstretched. She was a soft touch, a reliable source of loans never to be repaid. All of this was of course unbeknownst to Dad.

An avid reader, she occasionally put a new take on big word, by accident or for fun, I never was quite sure. Like the 'gymhanahana', as she insisted on calling it, that accompanied the annual summer fete the Protestant Proby family held for the parish. with an accompanying gymkhana. My embarrassment deepened as my spelling skills grew. I still sometimes use her pronunciation and laugh to myself. .

She had wonderful sayings to suit all occasions. On reading any information that she disagreed with her comment was 'Paper never refuses ink.' When anyone was loudly angry, her put-down was always 'You have to listen to thunder' and thunder was often very loud indeed in our house. When Dad was angry, or annoyed about something, he was always deemed 'a street angel and house devil'. 'Fancy living leads to fancy dying,' she often said – not that fancy living ever intruded on our lives.

Every Friday evening when I got back from Carysfort, Mam would start the weekly shopping list. I did the writing. Mam said it was good practice for me but I think it was because she had the beginnings of bad arthritis in her hands. Mam sat down at the dinner table and called out the weekly list, which inevitably began 1 Tea, 4 Sugar, 1 Butter, 6 Eggs. Other necessities were added in after checking the pantry.

When I began joining clubs and going to parish events, I think Mam felt she also needed to join in. She enrolled in the Mothers' Union. This was yet another club that was trying with great difficulty to rid itself of the whiff of Englishness, and was exclusively for Protestant women. I think Mam joined it just to get out of the house on the odd night during the winter.

The minister's wife was the head woman in the club. Under her tutelage, they ran jumble sales and cake sales to raise money for the school, the church and the ever-present missions. Mam used to attend a meeting about once a month in the Marlborough Hall where they'd have tea and cakes and the inevitable slide show of starving and then smiling children in Africa. Mam, I know, was largely disinterested, but was delighted one year to travel with them to Dublin to see Maureen Potter and Jimmy O'Dea in panto. Mam told me a lot of the women who went to the pantomime got a couple of drinks in the theatre at the intermission, but I didn't believe her. The Mothers' Union was another club that predominantly attracted country people and farmers' wives so that even to Mam the whole thing was a bit old-fashioned and stick-in-the-mud.

I don't think she ever walked into a public bar in her life, but she did love films. Once or twice a week, she went to one of the local cinemas with Connie or one of her neighbour friends. Robert Mitchum seemed to be a big favourite. A trip to the local hairdresser, exotically named Bluebelle's, usually preceded these outings. The arrival of television in the house seemed to put an end to all that.

Dad was a small dapper man with Brylcreemed combed-back hair. It came to a point in the centre of his forehead like a devil's cap. My earliest memory of Dad is of him singing into a mirror in the kitchen as he shaved and prepared for a night out drinking with his friends. When he got back a little late from work, if he was wearing his bicycle clips, he continued wearing them all through his meal and shaving, only removing them when changing into his going-out clothes. This always infuriated Mam.

He had an arsenal of shaving songs. He liked Bing Crosby, Frank Sinatra, John McCormack but by no means limited himself to artists like these. He often threw in a song he'd learned for one of his many stage appearances. He had a range of accents to authenticate these kitchen performances, the best being his attempt at Cockney for *All I Want Is a Room Somewhere*. Invariably Mam joined in quietly with the line, 'A room in a pub is what you need.' He was a baritone and when he sang, the lyrics seemed to expand to fill up the entire house.

One song featured more often than others. He referred to as the 'Sum Menchah' song. Initially this mystified me. I didn't know of any song of that name or even close to it, for that matter. Eventually Dad explained everything with a rousing rendition of the first few lines. The song was of course *Some Enchanted Evening*.

I began to notice during his exuberant preparations Mam often went out to the front gate to potter about. I think it was her way of saying she wanted no part in these antics. Remaining in the house would have been giving tacit approval to going out; by not being present, it was as if Dad was sneaking or slinking out. Mam was above all this and wanted to be apart from it.

He was given to wearing starched white shirts with sleeve garters on Sundays or special occasions. This gave him a lightly spiv appearance, reminiscent of a croupier in a gambling establishment. He wore glasses. These glasses were often self-repaired with a garnish of coloured tape which didn't always impress Mam.

Dad's contribution to the parish activities was wholehearted, but with one eye always on the possibility of getting a few drinks after with likeminded souls. Dad was an enthusiastic drinker who often confirmed this by declaring, 'It never rains in pubs.'

He joined the parish choir and sang each Sunday. Likewise he joined the Parish Drama Group both as an actor and for set construction. Mam and I didn't think it would last, due to the lack of committed drinkers in the parish. But things turned out well for Dad. His path eventually crossed that of a man called Harry Wilson, and they both had many pleasurable years together treading the boards in the Marlborough Hall and adjourning after the performance to the nearest bar. In her inimitable style, Mam referred to them as 'like peas in a pub'. I think they became saviours for each other. I frequently had suspicions that Dad's main ambitions in life were a pint of Guinness and a warm overcoat to protect him on the way home.

Over the years, Dad performed in musical concerts and had learned many of the songs from *My Fair Lady, Oklahoma, West Side Story* and of course *South Pacific*. These songs were very popular, well-known and the audience inevitably joined in enthusiastically.

Apart from musical revues and comedy sketches, on a couple of occasions he performed in serious plays. The one I remember best was *The Ghost Train*. Dad learned his lines every evening for weeks. Sitting in his armchair in front of the living room fire, he would fall asleep after just a few minutes. Despite this Man complained continually about Dad reciting his lines while asleep in bed. When he wasn't looking, I took a peek at his copy of the dialogue. His part was a character called Teddy, but all references to 'Teddy' were scored through and replaced by 'Ned'. There were other mysterious changes. Entire paragraphs were crossed out and replaced by the word 'song'.

By coincidence, a few weeks before the opening night, a film version of the play with Arthur Askey in one of the parts appeared in the local cinema. After we'd seen it, we were mystified how the Marlborough Hall was going to cope with the train scenes. I couldn't wait to see Dad's performance.

The play ran for three nights and somehow inexplicably was a sell-out each night. Mam and I went the first night. We had bought our tickets as soon as Dad was given his allocation to sell. That night the Marlborough Hall was jam-packed. Country people and town people sat cheek by jowl. Protestants and Catholics joined in happy expectation of a night to remember.

After a brief speech welcoming everyone and setting the scene for the play, eerie music came from backstage and the curtains parted. One by one the characters were introduced to the audience. When Dad made his entrance, a great roar went up mainly, it has to be said, from Fishery people and neighbours. It was a bit embarrassing, but it set the tone for the rest of the performance. Every time he spoke he was applauded. When he sang a duet with a lady who always carried a bird cage, the audience went into raptures. *All I Want Is a Room Somewhere* was the song they sang and it seemed to sum up Dad's philosophy on life. The story line wasn't exactly the same as I had seen in the movie. There were several references to employers in the town, council members and other well-known characters. The audience seemed to enjoy it.

During one scene Dad had to fall through a door from off stage into the middle of the onstage action. For a man his age, it seemed a slightly hazardous manoeuvre, but he managed it with aplomb; a fellow actor deftly catching him before he could come to any harm. On the final night however, things didn't go so well. He fell awkwardly and wasn't cushioned by his compatriot. Several broken ribs resulted and he was off work for about six weeks. Mam was livid. The thought of Dad hanging around the house unable to do anything was too much for her to bear; but bear it she did.

5

'Kids are the greatest fun'

The initial excitement of walking the length of the Main Street each morning waned. Occasionally to break the monotony we went the back way, up a lane called the Ditch. It was roughly parallel to the Main Street. High brambles lined this lane on both sides. For weeks in autumn we gorged ourselves on their bounteous blackberries. It was a time when if you saw anything growing on a tree you ate it, or stole it and then ate it. I began to realise that perhaps adults felt it was always good to be a little hungry.

We started school as near-wild sun-blessed children, but soon had rashes around necks, arms and thighs, where new shirts and shorts troubled and worried the summer's browned skin. The awkwardness of new shoes, stiff shirts and overly warm jumpers and coats disappeared gradually and imperceptibly as the weeks passed.

My satchel contents changed. An often-repaired Thermos flask was a noticeable addition and now had pride of place. Pens and pencils rattled when I ran and numerous ink stains pointed to frequent and messy use. Books that were acquired were carefully covered with brown paper or wallpaper.

One thing that did change noticeably was the weather. I learned that summer fades quickly when the school gates open. It was as if the sun was blown out like a birthday candle, suddenly and silently. The evenings' brightness leaked away, and the mornings seemed infiltrated by grown-ups in heavier and darker clothes. We tried to make the most of these last lingering days but realised that summer was almost over, fading like our tans.

Grown-ups embrace autumn and cold weather way too early. Parents' thoughts turned easily to winter coats, galoshes and rain macs. Children are different. Every morning, especially if the weather was good, a petty argument was inevitable with Mam over what to wear. No one wished to be out of step with what everyone else was wearing. The early wearing of a heavy winter coat was greeted with hoots of laughter. The English-type school cap that Mam insisted I wear, hail rain or snow, gave rise to regular arguments. She did not realise that this despised hat was consigned to my satchel each morning as I rounded the corner of the Back Lane and entered the Harbour Road. Or maybe she did and made me wear it anyway.

Autumn arrived with the usual splash of autumnal colours. Trees turned a cornflake yellow mirroring the new breakfast cereal I occasionally had. Soon there was nothing to be seen except the dry black branches of winter.

Sometimes it rained for weeks, and with it came a sly wind that blew the length of the Harbour Road straight out onto the murky river. This cutting wind always managing to blow sideways down alleys and lanes, rattling unbolted gates and disturbing loose dustbin lids. It swirled unraked leaves through the air and caused them to fall like yellow confetti around us as we tramped our weary way home.

There were the usual accompanying colds and coughs. Sally usually managed to have a very active bubbly head cold that sometimes bulged forward from her nostril as she spoke or laughed. In school the smell of damp overcoats welcomed me each morning as I pushed through the disrobing throng on the way to my seat.

Occasionally snow locked us out of school. This was not an innocent snow. The snow I remember was rarely gentle frolicsome fun snow, but more often than not a frozen icy version that lingered, wind-swept in dark corners and added to our winter woes. The only snow I remember seeing at Christmas was made of cotton wool and calico, neatly positioned in shop windows and draped with earrings and other gift suggestions

Moments of snow-caked mittens, attempted snowmen and the inevitable snowball fights entertained us till the harshness drove us indoors. Sitting around a turf and slack fire, we toasted our feet and hands in an effort to recover. The result of this of course was winter-long chilblains. I'm not sure if chilblains were a widespread problem among my peers; we never talked about it. We achieved temporary relief from this affliction by application of an ointment which had the fantastic name of Snowfire. If I close my eyes I can still remember the intoxicating smell of this wonderful stuff while squeezing it from the large tube to give an almost instant if temporary relief. It had a peculiar smell, one that got right up your nose. On one hand it reminded me of the whiff of tarmacadam that took your breath away when passing road repairs, but with a faint hint of lemon. It also was reminded me of the smell that came from a doctor's surgery It was simultaneously heaven and hell. Despite the constant use of this wonderful stuff, I eventually realised that the only real relief from this ailment was the warmer weather of spring and summer.

Soon after our first day we were introduced to Mr Poyntz, the minister, also always called Sir. I was also familiar with him and his wife. Mrs Poyntz looked a little like the English Queen Mother. She seemed a lonely woman who smiled a lot as if trying to convince her husband's parishioners that she really did understand them and that her husband meant well.

Mr Poyntz was a huge man with wavy white hair and a posh English accent. He was like someone from a film: the ones set in England during the war when everyone spoke with a strange accent and always dressed for dinner.

Despite this kindly image, everyone was terrified of him. As well as going on about the bible, psalms, prayers, hymns and commandments, he often rambled on about his times at school. I was never too sure whether he went to school in Ireland or England. The posh accent pointed towards England.

'The poor are our grief,' Mr Poyntz said frequently, but he didn't look like he knew what poor was. It was obvious to all that it was a long time indeed since he'd missed a meal, with ample flesh hanging over his dog collar to attest to this.

During that first visit to the school, he pulled up a chair in front of the class and spoke to us. He had a mesmerising tone of voice and held the attention of the entire room, while he examined at length his clasped fingers and spoke about the subject to hand. He continually made churches and steeples with his hands and fingers. He told us of the things we needed to learn: the catechism, the Lord's Prayer, the creed, the bible. It seemed a long list.

We had a bible in our house and it was very big and full of tiny print. I remember thinking 'That'll take a long time.' As if to confirm what I was thinking, Mr Poyntz mentioned that we should attend Sunday school each week in the parish hall to help us learn these important lessons. Also he planned to have classes each week in school. The visits of Mr Poyntz over the year were to prepare us for oral exams in May on our knowledge of the scriptures. He got ministers from nearby parishes to help him ask the questions. These examinations were also held in our parish hall.

He explained there were four different grades of test for four different groups of kids: Junior Juniors, Senior Juniors, Junior Seniors and Senior Seniors. It took me some time to understand the groupings. He plodded on.

Within these groups you could get a First Class pass or a Second Class pass. Nearly everyone in the school got a First Class pass. The prizes usually were a book with an inscription on it. I think they hoped that you might ask for a bible or a prayer book. If you paid the price difference, you could ask for a dearer book. Our parents encouraged us to keep within the price range. The prizes were presented at a games and picnic day at the end of the school year in June on the soccer field in Lamberton.

Not all of the kids in the school went to our church. Some attended the numerous little churches dotted around Arklow. Some were Methodists, some Presbyterians and others Baptists. Occasionally ministers from these churches accompanied Mr Poyntz to help with his weekly visits. Sometimes they invited us to attend events in their particular church. Mam warned me against visiting the Baptist church. 'I don't want anything to do with those Dippers,' she said mysteriously.

Other times we had guest speakers from the foreign missions. Lean men, emboldened by some happy reveal, bright-faced and eternally happy with some inner goodness. You could tell they were holy from the sheen on their faces. And smiling, forever smiling. Wearing shirts with cuffs that were noticeably frayed and suits with unravelling borders which we chose to ignore. Representing organisations called the Lantern or Lead Kindly Light, they invited us to slide shows in the parish hall where refreshments were provided, all for a small admission charge. Donations were gratefully accepted on behalf of lepers and starving people in Africa. Their demeanour was saintly; they constantly agreed with everyone and everything. They recounted long-waged wars against the heathens in Africa and informed us that through their endeavours, many were saved from eternal damnation.

The emphasis on our religious education predominantly centred on the Old Testament. I became familiar with the dead of Jericho, David and Goliath and the flight from Egypt. The parables were very popular. We learned about plagues and locusts. We were told about the plight of lepers and somehow understood the missionaries' messages. Mam however did not, and missionaries were summarily put in the same category as Dippers.

Mr Smythe sometimes joined Mr Poyntz at the scripture lessons. They were both big men and somehow they indicated the big world which we were edging towards. They represented the power adults had over children, not so much to harm them with this power, but rather to control their aspirations and hopes.

Over time our relationship with Mr Smythe becomes less one of dread, more one of snickering disrespect. Among ourselves we called him 'Jammy Mr Sammy' after a comic character, for conveniently we learned that his first name was Samuel. The earlier threat of six of the best dissipated into a rarity. Punishment came to those who did nothing rather than those who did their work badly. He did however have a tendency to knock on kids' heads with his knuckles as if trying to open some secret doorway to their brains.

Eventually the experience of going to school complemented our parallel lives. I formed friendships that were totally apart from the relationships in my day-to-day life in the Fishery. I knew kids that no one else in the neighbourhood knew. The surprising thing to me was that they were all normal kids. In spite of living quite isolated lives on remote farms in the surrounding Wicklow Hills, they liked and did similar things to me. They got the same comics, collected the same toys as town kids. They were perhaps a little more religious than us though; they had no distractions on Sundays.

Of course they did differ in many other ways. The kids down the Fishery were mostly called Seamus and Sean, Mary and Cathleen. Byrnes and O'Neills abounded. In Carysfort I came up against kids with more exotic names like Roy, Russell and Claude, Daphne, and Felicity, Isobel and Laura. The surnames of Pringle, Flyte, Ross, Blennerhasset and Hollingsworth together with a few hyphenated names like Hope-Kearon and Tackaberry-Kearon completed the picture of my alternative world. Even to speak of these names to my Fishery friends invoked laughter and merriment.

Friendships were built and discarded. Many lasted the duration of Primary school, despite our seeing each other only during term time. Most friendships ended, even the most enduring, the day I finished in Carysfort.

One such friend was Jack. He was as tough as an ear of corn with short blond hair the colour of the stubble left after harvest in his father's fields. A multitude of freckles lit up his face. Wise beyond our years, Jack professed to be able to drive a tractor and at times his father's car. I did not doubt this. The revelations just increased my admiration of this effusive boy. Jack's friendship came with added advantages. He had loads of other siblings, older and younger. Jack also had a bevy of sisters, all very pretty and protective. You were safe being Jack's friend.

Another was a big lad called Stephen, but we knew him affectionately as Bongo. We got to know Bongo as the arch schemer, forever concocting plans and campaigns to attack, banish and defeat other gangs in the school. In the dusty bleak playground, big children, by their size, were initially seen as much smarter than the small kids looking up at them in wonderment. He was certainly that.

Bongo commanded attention. He sported a wondrous mane of red hair, which seemed to have a mind of its own. He had a glorious cheekiness and an engaging manner when incubating one of his plans. Eventually when he divulged these plans, his face lit up, his voice dropped. His bright red hair flopped this way and that as if to accentuate the plans and details commanded.

Bongo was always reading Commando war comics, always lobbing make-believe hand grenades into doorways and windows. I swear to god if ever he laid his hands on a real hand grenade he would surely have used it on Jammy Mr Sammy.

He took to wearing a military gasmask to school. With his hair and height, it gave him a faintly bearlike appearance. Mr Smythe had to put a stop to it though. Younger kids were too terrified to come to school.

Terms like tracer bullets, Bren guns, Sten guns and silencers peppered his vocabulary. He always had walkie-talkies close by – the bean can and string variety. With Bongo's company, there was always a faint whiff of danger and cordite.

One Saturday afternoon, I decided to call for him at his house on the Coolgreaney road. I spotted him in his front garden crawling toward the fence. People were walking by on the road. Bongo had covered himself with branches and leaves in an attempt to camouflage himself. He loved camouflage. He was wearing a balaclava which he had covered in leaves and grass. As he crawled through this very overgrown garden towards the fence He raised himself up and with a peashooter fired off some haw berries at people passing by. He then immediately went low and disappeared into the tall grass. It was wonderful but I got out of there quickish. This was dangerous stuff...

Bongo lived a sort of Huckleberry Finn life. Rafts and boats featured heavily in his adventures. He talked frequently about building a raft to go to an island in a small pond near the Brow. I joined this particular adventure until it was scuppered by Mam because of complaints from the farmer who owned the land around the pond.

Nobody knew what they wanted to be when they grew up but all of us were convinced Bongo would end up in some sort of a uniform, possibly sporting a rifle and bearskin. I hope he did. A pity we lost touch.

I learned the alphabet and read well before I started school. That didn't provide any great advantage, as everyone in the babies' class was assumed to know nothing. However knowing anything at all put you firmly outside the pale. I learned to think about what a teacher was saying and whether an answer was required or advisable. I learned not to let my thoughts venture forth without some consideration.

Who taught me to read? I suspect the blame can't be attributed to my father. He was always too busy, too tired, sleeping it off or just not present. It was definitely down to Mam. Not that she indulged herself with the classics or anything like that. She was a Mills and Boon fan. You could rent them in small libraries in local grocery stores all over the neighbourhood. She was also keen on women's magazines; all the better if they had pictures of what Prince Charles was wearing. She got the idea for my school cap from one of these magazines. Once I saw a picture of Charles wearing a red kilt, and for weeks I feared the worst. It was reassuring that many of the boys around me were wearing fair isle pullovers of the kind he wore.

In Junior school, twice a week, just after lunch, we had sewing and knitting classes. Many woollen squares were produced; calico with button holes were lovingly worked on. The girls loved it, the boys less so but there was nothing else for us to do and no one to watch over us. This was perhaps our greatest and darkest secret in Carysfort; it was never mentioned outside the school walls. Even John, who had presumably suffered the same fate, was uncharacteristically reticent except for an occasional guffaw and rolling of the eyes.

So I learned to knit and sew. Embroidery was mentioned. I told Dad. 'Embroidery,' he said mysteriously, 'that'll come in handy in later life.'

6

'O mio babbino caro'

It is the way of the world; poor people do indeed work for rich people. In the early 1950s, it could also be reasonably said that poor Protestants invariably were employed by rich Protestants. My father worked for Kevin Kearon Ltd as a carpenter in their joinery workshop. When I was younger, I thought carpenters painted cars; what did I know?

Kearons owned a hardware shop with a small engineering workshop on the same site. Across the Bridge in Ferrybank they owned a grocery shop. They were also shipwrights and owners of several tramp steamers that plied a trade between Ireland and the continent. All of these activities put the Kearons in the rich Protestant category.

The yard and workshop where Dad earned his living was about a hundred yards from our house, on the way down towards the dock. This workplace played a big part in our lives. Dad had his own key and was allowed to go back at night and work overtime or work on jobs he took on privately. Because he had a key, he also was on-call for the Yard. Often we'd have people knocking at our door to get Dad to open up so they could collect completed work after hours. In this yard you could buy coal, turf, peat briquettes and paraffin oil. You could also sell scrap iron there. This was an easy way to make a bit of money as there was so much iron about from people getting rid of their old ranges in favour of the modern electric ones. Because Dad worked in the Yard, he didn't like me getting involved with scrap.

Although Dad worked for Kevin Kearon, the workshop was known locally as Jack Kenny's Yard. Jack was the foreman and also worked for

Kearons along with his son Pete. Jack was a kindly old gent whose pipe-smoking had taken over his entire face with many brown and red blotches, reminiscent of one of Rembrandt's later self-portraits. George Mates worked alongside Dad. Dad always introduced George as 'my accomplice.'

The workshop itself was a big corrugated-iron-covered building, cold in the winter and stifling hot in the summer. It was the most interesting part of the Yard and housed all the electric saws, drills and planes that Dad used for his work. Calendars advertising wood glue or paint brushes, decorated with ladies in swimming costumes, hung on nails here and there among ancient and rarely used tools.

Noise was a constant; from the most delicate sounds like the hum and whirr of the band saw and wood drills to the raucous drone of the rotary planning machine. In the lulls, Dad or George might start singing. Dad had quite a repertoire, but George seemed eternally obsessed by what was *Behind the Green Door*. It was a decent place to work; whether George or Dad were wrestling with machinery, or working on windows or doors, the atmosphere always was convivial, jokey and positive.

If the workshop was noisy and sometimes frenetic during work hours, in the evening, after tea, it was quiet and tranquil; the machines lay dormant, expectant and still. Hand tools lay abandoned where they were left when the work bell signalled the end of the day. As the sun set, the fluttering of pigeons returning to roost among the substantial rafters above broke the eerie silence

From an early age, I spent a lot of time in the workshop with Dad. If Mam went to the pictures with Connie or one of her friends, I'd spend the evening with Dad down in the Yard. I learned a lot and knew all the tools, where to get them and what they were used for. I had my own jobs such as mixing the Cascomite wood glue and waterproofing the joints before Dad assembled windows or doors. I'm sure my understanding of sums and figures had its foundation in this experience.

When helping, I was expected to follow him around and be available to run any errand or provide any help that was necessary. After I'd tagged along with him for so many years, he somehow treated me as someone who should be able to predict what he needed next, like one of his apprentices. I needed to keep alert to what he was doing: watching where he left his pencil or ruler, always to be ready to hand him the hammer or chisel as he needed it, or to provide him with a steady stream of nails. If I was slow or wasn't around, his impatience showed quickly. He could be a little unforgiving. He was however enthusiastic, optimistic and completely confident in his ability to do his job.

Each work area had its own trademark aromas; I remember them still. The sharp acrid smell of the metal work area I found the least attractive. The heady mixture of oil, abrasives, lubricants and metal dust was a challenge to my young nose. I much preferred the medical-like smells of the fine sawdust underneath the planer, the dainty, almost girl-like wood curls around the drill and the damp forest smells around the huge saws used for cutting entire trees.

Dad always seemed to have lots of work, and always with plenty of people watching him do it. He used to say, 'An artist will always attract an audience.' Men constantly hung around the entrance to his workshop, like anglers who have put away their rods; awkwardly, not really knowing what to do next. They stamped their feet and rubbed their hands in cold weather and lingered in the shade on summer days, while maintaining an intense interest in what he was doing; always willing to give Dad a hand when required or even sometimes to risk advice. Every morning, these men appeared. It was their routine, almost part of an accepted ritual, spreading out and forming a respectable perimeter around Dad's work endeavours.

For a man who displayed little patience at home with anything or anybody, my father was completely the opposite at work. He helped everyone in the workshop and always made time to advise anyone passing through. You could sense the admiration people had for him, and although he wasn't the boss, everyone came to him for help with their problems. I even got to understand Mam's 'street angel' quip.

In a single day he might deal with people as far apart as the local Protestant minister or nuns from the convent. He might just as easily have to deal with tinkers.

Tinkers' caravans were big business for the Yard. Dad built the caravans from the ground up, as he liked to describe it. This meant that he could build every part of the caravan: the wheels, the decorative windows and doors, the curved roof covered with the distinctive green canvas. He took great pride in this work and even arranged to have the caravans painted in the familiar bright colours. 'Carpenters, like artists, are born, not made,' he often said, adding: 'There aren't many left who can do this work.'

After leaving Primary school, Dad had served his time as a carpenter – he didn't like being called a joiner – and he had the reputation of being very good at his trade. He was in great demand for fixing antiques and other delicate work. He had a steady stream of private clients, including numerous old ladies who called on his skill when antiques were damaged and needed repairing.

Tinkers came from all over the country to get Dad to build their caravans. It was fascinating to see him talk and deal with them. Sometimes it was difficult to understand what they were saying, and they swore a lot. One day when my father was speaking to tinkers, I heard him use a curse word. I thought swearing was something only tinkers did, but it seemed to be all right to swear in their company. It seemed such a necessary part of the conversation. I rarely saw them with their wives, but when I did see any, like nuns, they seemed to travel in a bunch.

If Dad asked them anything, they had an incomprehensible conversation among themselves before replying. I wondered what they were discussing – still do. They lived life lightly, despite hardship, and the mystery of their lives was intriguing

Tinkers were very important customers and good payers. They counted out the cash on the workbench and always left lucky money for Dad on top of what the job cost.

Dad was a short man and not very broad, but his hands were large and powerful. Bigger men commented on his strength and he in turn was proud of these comments. He drank too much beer and smoked too many cigarettes and spent too much time sleeping off the effects. In pubs he was renowned for witty if somewhat barbed comments. I often heard him declare, 'I hate small men!'

In his younger years, he had spent three long years in hospital fighting tuberculosis. He never spoke much about it; neither did Mam. Bad food, bad lodgings, and bad health: he blamed them all. But then he wasn't the only one in Ireland to catch this disease in the Forties. This small, insignificant town had its own sanatorium, as did many other small towns.

In Arklow, the TB hospital was a wooden building in a lovely setting, framed by a wooded hill and facing out into Arklow Bay and overlooking the North beach. It undoubtedly had plenty of cold fresh air. With its grounds surrounded by high fences and locked gates, the hospital was one of those buildings that you might pass by without even noticing. I don't think I ever realised that it was a hospital until my parents started discussing one night that it was going to be converted into a hotel.

Mam said, 'It was a sad place, that hospital.' I asked her what she meant.

'It was a TB hospital,' she said, 'a sanatorium.' And then almost as an afterthought she added, 'Your father spent three years there with TB.'

Up to that point, I had no idea that Dad had ever been sick, never mind spending three years in hospital. Three years seemed like a prison sentence.

'What was wrong with him?' I asked.

'Like I said, he had TB, and the only cure then was a long stay in hospital. It was very common, before you were born. Nowadays it can be cured easily with all those wonder drugs.'

I couldn't wait for Dad to get in from work. What Mam described was as impressive as climbing a mountain or walking across the frozen wastes pulling a wicker sledge behind. To me, what Dad had done was the same as escaping from a German concentration camp.

When he arrived, I blurted out something like: 'Tell me about the time you spent in hospital, Dad.'

'You might not like to hear about it,' he said quietly.

He moved into the scullery and began washing his hands at the sink. I could see him watching me through his shaving mirror, which he'd propped up against the egg cups on the shelf above the sink.

Eventually he said, 'Well it wasn't a bed of roses. The first three years were the worst.'

'Were there many in the hospital with you?'

'More went in than came out, and that's the truth,' he replied.

'And how long were you in there?'

'The best part of three years.'

'God, what did you do all the time?'

'For the first couple of months I read till I was sick of reading, and then I read some more. The Vincent De Paul people were very good for the books.'

While I was digesting this, he went on. 'We used to make rings and jewellery out of silver coins. You know the three-penny bits with the rabbits on. We used to get one of those and stick it on a bit of wood to hold it firm and the pick away the middle with a hat pin.'

'It must have taken a long time to do it that way. Why didn't you use sharp knife or a chisel or something sharp?'

He laughed. 'Oh we could have made those rings faster, any number of ways. I suppose we didn't want to finish the rings at all really. We just needed something to be getting on with. We needed something that would last. Remember we were doing nothing else all the time except sitting out in the open air, winter and summer, chatting among ourselves and with the nurses and nursing our spit mugs.'

'What?' I said.

'We were encouraged to spit up hocks. They gave us these special mugs to hock into so the nurses could see if we were spitting up blood.'

'Yuck,' I said. I don't know why but Mrs Jacobs' coffee cup sprang to mind.

He added: 'You don't know the half of it, young man. It became more a way of life than a cure, for as many years as it took. It was like being in prison. Some, a lot, didn't make it. They called me Ruxton the Indestructible. I saw a lot bigger than myself go down.' He finished the conversation declaring: 'They only honour the horizontal man, never the vertical.'

I must say I always liked the 'indestructible' bit. It had a ring to it. Ruxton the Indestructible – SuperHero.

He often planned big projects for the house, which usually caught Mam by surprise and immediately worrying if it was going to be completed. One summer during his holidays he announced that he was going to build a porch onto the front of our house. During the winter, the gales blew across the river from the sea, with our row of houses feeling the unchecked onslaught of whatever the elements threw at us. The porch was a grand idea to provide one more barrier between us and the weather.

My mother was delighted that he was 'doing the porch' as she described it. The prospect of having the first porch on the row appealed to her. She said something about keeping him out of the pubs for the fortnight, and I suspect this was part of the reason that she was happy. I didn't know what to think. Sometimes with Dad the talking ran ahead of the doing.

The morning before starting the work – I was volunteered to help – we were treated to a fried breakfast. I was expecting Dad to comment on it but he let it go, maybe saving it up for another occasion.

He obviously planned out what he was going to do to put up this porch, but as usual didn't speak to anyone in the house of his plans. He showed me a drawing of the porch and the day's work seemed a little clearer to me.

He produced four or five bolts from his jacket pocket saying that these were to hold the porch in place. He then produced a small bag of cement and another bag full of sand. Within a half an hour, he'd mixed the cement and laid the foundations, setting the bolts into the cement.

'What are we building it with?' I asked.

'Pitch pine,' he said. 'The best of pitch pine. Great for withstanding the rain and damp. And do you know where this pitch pine came from?" he said with a mysterious smile.

I had no idea and said so even though it was always best to venture some sort of reply or solution when he was in this type of humour. I shrugged my shoulders.

'Across the river,' he said.

I looked where he was pointing. On the other side of the river there was a small inlet called the Back Guts. A road ran over the entrance to this small backwater; boats could pass under it to gain access to a small mooring area behind. For years an old wooden bridge carried the traffic, but had recently been replaced by a stronger iron and concrete one, to carry the heavier vehicles associated with the new fertilizer factory.

'They were going to throw all the wood beams away,' he said. 'The eejits didn't know what they were dealing with... The best of pitch pine,' he repeated. 'I got one of the council lorry drivers to bring a couple of beams down to the workshop ages ago. I've been cutting and preparing the beams for weeks now.'

He was obviously enjoying the story and especially the secretive part. 'I got some lovely planks, and tongued and grooved them. The door and window will have three panes each and have semi-circular tops. I've also started a gate with a curved top to match the door.'

He was in full flow. 'I've ordered glass special that I've seen in the catalogue. I got the girl in the shop to order it. It hasn't arrived yet, but hopefully it will be here before the holiday is over.'

He slowed down this excited speech, and got serious. 'The wood,' he said, 'it's beautiful pitch pine. You know, they were going to throw it away or burn it. It would have been criminal. But now the best part of it is that it's exactly facing where it was situated all these years.'

He looked over the rim of his glasses and said, 'Things were made to go round, you know. With all the strangers coming into the town and all the changes happening, we should start to look after what we have and who we have.'

He left it there. We were just about finished, he told me. 'We'll go down to the workshop and you can carry some of the wood up to the house for me.'

He never mentioned where he got the wood again or the reason behind using it on the porch, but I know that he valued what he was doing as a gesture against the changes occurring in the town and on our very doorstep.

7

'In a pew losing my religion'

While attending Carysfort I had to participate in other parish activities which complimented my new existence and contributed immensely to an awkwardness that grew relentlessly over the years. The most important of these was going to church and going to Sunday school. There seemed no way out but fortunately my older cousins were there to lead me gratefully astray.

Algy and John were in their final years in Carysfort, and had reached the stage where church and Sunday school had become a 'drag' as they called it. Algy in particular embraced wholeheartedly the prospect of soon becoming a teenager and rebelled against anything to do with the church, with a cool passion. In this drag department, I was an early bloomer.

If I set off with them, to church in particular, it was touch and go if I reached my destination. The distractions were many for the uncommitted soul on the rocky road to St Saviour's.

On the occasions after Mr Poyntz or Mr Smythe had mentioned our non-attendance, my father accompanied us on our walk. Going to church with any parent was a miserable event. Why did adults make out that church and the whole Sunday routine were joyful? I remember the horrendous and sometimes hilarious hurry of Sundays. Being dragged to church, forever late; always your fault, held by the hand, stumble running, always late, always trying to catch up, but still late, always late.

As churches went, however, St Saviour's wasn't that bad. It was bright and uncluttered. The interior was dominated by a dozen or so large columns of a bright white stone that had weathered well down through the years. It was almost spotlessly clean: more a testament to lack of use than anything else. The pillars tended to block the view if anything interesting was happening, but equally could give you some relief from the accusing stare of the minister during the sermon.

If the Catholic church was a frumpy grumpy pantomime dame, then St. Saviour's was a young lithe prima ballerina, *en pointe*, with arms stretching majestically upwards to heaven and happiness. Sprite-like, ethereal and urging the believers ever upwards; accompanied by the sound of joyous bells and surrounded by lush trees and foliage, the clusters of daffodils, bluebells and primroses waving in the shade as we trudged to our destination.

An impressive grassy verge with trees framed a grey crunchy gravel drive to the entrance of the church. This entrance had huge double doors that were opened on special occasions such as weddings and funerals. Just inside was a baptismal font of Notre Dame proportions. As these formidable doors were almost always firmly locked, parishioners normally used the side entrance.

Any newcomer attending Sunday service immediately noticed the bells. Bells always evoked a delicious response in churchgoers. I noticed bells were always used in old English films to let people know that all was well in the world and conjure a time long since disappeared. Close up these bells could be harsh on the eardrums but outside wafting across rooftops and the misty marshes below, they signalled that the day was going well.

The bell-ringing was a performance of sometimes heroic proportions. It began with a single note, a marker as it were. But this was no solitary tinker bell; this was no limp Angelus, summoning the hordes to confession and to renew their faith. This began a sweet hymn to praise and demonstrate the talents of the bell ringers in the belfry and their honed, practised skills. Other bells joined until an orchestration of sorts with all bells swinging. These were rock 'n' roll bells, a celebration of human endeavour and nothing at all to do with religion.

St Saviour's people were proud of their bells. They had a club dedicated to propagating the skills needed to achieve perfection. They recruited school kids to get them interested early. They had social and dance events for the bell ringers. Could anyone fail to pull at a bell ringer's dance? It often crossed my mind?

The belfry was a small room fifty-two steps up the tower. Its entrance was through a heavy wooden door in the cloakroom at the back of the church. It had benches along the wall to accommodate bell ringers and audience. I was there many times. There was a grand view of Arklow through the small windows directly under the four clock faces. The club encouraged youngsters to look around; their motives were entirely ulterior.

Along the walls of the church at intervals were brass commemorative plaques: long-forgotten donations from people with very English names. There was more than a hint of empire about the place. I'm sure there was a Union Jack here at some stage, but it had long since disappeared; the pennants and brocades had been banished to a secret part of the church. Occasionally you noticed a brass plate on a wall in some dark corner, proclaiming sympathy for some Smithers-Jones who died for king and country on some foreign field.

The church remained largely unchanged in my childhood except for one long rubber mat that ran the length of the main aisle. It was there to capture the rain from pious wet shoes and it added an extra bounce in the step, like floating on clouds towards the business end of the church... This plus the serenade by the bells and the deep serious organ seemed to encourage parishioners to their appointed seats. If the bells were entertainment, the organ was authority. Its voice was a command. The organ seemed to rise to meet the bells, then dropped away in a moment's silence before the minister rose to his feet and declared, 'Let us pray.'

My mother once told me the particular smell of the church was of course frankincense and myrrh, to be sure. Certainly the mix of dust, polish and old prayer and hymn books suggested something ancient, something unsettling. On summer days the sun shining through the stained glass windows picked out this smell in the form of magical colourful molecules swirling in the heavy air – our very own transubstantiation, to be sure.

Families had their own pews, chosen by whim and perpetuated by habit. My family's was toward the back, slightly more than midway from the altar. Dad often referred to it as 'the sinners section.' However, when I went to church alone with my cousins, we sat in the last pew nearest the side door. Last in first out was the plan.

The regulars were ruddy red-necked men struggling with unfamiliar suits and starched tight shirts, accompanied by pale-faced women in their best frocks or suits – pew after pew of them. Good tweeds abounded. These were people who bought clothes for the long haul. Frayed edges were discreetly sewn and mended. Shoes shone at a level and standard only achieved by those who did it themselves for themselves.

What they wore very often gave some indication of what they achieved in life. Some wore lighter-coloured suits indicating careers in warmer climes. Several wore nautical-styled blazers. Many women wore watches pinned to their lapels, as nurses might.

Among them were the organisers of church events, the small ladies who oversaw these smug occasions like they owned the church, giving the impression that we children had no place here. They sat in a line with colourless hats and fixed stares that said we were interlopers to be barely tolerated. At Christmas and Harvest Home, these busy ladies decorated the church with more food on display than we saw all year. They were always called Miss – Miss this and Miss that – when primarily I suspect they missed love most of all.

The sermon came towards the end of the service. As the minister adjusted himself and walked slowly towards the pulpit, we knew we were on the home stretch. But we still had to endure the sermon itself. Obedient silence reigned as the minister advised, threatened and cajoled the congregation on lofty religious ideals, behaviours and conundrums. Then someone would have a bout of coughing or would knock over their walking stick. After that the jury's verdict would be that the minister had lost the moment and should cease the performance.

Last came the collection. This was no retiring collection. During the last hymn, a brass plate, supremely polished, was passed under everyone's nose for their contribution. To us it seemed like money ill-spent.

'Metal washers,' whispered John as the plate neared. 'They sound like money.'

'D'you have any then?' He didn't.

'Just rattle the money on the plate,' said Algy. 'Or pretend to put in a shilling and take sixpence change.'

'D'you have a shilling?' She didn't.

John frowned. 'Anyway, they watch like hawks. They pretend they don't but they do. We'd never get away with it.'

It was the same theme and variation every week. The plate arrived and swallowed up our meagre offerings. It always did.

At an early age, I decided Sundays and the whole experience of service and sermon were not worth the breath it takes. Tedium became a sort of recreation, a way of life. We were martyrs to monotony. Time did not just pass; the hours just seemed to decay and leak into each other.

It was difficult to pinpoint where exactly the church and religion figured in our lives. It was always present, in the background like a dark shadow. The church had a huge influence where schooling and marriage were concerned, but in fact we treated religion with ridicule and humour. I'm sure BBC radio programmes help developed this attitude; it certainly rubbed off on me.

The church became an entertainment of a sort, with eccentric characters, funny rituals, comic incidents and frustrating rules. I think we got more fun from the crazy incidents that happened in this church than in any other part of our lives. In some way they mirrored my favourite programmes on the radio.

On Sunday afternoon, always in the distance, somewhere and everywhere, a manic Mícheál Ó hEithir could be heard on a radio commentating on some GAA match. His screeching voice, rising and falling with the run of play, formed a familiar anthem for our boredom. His commentary was interjected now and again with something incomprehensible in Gaeilge. Not everyone understood these '*cúpla focail*', but of course this was never acknowledged.

I never listened to Gaelic games on the radio in our house, a decision that probably saved my sanity. Radio on Sunday for us consisted of *Two Way Family Favourites, Beyond Our Ken, The Navy Lark* and latterly *Pick of the Pops*.

It was always dinner, then tea, then the weather forecast. I'm not sure why in our house everyone listened to the weather forecast, despite our having no connection with the sea. I became familiar with the peculiarly named sea areas, to such an extent that many years later I immediately got the joke in the film *Kes*. Perhaps it was a family thing but it seemed we were threatened by the weather all of the time. We were landlubbers, frightened and in awe of the sea. Foghorns and lifeboat rockets aroused a sense of dread in us.

My friendship with Jack and Bongo also spilled over into activities outside school but always very much tied up to the parish. We were all members of the Life Boys or Boys' Brigade. This was a club for Protestant kids and to some extent was an extension of Sunday school. The uniform was reminiscent of the Royal Navy topped with a cute flat sailor's hat.

When I started attending the Life Boys with John, it was run by a man called Mr Bury. He was very old and posh with a distinct English accent. There was more than a faint whiff of the Army about him and he treated the Life Boys as his command. He occasionally wore a black beret with some kind of winged badge on it. We met at the KB hall in Ferrybank and did a lot of saluting and marching: up and down, criss-crossing and doing complex movements. We learned to stand to attention at an early stage. We mastered that peculiar skip that got you back in step. The only thing missing was someone carrying a flag, but Mr Bury always managed to produce one at the yearly jamboree.

When we practised marching, Mr Bury dug out from somewhere in the bowels of the KB a hamper full of wooden sticks that vaguely resembled rifles. At some time years earlier, they had been painted white, but like everything associated with the KB, they had aged badly. However they were a popular accessory, and we used them in all sorts of mock hand-to-hand combat.

Mr Bury ran the Life Boys as if we were living in England in the 1950s. He was a complicated and controlling man. I think he hated children. He was very severe with us, to such an extent we were more afraid of him than Mr Smythe.

The KB Hall was a tumble-down shack of a place, faintly reminiscent of a railway carriage, and looked every inch the dilapidated cricket pavilion that it was. Felt-covered, tarred and precariously raised off the ground on stilts, it had seen better days. When the troop stood to attention, we could feel the hall wobble.

Inside the KB was the detritus of long-forgotten cricket games and former Life Boy glories. Keepers' pads and assorted sports equipment lay scattered hither and thither as if left by someone who had been searching for something. The walls displayed faded photographs in dusty frames: past teams, past memories, now irrelevant, forgotten and unwanted. Mr Smythe featured in one photo. It was a picture of a cricket team he had started, with a group of moustachioed gentlemen with similarly sounding Protestant names. 'Arklow Cricket Club rises from the Ashes', read the inscription.

In the fine weather, Mr Bury assembled everyone on the field in front of the KB Hall and tried to interest us in playing cricket. It goes without saying that most of us, except the few who were at boarding school, hadn't the foggiest about cricket or its rules. Everyone just wanted to play rounders. Occasionally we erected ancient canvas tents and sat around a pretend campfire singing songs.

It all improved when Mr Bury retired and his second-in-command, Roy Keegan, took over. Roy worked in the pottery and was an active member of badminton, bell-ringing and general upkeep of the parish. He and Dad were two of those people who the minister could call on for repairing, collecting and organising. They kept things ticking over in the parish with little or no credit.

Compared with Mr Bury, Roy was a fairly likeable man. He was also a bit more modern than Mr Bury, and on his own was able to provide the games and activities that appealed to the entire troop. Once a year we all went on a bus to the Mansion House in Dublin for a national Life Boy jamboree. We'd get the chance to show off our marching and drilling skills and end up the night singing with all the other troops. Parents loved coming along to this show.

The Life Boys had their own songbook, which contained a mixture of religious songs and old favourites like *Ten Green Bottles*. The one we always seemed to be singing was *A Life on the Ocean Wave*, which really was quite strange. As long as I was in the Life Boys, we dressed like little Royal Navy sailors, sang seafaring songs, learned to tie sailors' knots, yet I never set foot on a boat. But I never forgot the words to that song, so I guess that's a win of sorts.

When I got to the Boys Brigade, meetings were in the Marlborough Hall, which was just as well, as the KB was almost derelict. The Marlborough was an impressive building with a high vaulted roof sweeping down to splendid windows. Inside it had the appearance of a place built for grandiose schemes and events, but never achieved its potential. The Marlborough Hall was next door to Mr Smythe's house and almost joined to it by a peculiar raised room jutting out from the master's house, almost forming a bridge to the hall.

The word I most associated with the Marlborough Hall was 'dwindling'. It was home to a dwindling coterie of clubs and endeavours; a dwindling badminton club, a dwindling Life Boys group, a dwindling theatre group... Its most popular activities, attendance-wise, were the yearly Christmas bazaar and jumble sale. Unsurprisingly all denominations were welcome.

The Dramatic Arts Society in the Marlborough Hall mirrored the Marian Arts Society in the Catholic community and was also immensely popular. They performed fund-raising shows each year, with sometimes a play and sometimes a series of sketches and musical turns. After awhile I noticed there was an element of repetition in the sketches, but nobody seemed to mind.

The Dramatic Arts Society attracted a peculiar bunch of people. They called each other 'darling!' in a particularly dramatic way, as you'd perhaps expect. At one time it was run by a lady who Connie addressed as 'Cousin Cosy', due to some family connection. This woman looked like the film star Margaret Rutherford and spoke like her too, which was exciting. She had been a founding member of the National Movement for the Abolition of Theatre Queues in The Civilised World. I'm not sure this meant very much in the Marlborough Hall though.

The hall itself was a huge building. As you entered the main door, to your left was a stage; to the right was a function room running the width of the hall. The stage seemed a proper stage with steps on both sides so actors could 'Enter, stage right', and 'Exit, stage left'. Underneath the stage, the props and detritus of past productions gathered dust.

They held the badminton in the main hall and the table tennis and beetle drives in the adjoining room at the back. Presumably the architects had badminton in mind when they designed the high roof with its criss-crossing beams and rafters and black metal stays. They couldn't have been thinking about cleaning it, so the remnants of balloons and party stuff that people had thrown up there stayed put.

A man called Reeves decorated the stage. His daughter, Frances, was in Sixth Class with me. Mr Reeves had come to Arklow from England and started a factory that supplied shops and supermarkets with pre-packed vegetables and fruit. People said his idea was ahead of its time.

Above the curtains on the stage was a huge blue partition all the way up to the roof, which sort of boxed in the stage from the rest of the hall. Mr Reeves was a bit of an artist and painted two masks on the partition before it went up. They were like the masks you often saw during the credits at the end of a film: one laughing and one crying. Whatever was going on in the hall, 'Sock and Buskin' stared down as if commenting on the state of affairs below.

8

'Everybody needs good neighbours'

In spite of all those religious activities impacting on our day-to-day lives, we were a close-knit and friendly community. Protestants and Catholics rubbed along well, sharing best crockery, tea and sugar when the respective clergy paid a visit, sharing bed linen when unexpected visitors arrived, and sharing food when the need arose.

Our next door neighbours were the MacKays. Bill and Maggie had lived beside us for as long as I could remember. Bill was from Glasgow. Maggie originally came from Arklow and had a lot of relatives there. She'd married Bill in England during the war.

They'd lived for a while in Glasgow and moved to Mitcham in Surrey for a few years, before finally buying the house next to us. Two of their grown children, Billy and Sheila, came with them. Billy quickly got on in Avoca mines. He bought himself a scooter to get to work. It caused great commotion on the road, as Maggie insisted that Billy parked the scooter in her hallway. To get it up the steps each evening took much pushing and shoving, usually with help from passing neighbours.

Sheila also had no difficulty finding work. She became a secretary in a company alongside where Dad worked. Sheila had lovely black hair and wore the brightest red lipstick that I'd ever seen on a girl. Soon she was walking out with a boy called Aiden from the top of the town.

The MacKays had another son called Kenneth in England who was a police detective. Kenneth was a big, big man with a beard who looked like an actor who might play the bobby on the beat in British films.

The MacKays were nice people, as all English people seemed to be. We got on well with them. When I was very young, I spent a lot of time in their house. I'm not sure whether they were babysitting me or if I was keeping them company. Either way, I really enjoyed it.

Maggie and Bill were great story-tellers and had a lengthy tale permanently on the go for me. Settling down in front of their fire, me on a small chair with Bill and Maggie in their armchairs, the continuing adventures of Anne Fennackapan unfolded. Anne seemed to spend an awful lot of time escaping from the clutches of the Maulacoons and the Fleurakeens who were intent on imprisoning the poor girl for some unclear reason. Over the months, Bill and Maggie introduced leprechauns and Darby O'Gill into their story. It seemed their characters had relocated to Ireland along with the MacKays. Anne was often chased down the quay to the dock. She bumped into pottery workers crossing the dock bridge as she leapt onto a fishing boat to escape. As the tension grew to a climax, Bill occasionally removed his false teeth with a deft hand, and at the crucial moment made one of his toothless funny faces, which had all three of us screaming.

When these stories dried up or when I was too terrified to listen, we'd play cards, or drink tea, or make tapers from old newspapers. It was an art and I became quite good at it. Many a cold winter's night we passed folding newspapers into the tapers that Bill and Maggie subsequently used to light their cigarettes or the gas cooker. She kept them at the ready in a jar by the door.

Bill was a great man for using old newspapers wherever he could. He had some sheets of newspaper hanging up in the toilet where the toilet roll should have been. Mam said English people developed the practice during the war when they had no proper toilet paper.

Billy and Sheila came and went as I spent time with their parents. I was quite interested in them as they were the oldest youngest people I knew, and they had lovely posh English accents. Bill and Maggie had Scottish accents. Sometimes I couldn't understand what they were talking about.

Billy was a great footballer and played Gaelic football and soccer equally well. Bill and Maggie took me several time to the GAA Dog

Track to watch him play. Soccer was his greatest love and when he transferred from the local team to Drumcondra, he became the most famous athlete – alongside Ronnie Delaney – to hail from Arklow. In a game against Sligo, he kicked himself into the record books and into our hearts.

Bill and Maggie were like chalk and cheese at football games. Bill would make no comment, no matter what happened, even if Billy were injured or fouled. Maggie on the other hand screamed and shouted, using the word 'Gorbels' a lot.

Sheila was friendly with a young nun whom Mam, Dad and I got to know as well. Sister Assumpta was a small pale girl with a tuft of red hair peeping out from her white head band. Her father was a farmer in the West of Ireland.

One day I arrived home and found the nun talking to Mam and Sheila in our hall. Mam said, 'Sister Assumpta's going away.'

'Fair enough,' I thought to myself.

When Mam didn't get the reaction from me that she expected she said, 'Sister Assumpta's going away to Africa for fifteen years.'

'You'll be in your twenties when she gets back,' Sheila added.

'Fifteen years,' I thought. 'That's her duration. Just like me. Stuck somewhere for what seemed like a hundred years.' I thought this was very sad and worrying. Sister Assumpta was not someone you would have immediately associated with missionary work in darkest Africa, as we called it then, yet off she went. We never heard from her again. Maybe she got converted by Africa.

Maggie and Bill eventually returned to England. I heard Mam saying that the social benefits and pensions they got in Ireland weren't a patch on what they could get in England. Their house went up for sale and gradually all the MacKays moved back to England. I never saw Bill or Maggie after they left Arklow, but Sheila and Aiden, who was by then her husband, came back for short visits. She always brought me a present – mostly Airfix models of planes and boats – but one time she brought me a stick-together model of Buckingham Palace and another time she brought me a Tommy gun.

A Dublin family called Martin bought MacKays' house. Billy Martin was an engineer with the Posts and Telegraphs and had been promoted and transferred to Arklow to take over the Engineering Department. His wife was called Marion.

The whole family arrived one Saturday morning with all their belongings in a huge dark blue van that looked like a shoe box on wheels. Dad told me it was a special van for transporting furniture and it was called a Pantechnicon. Pantechnicon! It was the loveliest word I'd ever heard. I kept repeating it over and over. With all the excitement of the new arrivals, I soon found myself running up and down the quay, arms outstretched like airplane wings, shouting 'Pantechnicon! Pantechnicon!' Soon I had a squadron of local kids doing the same. 'Pantechnicon! Pantechnicon!' we screamed. I held onto that word for days until one day it just seemed to vanish.

It was obvious when they arrived that they were a modern young couple. Billy had a brand new car that he washed every Saturday just like the English did. As soon as he moved in, he set about building a brick garage in their back yard, immediately putting to shame the half-finished rust-red tin shed Dad had started several years earlier. Billy was also a great gardener and after a month or so his work had put our garden to shame as well.

Marion made a lot of changes to modernise the house. Where Bill and Maggie had had dark gloomy colours, Marion painted all the rooms a kind of white and put up Venetian blinds. Mam and Dad said that Marion 'would never keep them yokes clean,' but I never saw the blinds dusty or dirty.

It turned out that Marion was a talented singer of opera and Gilbert and Sullivan. She soon joined the Marian Arts Society, the Catholic choral club that put on occasional shows in the Ormonde Ballroom and sung on special occasions in the Catholic Church. She was such a good singer that she became their lead female voice, much to the annoyance of some of the local ladies.

Marion had a knack for making friends. She was soon inviting her singing acquaintances around for 'coffee mornings'. She invited Mam and our other neighbour, Kitty, to the first one, but I think they felt a bit out of place among the younger more modern women, most of whom were newly married – and some even owned their own cars. Once was enough for Mam and Kitty.

Tupperware parties were another of Marion's new ideas. Mam and Kitty went to the first one. Mam bought a plastic drinking glass with a self-seal lip. 'This will be good for taking your drinks to school,' she told me. What she couldn't have known was that it gave the drink a nasty taste of plastic. It stayed in the cupboard for years, occasionally getting used for cleaning paint brushes and mixing wood glue. Mam admitted there wasn't much point in buying Tupperware to preserve food, as food never lasted that long in our house.

As their kids got older, the Martins became more and more like the television family I always thought they were, introducing new fashions and behaviour to the our somewhat humdrum lives. Fly fishing was one of these. Dad had always wanted to take it up but never seemed to have the time or confidence. Billy seemed to be an accomplished angler. Actually he seemed to be good at everything. He'd drive off early on Saturday or Sunday and stay away all day. When he returned, inevitably he shared the day's triumphs with us for the dinner next day.

Dad couldn't hide his interest. Billy must have noticed, because before long he invited Dad along for a day's fishing. Dad got a loan of a rod and the rest of the gear from Jack Kenny.

And so the Martins settled in beside us, changing our lives in minute, imperceptible ways with their new ideas and styles. They grew to become friends as well as neighbours. We exchanged gifts at Christmas, Mam helped out when the babies were born, Dad and Billy loaned each other tools. Billy didn't drink but despite that I think Dad thought well of him. The Martins got to know the rest of our family too and just as they affected our lives, our family dramas eventually spilt over into theirs and showed us their compassion and concern as neighbours.

On the other side of the Martins lived Ben and Kitty Coburn, who over the years were easily our closest and most dependable neighbours.

Ben and Kitty had a stack of kids: three girls and five boys. Ben worked in the pottery, in the clay end.

Birds of all sorts were his hobby and to some extent his life. He had a pigeon shed in his small back garden with about twenty residents that constantly perched on his roof and noisily took flight at random times. He was a leading member of the local Cage Bird Society, frequently winning prizes for best bullfinch or best linnet. Kitty was always in and out of our house, having a cup of tea when the kids went to school, or maintaining the weekly comic swap.

9

'Bells were ringing out for Christmas Time'

Christmas was an exciting but surprisingly stressful time. Festive season? More like restive season. It started weeks before the blessed event with Mam nagging Dad to do work around the house. To be honest, the nagging was a weekly drama. It just heightened in intensity as Christmas approached and the hated painting and papering grew in urgency. These were jobs that Dad started fine and well, but then proceeded with in fits and starts. The work dragged on, hours snatched here and there, with Dad more often than not opting for the distraction of overtime or a drink in the pub.

To further complicate my mother's ambitions for the house, this was the time of year when Dad was busiest with the parish dramatic arts society and church choir. My father thought of this pastime as helping the parish and providing money for the upkeep of the church and for charity but Mam harboured a different opinion. She viewed it as just another excuse to get out to the pubs. As with everything involving my father, there was some truth in both arguments.

The carol service was a big event in the church calendar. In preparation, the Mothers' Union, together with the good and the great of the parish, decorated the church handsomely. The centrepiece was a huge Christmas tree positioned just in front of the pulpit. This tree was always donated by one of the rich farmers or businessmen from the parish, who naturally got a mention from the pulpit.

During the service, all the primary school kids sat in pews allocated at the front of the congregation. At a point in the service, we all trooped to the tree and put presents under it for the needy children, in particular for Avoca Orphanage. The idea was for each child to give something of their own that they didn't want anymore. Mam didn't like the idea of giving something that was used or broken, so I always had a newly bought colouring book or water colours to give.

The choir had been practising for many months. Their renditions of all the favourite carols really made Christmas come alive, that is of course until Sally gave one of her performances. Sally had the voice of an angel. No one knew where she got it from. Most of the family hadn't got a note in their heads.

Her interest in singing all started quite gradually, singing her times-tables as she hopped and skipped her way to school. Soon she was singing songs she'd picked up off the radio.

Eventually this voice was noticed by Mrs Jacobs who chose her to sing a solo in the Christmas service. They practiced for weeks, sometimes next door to the school in Mrs Jacobs' house where, accompanied by Mrs Jacobs' daughter on piano, Sally perfected her delivery. We could hear her through the adjoining wall, the whole class going silent in wonderment.

On the night of the carol service, we trooped into the church a little earlier and a lot more enthusiastically than usual. Sally's performance was towards the end of the service; first we had to get through an awful lot of boring stuff. Everyone was impatient. Bobby in particular was fidgeting more than usual.

We thought Sally's time would never come, but eventually it did. A hush came over the congregation, interrupted by a deep bellow from the organ. Sally got the nod from the organist and walked to the front of the church. She was wearing a red Christmassy dress and looked a little like Hayley Mills in her youthful prime. She appeared to be walking on tippy toes, smiling confidently at the hushed audience.

Connie and Mam were in raptures, as was the whole family. They both cried, as women do at weddings, silver tracks of tears flowing down their cheeks. Sisters united in pride.

Sally sang *Silent Night* in that high voice we had become so accustomed to. Everyone in the Fishery had known about this for weeks. After the service began, all our Catholic neighbours squeezed into the back of the church to hear her sing. They self-consciously edged into vacant seats in a place they only visited for funerals or weddings.

There's a pure silence you only get in churches, and it surrounded Sally as she sang. No one even coughed. The song rang around the church with a strength that really shouldn't have come from this ten-year-old girl. When she finished, all the Catholics at the back clapped and cheered. This raised a few eyebrows among the congregation, but we didn't care. It was Sally's night and the Fishery's night.

Dad summed it up in his inimitable style. 'There wasn't a dry eye in the house that night.' We talked about it for years after and the story became a regular feature of quiet seasonal nights sitting around the fire.

The town traditionally made few preparations for Christmas. Occasionally a band played Christmas carols to passersby and received universal sympathy in the bitter weather. There was usually a tree with lights outside the courthouse which the elaborately decorated tree in St Saviour's put to shame. Individual shop owners in the Main Street made an effort with mangers and Christmas trees in their shops and windows but it never seemed sufficient.

One Christmas, however, Gorey – the nearest town to Arklow – put up lights the length of their Main Street. People from Arklow travelled there to gaze in wonderment at the colours and bedazzling array of blinking lights, yes blinking lights. This was surely how a town should celebrate the festive season.

The Gorey lights somehow shamed the council and Junior Chamber into stringing lights along our main street on a single cable zigzagging from the Fishery end to the top of the town. They stitched the sides of the street together in an almost psychedelic lace, adding vibrancy to the street and attracted other seasonal innovations, like the pipe band and a newly formed brass band competing for the attention of shoppers rushing by.

It was a big job to get these lights in place for the first year, but it was an easy job thereafter. The lights were in no way spectacular. They didn't blink, but nobody seemed to mind. They certainly added to the feeling that it was Christmas. They were left in place until the New Year and had a peculiar unsettling affect on me when the shops were shut and the street was deserted.

My parents were always short of money, so an occasion like Christmas called for precision planning. My mother joined a savings club each year run by a woman called Miss Murphy. She was a regular visitor to our house for as long as I could remember, but I never heard her called anything except Miss Murphy. She was one of those 'Misses' that seemed to abound in our community; an old Protestant woman with a catholic surname. The way she ran the club, any religion could join. She banked the savings each week and gave any interest to the Missions for Seamen, which of course was a popular choice in our seafaring community.

A week or two before Christmas, Miss Murphy visited all the club members with their money. From each she received as a present – a ten bob note or maybe a pound, which no one begrudged her. The club money was a lifesaver, and I suppose it was the only way that families like mine were likely to get through Christmas.

It also gave my mother the rare opportunity to spend money on simple luxuries that otherwise might not be affordable. The sight of my mother buying new saucepans or a mat for the fireplace or front door brought a sort of sad pleasure to the proceedings.

Nearly every shop let you buy presents by putting a deposit down and paying off by the week or month. Everything for Christmas was paid for this way, sometimes beginning as soon as I went back to school in September.

The one thing that was left to my father was the drinks. Dad usually left it till the last minute, having them delivered after closing time on Christmas Eve. As much as Dad liked drink, my mother hated it, so he paid for it himself or else it wasn't bought. Every year he managed to accomplish this single important task.

Equally miraculous, he used to finish the jobs in hand by Christmas Eve. He was always allowed out for a drink on Christmas Eve, but always came home early and relatively sober.

As I got older and allowed to stay up later, Christmas became even more exciting and a time to treasure. While Dad was up having a drink, Mam started the Christmas dinner, making the stuffing, boiling the ham. She dreaded dad coming home and falling through the door drunk. I can't ever remember him letting her down on this night, but it was always in him to do it. When he did arrive home, he did the jobs that were traditionally his. He liked cleaning the turkey and stuffing it.

Our neighbours went to midnight mass, which meant they didn't need to go on Christmas Day. On their way home from mass, many of them called in to our house for a Christmas drink, bringing the house come alive with talk and chatter. Staying up late showed me a different side to my parents, one I hadn't known before.

I had noticed my mother filling a cardboard box with groceries, tea, sugar and canned foods and the like on Christmas Eve. For years I asked who it was for and usually she said, 'It's for Santa of course.' Well the Santa story didn't last forever, and I eventually discovered the story behind the box of groceries.

By the time the neighbours had left after grabbing a quick drink and a round of Christmas wishes, it was around two o'clock in the morning. Dad went out to the front and opened the door, returning and leaving it open. 'He said he'd be here about two o'clock,' Dad said.

She replied, 'He'll come in his own time.'

There was a quiet rap on the door. I suddenly thought I had been perhaps wrong about Santa Claus all these years.

Dad said, 'Come in Peter, come in.'

Peter turned out to be Peter Kelly who lived in a small cottage behind Aiden Doyle's pub on the Brook. He did odd jobs, clearing hedges and digging ditches, but he didn't mix with people. I always had thought of him as odd or simply different. He had matted curly hair, a beard and a long coat tied up with a length of rope. In spite of this rough appearance he spoke very gently.

Dad offered him a drink, and he took a bottle of Guinness and a small whisky, He didn't sit down, taking his drink standing by the table. Mam and Peter were standing in front of the Christmas tree when she gave passed him the box she had prepared.

Listening to their conversation, it was obvious that this happened every Christmas –something of a tradition. I discovered that he'd worked with my mother in the clay end of the pottery before she got married. Peter left the job because of nerves and moved into the shack away from everyone.

He drank up and gathered up his Christmas box. In the box I spied a small cake and a pair of woollen socks that Mam knitted before Christmas.

Loud good nights and enthusiastic Happy Christmases were exchanged in the doorway. We watched him walk up the quay and disappear behind the shipyard. Stony faced, my father went inside.

My mother said, 'I've known Peter for years. We've been giving him a few things every year since you were born.'

Christmas day used to mean early church service and Holy Communion, but as I got older, I only went to church on Sundays, and as long as I went this one day there was no problem at home. Our Christmas visitors would start to arrive around twelve o'clock, which gave us time to get ready for them after exchanging presents, Dad usually got a jumper or socks for presents. I usually gave him a presentation box of Woodbine cigarettes, which had a seasonal picture of happy smiling smokers with very Christmassy jumpers on.

Christmas day and Good Friday were the two days in the year when Irish men had to survive without a trip to a public bar because they were all closed. It was of course a heavy burden for them all to bear. Arklow was no different; Arklow also felt the pain. On Christmas Eve, there were whispered discussions among groups of distraught men as to which pub might flaunt this pagan law. Back doors and side entrances were mentioned. 'Aiden's won't let us down... John Joes will see us all right...' were the sentiments of men obviously grasping at straws. Every year their hopes were dashed. Publicans caught open on this day faced heavy fines.

The alternate plans usually involved visiting a friend's or a neighbour's house, getting a drink there and then moving on to the next port of call, with the man of the house swelling their number.

The possibility of endless and unfettered drinking for the entirety of Christmas Day was a godsend to the men, but not to their wives

Christmas morning in our house could be a quiet, calm affair, with Mam and Dad getting on with the small chores that would lead to our Christmas dinner, all of us happy that we had got this far into Christmas without any major arguments or problems. The day was sure to liven up when there was a knock on the door

Regular visitors to our house were a trio of brothers who had grown up with Mam and Dad. They were the Bermingham brothers Jim, Jack and Tom. If there was a pecking order between them they were comfortable with it. They were fishermen and easily the most fashionable men that visited our house, dressed in sharp shiny suits with hats like the one I noticed Frank Sinatra wearing in one of Mam's magazines.

My parents welcomed these brothers into our house as close friends. They were also drinking partners of Uncle Billy who inevitably turned up with them. Their arrival transformed the apparent tranquility of the day as loud camaraderie and infectious boisterousness took over. Both my parents brightened up. Amid declarations of 'Happy Christmas' and 'Give us a kiss Sally', off came the coats and out came the drinks. Cigarettes were lit and glasses raised to all in the house.

I dreaded the inquiry 'What did Santa bring you this year for Christmas?' but by now had learned to deflect such questions with vague answers.

One Christmas, Jim the eldest brother noticed I was assembling an Airfix model of a German U-boat. The sight of the grey plastic spurred Jim to recount one of the strange maritime stories that occasionally floated to a berth in our house.

It seemed a First World War German submarine had come to grief off the coast of Arklow for want of local knowledge. 'You'll be knowing about the sand bar that stretches the whole length of Arklow Bay,' said Jim. I didn't but agreed with him. 'We call it the Arklow bar' – that's original, I thought – 'and it's taken many a ship, large and small.

'There's a narrow passage that those of us who sail from here know about – we call it the Squash,' he said. To negotiate through the bar, the helmsman aligned the spire of the Protestant church with the cross of the Catholic church – a most serendipitous arrangement of interdenominational cooperation.

'This U-boat was on a mission to bring weapons for the Irish nationalists. She was sailing blind – didn't know the tides or the position of the Squash – and she ploughed straight into the bar. All hands on board was drowned.'

As far as Jim knew, there was no attempt made by the lifeboat or others to save the souls on board simply because no one knew of their existence. Weeks later, at low tides, the submarine was spotted by local sailors navigating the Squash. Eventually it became a war grave.

'Even now,' Jim said in a half-whisper, 'when the wind and the tide and the light are just right, you can just make her out, lying on the bottom half-covered in sand...' Intriguing though it was, this story simply added to my dislike of the whole seafaring and fishing culture.

While everyone drank, they discussed the weather, the cost of living, people who had passed and people who had married and the year in general. It always seemed to have been a bad year for everything but those present were also always optimistic that the coming year ought to be better even though it might scupper their baleful end-of-year musings.

Soon moves were made to go on to the next destination. The question 'Are you coming with us Ned?' hung in the air. At this stage I knew that if Dad went with them, Mam would be upset. It was happy days when Dad declined the invitation. So they set off to their next port of call, ensuring by the time they had dinner they were full to the brim with Christmas cheer.

Christmas seemed to bring out the angel in people and prepare us for the hardships of the harsh months of winter. It was a season revolving around small pleasures and small kindnesses.

Bits of that goodwill might have been lurking in corners when the New Year arrived. Mam traditionally welcomed it by opening all the doors and windows and shooing out the remnants of the previous year, eradicating its bad luck and bad memories. I'm not sure this ever quite worked for her.

10

'It's hard to bear'

Small communities like Arklow cultivated death and its traditions. Grief was raised almost to the level of recreation. Terminal tragedy appeared to come early and frequently. When times were particularly bad, there seemed to be a funeral every other day.

When I was very young I was dragged to the funerals of people I didn't know. I began to realise that no one in a small town ever really died. People went to the funeral, took part in the ceremony and then kept the deceased alive forever in their conversations. Death didn't seem to mean much. People remained whatever they were remembered for. Somehow I began to get the gist of it all.

Some deaths, however, were more memorable and poignant than others. One summer a local boy went missing. The Gardai searched in vacant properties. The Civil Defence combed open spaces, beaches, and nearby farmlands – all the usual places. Mothers gathered in groups offering each other consolations and nuggets of the latest developments. Chinese whispers replaced rational conversations.

The boy was eventually found hanging from a rafter in his grandfather's garage. It was a tragic accident or a game that went wrong, people said. A funeral of desperate proportions ensued, attended by the entire town. This death was a mystery and we were unable to solve it. Religion was meant to protect us from hell but what happened when hell visited us? An incomprehensible tragedy became a dark cloud in our otherwise carefree life.

In our little town with its dock, river and beaches, summer had ample opportunity to inflict emotional pain. The occasional swimming or boating accident united everyone in grief for months. For the rest of the summer, there was a muted presence on the beaches. Sometimes summer smelled of tragedy, or was it the other way around?

Mam readily acknowledged that real life was full of such tragic events that could happen any time. Tragedies had a great effect on her and she lived with them constantly. It kept her going through normal times. She managed to work overtime on her worrying. She was prone to be overprotective of me – a price I paid for being an only child.

The dock and river were busy at times, lonely at other times. Saturday mornings were very busy indeed. The area attracted all those with an interest in fishing or boats. The crews prepared for the Monday morning sailings, repairing nets, loading up with fuel and food. It also was a haven for those who had retired from the sea; old men dreaming of times gone by, nothing to offer but grudging advice.

By Saturday evening it was a different story. The work was completed, and the dock gradually became devoid of human activity. Stragglers often drifted away simply because it became an uncomfortable place to linger, this cold deserted space, with just the seagulls for company. The call of pints in the nearest pub became very loud the closer the clock got to the Angelus.

On one such Saturday evening when I was just eight years old, I was playing marbles with a gang of boys. We congregated on a dirt patch opposite the harbour master's office. Marbles was a serious business; like a religion. It was one of the rites of passage we all went through, hopefully coming out the other side unscathed

We tried many games and activities with marbles. Sometimes they were horses or cars racing down inclines, sometimes colourful soldiers advancing on an unseen enemy. Somehow it always came back to the circle in the dusty dirt, the start line and the practised throw.

We played marbles all afternoon, shouting the magic words 'Brantents' and 'Derlings' when necessary, to change the direction or angle of the shot. As the afternoon wore on, new boys joined the game and others left. Coming up to six o'clock, everyone began to drift home.

Presently I heard the Angelus bell reminding me that I should be making my way home as well. To confirm this, I saw Mam come to our front gate waving a tea cloth in my direction. I gathered my remaining marbles and headed up the road.

It went quite chilly and a sharp breeze was chopping up the river water. In spite of it being quite early, it was quite dark under an overcast sky. I looked back. I thought I heard a loud 'Brantents' where we had been playing but couldn't see anyone. It suddenly seemed to be a scary and evil place.

Soon I was sitting at the table for my tea. A bath followed and I was settled down for a typical Saturday night. Dad was reading the paper while Mam prepared the Sunday dinner: steeping the peas, stuffing the chicken and starting the apple tart. I was in my pyjamas reading a book.

At nine o'clock, Mam said, 'It's time for bed young man.' This meant that I had go up to my room and read there instead. I didn't mind that. Dad was shaving and getting ready to go up the town for a pint. He was singing and in a good humour.

'Don't forget your prayers,' he said to me looking through the mirror, giving me a mischievous wink.

I was about to say goodnight to Mam and Dad when the front door burst open. Kitty our neighbour put her head around the door and said, 'Sally, it's that little boy from down the road. He's missing. He didn't turn up for his tea. They're getting up a search party to comb the Brow and the Links; maybe he went up the town, up to the chapel or something.'

Mam was holding a teacloth up to her mouth. 'God it's very late,' she said. 'You'd think someone would have spotted him by now and run him home.'

I silently agreed with Mam. When I strayed a little too far from home, often someone who knew my parents challenged me. They'd say, 'Well you'd better be making your way home. I'll follow along behind and have a word with your father tonight.'

Mam and Kitty walked down toward the harbour office. The Gardai arrived in their new patrol car, a blue light flashing ominously. Eventually a woman asked one very young Garda whether they'd contacted the Gardai divers' unit. The reply was the boy had only been missing for a few hours and he might turn up anytime soon. The fact that it was a weekend was also mentioned.

A groan went up from the women. 'He must have fallen into the river,' one of them said. 'We should start dragging it now.'

The Civil Defence men were sent off to search the golf links out as far as Arklow Rock. Fishermen were asked to get their boats and begin searching the river. Women's tears pointed to a growing but unspoken realisation. Every couple of minutes someone tried hopefully, 'He'll turn up.'

In fact the boy didn't turn up all that weekend and as Sunday stretched towards Monday there was an increased uniformed presence. Searches were organised further and further from the little boy's house. All weekend, everyone I knew helped to look for him. Derelict houses were entered and searched. Locked-up holiday boats were forced open and examined. Faraway fields were combed, but to no avail.

On Monday, a team of Gardai divers arrived. This caused great consternation among the women and morbid excitement among the kids. We watched the divers slip into the deep dark waters of the river. Within five minutes one surfaced and gave a signal to the Gardai on the water's edge. Quickly they sent a boat out to the divers. Eventually we saw them transfer what looked like a bundle of clothes on to a boat. Children were safely gathered in and doors slammed shut.

I learned later that some time Saturday evening the boy must have somehow fallen into the river and drowned. I heard Dad say he was still holding two marbles in his hand when they pulled him out of the water. I could only guess how the little boy's parents coped with their heartbreak.

One summer a tragedy – or at least a near miss – struck a little closer to home; too close in fact, and it affected my day-to-day existence for years. My childhood was full of the good times when my parents were rubbing along quite well. However, events occasionally occurred that put Dad in the doghouse for years. This was one of them.

August Bank Holiday was an exciting time, attracting hundreds of visitors to our small seaside town. For the entertainment of these new arrivals, a circus and a road show usually spent the three days in the town giving morning, afternoon and evening performances.

The main attraction, however, for the locals at least, were the celebrations centring on the river and dock. The annual Blessing of the Boats was the big event. In preparation, the fishermen decorated their boats, painting everything that could be painted and polishing every bit of brass in view. Around the dock and in the streets leading to the river, all sorts of decorations were put up. Bunting, plants in beer barrels and lights temporarily borrowed from the council's Christmas decorations all added to the importance of the occasion. The centrepiece of the festival came on Sunday afternoon when the parish priest was transported from one boat to another in the lifeboat and with great ceremony blessed each boat and its crew.

The local pottery shut down for its summer holidays after this festival and there was a great air of relaxation about the town. Dad also took his holidays at this time as the Yard was closed for two weeks.

This particular Bank Holiday Saturday morning, sitting at breakfast, Mam said, 'Can you take him down around the dock for a walk, while I do the washing?'

This was not really a question, more a declaration of what was going to happen. I looked over my toast at Mam and them across to Dad. He was reading the newspaper which was full of details of the weekend festivities.

'Fine,' he said, although I felt that what he meant was 'Oh bother' as some preferred activity was about to be thwarted. 'Fine,' he repeated. 'When will we head off then?'

I got in first and said, 'If we go down too early there'll be nothing to see. How about eleven?'

He looked at the cuckoo clock. 'That'll give us a couple of hours to get ready,' and winked at me.

I wasn't too sure what this wink meant. Did it mean that in the next two hours he'd concoct some story or other to get out of it, or that he had plans for something exciting, that Mam shouldn't know about? I shrugged my shoulders. I'd get to know about it sooner or later.

I finished up my breakfast and went up to my room. Mam had bought *The Hotspur* and *Victor* for me on Friday and I needed to finish them off before I swapped them with Brendan, who lived beside us. When I'd read both comics, I went next door to find Brendan. His dad, Ben, was lying over his front wall, looking at all the activity along the river.

'It's a great day for it, eh Richard.'

'Sure is, Ben?' I said as maturely as I could.

I liked Ben. I think he always pitied me for having no other kid in the family. He laughed. 'These fishermen get an awful lot of painting done on the Saturday morning, don't they. Many a good suit and dress will get ruined during the blessing tomorrow, eh.' I had to agree. Every year this last-minute painting never dried in time and invariably ended with white or black bums for everyone.

We shared a quiet moment watching the goings-on. The river was jam-packed with all sorts of boats. Some were loaded down with people. Ben said, 'They've started taking trippers out early this year.' It was a tradition that the fishermen ran trips ferrying townspeople out into the bay for a distance and back home again. The good weather had attracted people to the dock early.

'Will you be going out over the bar yourself?' Ben said again without looking up.

'I expect so; Dad's bringing me down around the dock to see the sights in a couple of minutes.'

Dad walked towards us lighting up a cigarette. 'How are you today, Ben?' he said. 'Fine, Ned, fine,' was the reply.

'C'mon junior, it's me and you,' he said, 'we'd better get this show on the road, before our dinner's ready.'

The road was suddenly full of people. The pipe band passed us, marching to a solitary drum beat. They were keeping their powder dry for the ensuing battle. Numerous couples walked by holding hands. Kids with mothers and prams competed for space on the road.

Distracted, I didn't notice my father wandering over to the Yard where he worked. Something had caught his attention. The gate was open despite the holidays. A car and trailer was parked just inside the big gates.

He was a little ahead of me, and I could see he was talking to someone. I also noticed a lovely white dinghy on the back of the trailer. Roy Kearon came out from behind the gate. Roy was the brother of the owner the Yard, and good friends with my parents. He was Bongo's dad and had all those traits that are endearing in a child but tiresome in an adult; gushingly enthusiastic about projects that he was ill-equipped to carry out.

My father continued his conversation. 'So you got it then.'

'Yes,' Roy replied. 'And he knocked a hundred off to take it away this weekend.' They both stood back and silently admired the boat. Roy eventually noticed me. 'Hello Tarzan,' he said.

'Eejit,' I said silently to myself.

'Will you be sailing it today?' Dad said as he ran his hands over the curves. He hunched down and with one eye closed checked that all the straight lines were straight. 'It's well put together,' he added.

After a while Roy said, 'I think I'll check it over this afternoon and take it for a bit of a spin tomorrow afternoon. Are you on?'

'Well I'll have to get to church first and maybe I could get away in the afternoon,' Dad replied fairly unconvincingly. That seemed to be the end of the conversation, and I walked ahead of Dad out of the Yard towards the river. I looked back. Roy and Dad were still talking. Dad caught my eye; I thought I caught a bit of a guilty look.

Ahead of me in the river, a large motor launch was manoeuvring into a berth on the North Quay. The boat looked majestic in the calm waters. Five or six uniformed sailors stood to attention on the bow. The windows of the wheelhouse were made of darkened glass, which gave the sleek, modern-looking boat a touch of mystery. It was completely white except for those windows. Its wheelhouse was made of rounded fibreglass that gave the impression of floating through the water. Out at sea, in the distance, I thought it might look ominously like a cloud on the horizon.

'What's that?' I said to Dad.

'That's the Rowntree boat. It's famous.' He whistled and added, 'Isn't it beautiful?'

Occasionally the Blessing of the Boat weekend attracted maritime visitors; perhaps a navy corvette or a famous locally built yacht. This year it was the Rowntree boat. There was a rumour that this fabled visitor gave out free chocolate all weekend.

By now the sailors were fore and aft mooring the boat and lowering an impressive gangplank. 'I'll find out when they are allowing people on board and we'll go over,' said Dad. Off we went, down towards the harbour master's office. Dad called it the 'Youth Club' because it was where all the old fishermen used to congregate. Today it was packed; a hive of activity. All the old boys were present with their polo-necked navy gansies and peaked caps. Some had rubber boots with the tops turned down, like Santa Claus. People were collecting money with cardboard models of a lifeboat.

Away on the other side of the dock, members of the pipe band were standing in a circle practising for the big event. At the entrance to the pottery, a group of teenagers with guitars and drums were singing 'I walk the line' with cowboy accents. I knew them. They were the Red Seven, which was pretty mysterious as there were only five playing today and none wearing red. The lead guitarist was my cousin Freddy. We sort of waved to him and continued on our way.

The day's excitement soon petered out and lapsed into an ordinary Saturday evening. This meant a bath for me and bed by nine o'clock. For Dad it meant a shave and wash in the scullery, and an early escape up town for a drink with his friends.

I awoke the next morning to find that Mam was at the table by herself. 'Is Dad still in bed?' I asked?

'No,' she said, 'Roy Kearon called for him early and he's gone somewhere with him. He didn't say where.'

I mentioned the boat that Roy had bought and said, 'Maybe Dad's helping him get it in the water,' but secretly thought he had invented something more urgent than going to church. With Mam, attending church was still a big issue even though she only went occasionally herself.

'Ah well,' she said with a sigh, 'maybe he'll take you to Vespers.' I hoped not. I hated the evening service and even its name filled me with dread. Usually only a handful of people turned up and they seemed to feel an obligation to sit near the top of the church under the full scrutiny of the minister. I'm sure he was annoyed when so few people turned up. You could sometimes feel his annoyance in the air.

We had breakfast and Mam was just about to wash up when a loud bang on the door startled us. It was Uncle Billy.

'Sally,' he said as he burst through the door. 'Sally, the lifeboat's being called out for a boat in distress, and we think it's Roy Kearon's.'

Mam went white and sat down in her chair by the fireside. 'Are you sure?' she said.

'Well not completely, but no one else is out in the bay as far as we know.' Uncle Billy was one of these men who actually had nothing to do with the lifeboat, or any boat, or fishing or anything to do with the sea, but spent most of the time wishing he had. Within minutes the house was full of neighbours and family. The parish priest soon arrived, despite the fact that we weren't Catholic. They said he could smell a good tragedy before it happened.

The information about the boat was sparse, but nearly everyone seemed to agree that it had capsized, throwing those on board into the sea. The running commentary informed us moment by moment of the progress of the lifeboat towards the capsized boat. No one knew whether those on board had stayed with the craft or if they were wearing lifejackets. I found out from the conversation that Dad or Roy couldn't swim a stroke and that their predicament had been spotted by someone down at the South Pier.

Some drink materialised and Mam was asked if she might like a sherry or a drop of whisky. Mam bristled and said something to the effect that it was probably bloody drink that got my father into this mess. Those offering backed away and sort of hid the drinks they were holding, for a while at least.

Eventually word got through that both men were okay and that they were indeed Dad and Roy. It was then that Mam started crying. Aunt Connie, seizing the moment, started shushing people out of the house. Out they went, downing drinks quickly and saying as they left, 'Thank God for that' and 'Merciful God and His Gracious Mother'.

Dad soon arrived, with a lifeboat blanket draped around his shoulders. He walked up to Mam and kissed her. She tried to turn her head away and failed, but she did say, 'You complete fool, what kind of an eejit are you? And at your age too. And you wanted to take the child with you.'

Even at a young age, you notice moments when things change forever and for me this was one of them. It was a sinking moment for Dad in more than one way. I could see from his face that he realised just how much trouble he was in. He knew he wouldn't get over the repercussions of this adventure for a long while.

We never did get to visit the Rowntree boat that year, and it never returned to Arklow, leaving the legend of the free chocolate intact.

11

'Riddle of the Sand Dunes'

The life of an only child was difficult at times but overall it had some benefits. The sporadic loneliness, being the centre of attention, having never to compete for anything were normal for me. The best thing was I always had my own bedroom. It may have been a small and badly lit room but I loved it because it and everything in it – the knick-knacks, treasures and secrets that were important for my existence – were mine.

Childhood could be sombre, but I began to like the quiet unpredictability of days spent alone in this room. It was my sanctuary. As an only child, you get drawn towards activities that don't depend on having someone else around. Reading had a natural attraction; it started with the weekly English comics and gradually moving on to the Dells and Commandos, which got swapped around the neighbourhood as needs dictated.

One morning I awoke to find a newly built bookcase in my room. Dad had noticed me engrossed in a book. I remember it still: it was *Carib Gold* by A H Verril. A boy named John Tyndall at Carysfort had loaned it to me. It had everything I needed: treasure maps, treachery and suspense – a new world of excitement and adventure. I think I read it at least ten times. On my new bookcase was a copy of *Treasure Island* standing proudly on the middle shelf. In the ensuing months and years, other books mysteriously found their way onto those shelves.

A collection of Airfix models – Spitfires, Hurricanes and Stukas – hanging on strings from the ceiling were further testimony to my only-child existence. Dad said he used to make planes from balsa wood when he was young, so my endeavours in plastic were a progression of sorts. Pride of place went to a box kite. A joint effort between me and Dad, it had yet to complete its maiden flight.

I took to stamp collecting, but rarely came across interesting stamps from foreign countries. Occasionally we got a letter from Uncle Ronnie when he stopped over in a far-flung port but these were so infrequent that my collection remained somewhat static. I noticed however from an advertisement in a comic that English stamp collector clubs conveniently sent books of stamps 'on approval'. I embraced this idea wholeheartedly and soon had a steady stream of stamps arriving at our house. Occasionally a letter would arrive reminding me of the principle of 'on approval', but these were so meek and mannerly that I disregarded them and burned them before Mam saw them. Eventually these stamp people just gave up and I was left with a sizeable collection that might have been the envy of the Fisheries, but of course it was yet another solitary hobby.

The long hours I spent in this room reading anything that came my way had a profound affect. I was reading magazines and books that perhaps were a little too adult for me as they became available and somehow found their way into our house. I sampled Anne Frank's diary, *Fahrenheit 451, Exodus* and many others.

Books like these had that wonderful quality of showing you other peoples' lives. As I read, I sometimes noticed from my window a scene being replicated outside on the quay: the hunched up workers shuffling to their drudge; the courting couples bumping into each other, hand in hand; the wind-swept water; the postman overwhelmed by his load. I began to wonder, 'Is all life like this, repetitive, duplicated and predictable?'

It was similar to taking the same way home day after day, and how everything became so familiar and monotonous. I tried to imagine what it would be like to step into someone else's shoes; silently watching and listening; hiding in other peoples lives. It was my way of escaping from the greyness that tainted our lives. It was like I was experiencing my own personal pages.

Directly across from my room, on the other side of the river, a wooden bridge spanned the entrance to a small backwater called locally the Back Guts. Jutting out from this bridge was a small jetty used by locals to moor their boats. Beyond this small bridge lay the derelict remains of what was once a thriving munitions factory. Huge red-bricked buildings in a severe state of decay blocked my view of the beach and sea beyond. Sharp beach dune grass waved at me from gaps and windows in these walls. Through these same gaps I saw ships easing by the coast; at night their flickering lights friendly like the stars above, in the daytime distant and aloof.

The ruins, a symbol of past ambition, past promises and past lives, were now a fallow area inhabited by feral cats ruling over a kingdom of tunnels, cellars, briars and thistles. Without realising it, I lived in close proximity to the detritus of a sort of history. The past was everywhere to be seen.

To the left of these ruins lay the town municipal dump, bane of those who lived nearby, especially those living facing out onto the river. To the right were the moorings for large ships that were used to export ore from Avoca mines and pit props from local forests.

Winter or summer, high or low tide, when I opened the curtains the river was a pervasive influence. At high tide and in the winter storms, the river slowly eased its way past our house, prowling largo-like towards its predestination, with the certain knowledge that it could take anything or anyone with it, given the opportunity. The wind and rain occupied the whole scene in front of me, sweeping across from one bank to another, barely stopping at the metal window frames of my room. The mists and river fog dissolved into one. The damp air had the capacity to corrode your very spirit.

My white window sill was covered in a constant layer of dust, probably from the dump across the river or perhaps the loading of ore from the mines. I sometimes wrote the word 'dust' which left a grey smudge on my finger. Eventually the word disappeared.

The dust was grey and the days were grey. In winter the formidable wind blew grey freezing water on to the road. It seemed that the world could drown beneath this banal greyness.

The road was without sympathy for people passing by; workers in a rush clutching their jackets to their necks and hats to their heads; small men riding big bikes and big men riding small bikes racing to beat the hooters that ruled their lives. Dad daily wove his way to the workshop, whether walking or on his bicycle, battling the unrelenting gusts. We were a society that lived under clouds and were summoned by horns and bells.

Yet even in this dullness there were smatterings of bright colours. The rain-swelled river pushed the bright yellow soon-to-be-laden boats against the quayside. It was as if the river was physically trying to reject this too-bright intrusion. To me, it soon became obvious that the river somehow dictated the mood of those living nearby. A girl who lived down the way, seemingly always dressed in black and white, walked by like a penguin but carried a colourful umbrella that in the rising wind interrupted the grey monotony. Darkly attired workers passed by, their rain macs and southwesters blurring into the grey eternity on these days when night seemed to fall in the middle of the afternoon.

In all weathers the fishing boats came and went; always the fishing boats. Black-painted trawlers slipping slowly and silently down the river from the safety of the dock. There was no one to be seen on deck, no activity. They were like hearses on that final journey, sailing away from a dark and dismal country, to the bright and silver yonder.

Quietly plying their trade, in all weathers, these fishers – brave men in small boats – lived and died for their living. Yet not everyone was so brave. One owner-captain was so averse to fishing in bad weather he earned the nickname 'Smoothie' and was relentlessly ribbed by other fishermen and by the community at large.

At the lowest tides myriad barnacled ribs, the mangled skeletal remains of ancient hulks, stuck out above the water. Languishing and embedded in the river for decades, they were fighting a losing battle with the storms and floods. Each spring tide, the river devoured more large chunks of the slimy structures. Cormorants collected like mourners on the remaining dark wooden shapes protruding the murky stillness. Heads hanging low, seagulls hopped and complained at the intrusion of the cormorants on these favoured resting places.

And among these dreary grey-filled days, there was activity and human endeavour to be seen. If the rain and wind were particularly heavy, the swollen river uprooted trees from the riverbanks above Arklow, and swept them past our house and out to sea. The river also invariably flooded Avoca mines, and coloured the water with a copper brown-yellow. From there, pit props and other timber were dragged downstream. Sheep and cows, the victims of the flood, were a grotesque comical sight rolling and tumbling with the flow of the river; legs appearing and disappearing like synchronised swimmers.

Brendan, one of our neighbours, captured trees as they floated past the slip with the help of a long rope with a metal hook. He pulled the tree in towards the shipyard slip and eventually got it up on dry land. We would all lend a hand to pull the logs the short distance from the slip, up the road past our house and stack them outside the house of Kitty, his mother. The pile of logs grew throughout the winter. On weekends the entire Coburn family attacked the pile with bush-saws, cutting the logs into fire-size lengths. Mam often said Kitty's log pile lowered the tone of the place, but she kept that to herself.

In high summer the river smelled to high heaven. An ancient system spewed raw sewage the length of the imposing quayside.

During these years, my serene solitude was interrupted by the arrival of my cousin Sally. She came to live with us. During the summer she had become a little run-down, as Mam put it. She and Connie decided Sally should stay with us for a while, until she got back on her feet. She was with us until the following May.

I'm not sure what part Dad played in all this, but I never heard him complain. Perhaps he liked having a part-time daughter. In any case, Sally soon became the younger sister I never had. We continued to go to school together, meeting her brother and sister at the corner, as I did daily for several years.

Her younger brother Bobby began school about the same time as we crossed over to senior school. Bobby was no angel, despite his cherubic white locks. He attracted attention like a flame might attract moths. He suffered seriously from being the younger brother of much older, sassy sisters. The lack of a permanently present father didn't help at all. By the time he reached school age, he was fairly well out of control. One parent spoils you with too much lack of attention, but two parents mean discipline.

As John had explained the pitfalls and rules required to survive Carysfort and Mr Smythe, so Sally and I in turn tried to put Bobby on the straight and narrow, but to no avail. Easily riled, he was particularly averse to anyone singing *I Want to be Bobby's Girl* which was popular at the time. In time he outgrew this affectation, but he was constantly trouble-bound in school. Bobby was unable to cope with authority.

He lived for television. Before Connie got their own set, he developed relationships with neighbours who owned a magic box. Every night of the week he could be found squatting in some house, almost unseen and unnoticed, watching whatever programme was available in silence, his face lit up by the blue glow of this wondrous invention.

Bobby was particularly taken with an advertisement for a nylon shirt: the 'Raelbrook shirt with the London Look'. He chirped up when it came on. I think he began to think of it as his advertisement. This gave Connie a problem when he demanded a Raelbrook shirt for Christmas. He got his nylon shirt but it wasn't a Raelbrook. Connie went looking for one on a trip to Dublin but couldn't get his size.

Bobby became a little demon among children of his own age. Mam would write off his antics with her own TV quip, 'Leave it to Beaver'.

Almost a year to the day when Mr Smythe had surprised me with a most unexpected prize – of which more later – he called Sally up to the top of the class and went through almost the same speech. It seemed that Sally, while living with us, had gone the entire year without any absence. 'You should be grateful to her auntie for achieving such a great record of attendance,' Mr Smythe told her.

The prize that year was a box of biscuits. Sally was beside herself with delight. She skipped and sang all the way down the main street to our house. We parted company with Bobby, who told Connie about Sally's good news.

Aunt Connie, who was perhaps having a bad day, was miffed that Sally hadn't taken the biscuits directly to her. She stormed over to our house and had words with Mam. Never mind that Mam and Sally were on their way to take the biscuits over to Connie: she had all guns blazing.

Mam and Connie fell out for a while, or as Mam described it, they had a 'cooling' because of the box of biscuits. For me, the upshot was losing Sally, who promptly left our house. Once again I was on my own.

When John moved on to the Technical School or 'the Tech' as it was known, I took over as the oldest in our school-bound group. Even though the Tech was just across the road from Carysfort, John didn't walk up with us anymore. As a matter of fact, it seemed that John never went to his school at any time. He said he didn't have to attend all the classes and that he was only interested in wood-working and metal-working classes, but I'm not sure he was telling the truth. Dad said that if John was so interested in woodwork, he could have served an apprenticeship with him, but nothing ever came of that.

John hung out with a funny crowd. They were interested in odd things like rearing pigeons, catching wild birds, poaching in the river with gaffs. One of the older ones owned a boat and fished for herring during the season. They found lost golf balls and sold them on. They were always collecting scrap and owned a barrow to take it down to Jack Kenny's yard. It was one of their many money-making schemes.

You never knew what John was going to say to you. He had a lot of peculiar catch phrases. 'Hello Rodney, Hello Charles' and 'Left hand down a bit' were two he picked up from his favourite BBC radio shows. He had a special word for any event that impacted badly on our sunlit days. Anything that fell into this category was deemed 'Bizzastrous'.

John had truly grown up fast, helped no doubt by the continuing absence of Jack. Before he emerged as a secondary schoolboy, he was our constant companion and guardian, forever instructing us in the skills and crafts deemed necessary for life in the Fishery.

He introduced me to the art of catching wild birds, helping me to set up an aviary in a shed in Mam's back garden. There were different ways to catch birds and I'd learned all the tricks needed from John.

One way was to use a bird in a cage as a lure. It was a special cage with a false roof that was spring-loaded to close quickly over the bird when it landed on top to feed. You could also use a bird on a tether and spring-loaded nets to catch the bird.

The most common way was using birdlime or Dak as it was called. Dak was slightly illegal, but it was sold openly in Annseleys hardware shop. Dak was a type of thick glue that you smeared on branches or twigs where you knew birds came to feed. When the bird landed on Dak it immediately became stuck. Eventually through struggling the wings and tail feathers got caught and required cleaning with paraffin, which was quite distressing to the poor bird. No matter how you caught the bird, it frightened the life out of the poor thing.

Building fires, making bows and arrows and catapults, gaffing trout, John knew it all. Each summer he honed our skills in blowing up frogs and discovering birds' nests on the golf links. With the help of our Bowie knives – another thing he introduced me to – he showed us the mysteries inside golf balls; I was amazed to discover the amount of elastic they contained and the handy little bag of paint at their centres.

You didn't have to invent childhood back then; it was all about you – at the river and dock, in the fields and open spaces and of course on the streets. Older kids taught younger ones the art of making daisy chains, and they wore them with a casual ease in those amber-tinged days.

Then there was the peculiar local sport of 'catching bees.' This entailed the use of a jam jar, cleaned and dried, with a secure lid with air holes punched in it with a nail and stone. The idea was to catch bees of the bumble variety in these jars. Some flower blossoms were added to make the poor bees feel at home. This simple endeavour occupied hours, everyone competing to catch the largest. When you had a big one, you exclaimed, 'Look at the slunger I've caught!'

This childhood centred on familiar places, visited regularly and almost by rote. Adventures often began at the beach behind the Pottery. If Mam twigged that I was likely to be gone all day, she gave me sandwiches, wrapped in grease-proof paper. It was a bit embarrassing when she did, but four hours later these apple or sugar or fresh air sandwiches were more than welcome.

Along the South Beach just down from the Pier Head, was a stack of immense concrete stone blocks about ten feet high and totalling perhaps a hundred feet in length. Climbing to the top was difficult, but once there and hiding low in its convenient recess, you could observe unobserved all that happened below.

The Blocks, as they were always called, were tall enough to hurt yourself if you fell. 'Mind you don't fall off,' Mam worried.

'I won't,' was my reply, and I didn't through the course of an ordinary and uneventful childhood. I never broke a leg or an arm. I was never rushed to hospital with appendicitis or tonsillitis. I never sported those blue blotches on legs and arms to combat boils. Summer after summer, I survived the Blocks, the Brow and the seaside without incident. I was well into my teenage years before I even saw a dead body. Sometimes I think I missed a great deal.

With a modicum of imagination the Blocks became a spaceship, an ocean-going liner, or even a cash cow. From the top, you could see golfers playing in your direction. You got a perfect view of where their balls landed and you could see if they found them. You could make money from reselling these lost balls.

Our next port of call often was the Grotto at Arklow Rock. This was a Catholic shrine to the Virgin Mary. I was always a little nervous of hanging around it. I knew I didn't belong there and felt I was trespassing. It did however have a tap with drinking water. I got it into my head that it was holy water on tap. On torrid summer days, I summoned up the courage to partake. John reassured me it was okay to drink.

'Don't worry,' he said, 'you won't die, it's not poison.'

Between the Blocks and the Grotto we traversed a impressive line of sand dunes which formed the boundary of the golf links. These dunes were scalloped from the ground and gave an indication that the entire area at some time was covered by the sea. They ranged in size from head high to one particular dune, a huge one that was like a huge side-on oyster shell, full of golden sand and ringed by wavy beach grass.

Mam told a story about these dunes. She had a habit of telling stories sitting around the fire on winter nights. She seemed to relish stories that involved people she knew and had a frisson of mystery about them. As a result you never really quite knew if she was making them up. One that especially intrigued me and that deserved to be in a mystery novel concerned a woman who lived in the middle of the golf links in Arklow, eking out her income by searching for lost golf balls along the fairways and selling them on. She haunted the fairways long into the evening when the golfers were still in the bar celebrating their birdies or had gone home to forget their double-bogies.

'One evening,' said Mam, 'she spotted a man in the distance. He was behaving oddly and carrying a large hold-all. She ducked down behind a dune and watched what he was up to.

'The man made his way to a small, distinctive sand dune. He took some care in choosing a spot in the sand. Then he sank to his knees and began to dig a hole with his hands. When the hole was deep enough, he placed the bag in it. Then he covered it up. He brushed away every trace of his activities and with a cautious look around, he went on his way.

'The woman stayed low until she was sure he was out of sight. Then she quickly dug up the holdall and looked inside. It was full of money.'

According to Mam, she took it back to her house and that was the end of the matter, especially when soon after the owner of the bag passed away. How Mam came by this information, I will never know. The woman subsequently showed no signs of having come into a fortune, and I can verify that she was never seen again searching for lost golf balls along those dunes.

If any of us had any money, our next port of call was the Rock Shop. By this time, we'd be tired and losing interest, so the stock of sweets, ice-cream and lemonade at this little shop in the middle of nowhere – itself a novelty – tended to perk everyone up.

On our way back, our route took us past a pond in a small area within the golf course called the Warrens. The Warrens had a house in the middle and it often seemed that the golfers played through the garden, over the house and past the front door. The water in the pond was stagnant virtually all the year round. Planks of wood stopped the sandy perimeter caving in. There was no visible inlet, but I had my suspicions that it was fed by a small stream which flowed from the Sconce.

Our fascination for the pool centred on its wildlife. Dragon flies, butterflies and bumble bees, as well as mosquitoes, frequented its slimy, murky water. Our parents didn't like us going near this pond; they saw it as potentially a breeding ground for every disease known to the medical world and a few more besides.

In early spring, this pond was full of frog spawn. I marvelled how this arrived in the pool, taking into account the size of frogs. It was like a giant sago-filled crucible, and with some fascination I scooped out the spawn, letting in run back into the pond through my fingers.

The tadpoles that abounded a few weeks later offered us a new interest. We made expeditions to the pool armed with fishnets and jam jars and brought home tadpoles by the hundred hoping to observe them change into frogs. Alas, the mortality rate of these little animals was terribly high; few if any ever made the magical transformation.

Not so the tadpoles left in the pond, which produced a crop of big friendly frogs. In the long and hot summers that followed, I hate to admit that everyone at least once experienced the cruelty of blowing and inflating a frog with a straw.

The next leg of our adventure took us past the Sconce, a small waterfall, past the golf clubhouse and down McCarthy's Hill. This hill was more of a road with a gentle incline. Halfway down, a path forked off to the right and led to an open green area perfect for football and other childhood activities: playing shop when we were younger and throwing knives and making shapes in later years.

I associated McCarthy's Hill mostly with soapboxes. We built soapboxes just about as often as we could find two sets of pram wheels. We scavenged them off the dump or stole discarded sets from back gardens. These we fashioned into a design that was straight out of *The Beano*, often using a wooden fish box which were everywhere about the dock.

One summer we made various attempts, all unsuccessful, to build a tree house in a secret copse near the Brow. This construction was a step beyond our skills at the time, and we eventually gave up on it.

During the many lapses of interest when the days were long and languorous, John introduced me to the secrets of the dark recesses of this overgrown copse, where the smell of wild garlic was overwhelming. He showed me where I could find the biggest blackberries and the largest hazelnuts. He imparted this knowledge as if it were his legacy. John grew up, matured, and left us behind long before we all eventually lost interest ourselves in these pastimes.

As the summer months passed, we turned to making bows and arrows and the occasional spear and shield. It took days to find the straightest and most pliant saplings for these endeavours. Our arrows improved vastly after John Greene returned from holiday in Kildare and informed us that in that far-flung province he had observed flights being added to the arrows. Further, they could be made of feathers, cardboard or plastic and were simple to apply. When we saw how the flighted arrow travelled straight and true, we readily embraced this modification. The arms race now truly meant something to us in the Fishery

One summer the inevitable happened, I and one other boy, David Rees, somehow acquired air rifles. These were known as pellet guns locally, but as everyone knew, they were BB guns in Dell comics. I got my airgun, despite serious misgivings from my parents, from Annseleys Shop in the Main Street. I paid for it by 'leaving it by' and putting money off it for what seemed an eternity. Selling golf balls, returning lemonade bottles, gifts from relatives all paid their part in this almost never-ending process. After I eventually paid it off in full, I travelled the local haunts shooting at anything and everything.

This came to an abrupt end the day Bobby was accidentally shot in the head, thankfully by David's gun, as we climbed over a fence. Bobby fell off the fence like someone shot in a cowboy film. He was rushed to hospital for an x-ray on his wounded head. It turned out well for him: no permanent damage. Not so the airguns, for which the episode was fatal. I hid my rifle, but eventually had to surrender it to Mam and Dad.

Perhaps the best information John passed on to me was how make bombs with gun cotton from the Kynoch's ruins. The old factory buildings gave us a fantastic area for playing during the summer months. The ruins that we most frequented backed onto the north beach right up to the north pier, but the ruins of the whole factory stretched all the way from the north pier to the headland know locally as the Spion Kop.

Kynoch's made munitions and had been a big employer in the town for many years going back to the Boer War. Almost overnight, they transferred their operations to South Africa, leaving behind an area along the north beach full of buildings, railway tracks, tunnels and bunkers.

The building soon became dilapidated and collapsed due to coastal erosion and neglect. Sand dunes encroached and over the years buildings were undermined by the tides and the exact location of the different buildings became blurred. The whole area became one big site of red bricks, concrete floors, small railway lines and paths leading nowhere.

Of course we soon found out that Kynoch's had left behind more than buildings. In the process of making ammunition, the factory produced what we called gun cotton. If you knew where to look, you could find any amount of gun cotton.

John introduced me to the mysteries and excitement of this substance. Gun cotton was like ordinary cotton but obviously tainted by gunpowder. When we found it, the cotton sometimes was dry but usually was damp. John always took it home and dried it under his mattress. He said that it was the best place to hide the cotton because it looked like fluff you got under any mattress. I wondered if perhaps that wasn't the smartest thing to do, as I knew for a fact that John often smoked in bed.

John had a favourite way of making these bombs. He liked a nice big can that he could seal tight. Normally a Brasso bottle was sufficient. He knocked a couple of holes in the container with a nail and a brick for the fuse which he made from a thin piece of twine that he'd soaked in paraffin. He'd light the fuse and hide behind a wall or something for protection. It was quite frightening when the bomb went off, more frightening if it didn't. In those cases, we'd leave it a couple of days before we went back to it. We had a lot of respect for our bombs.

The bomb-making was quite technical and John impressed on me the need to follow his instructions to the letter. Of course there were boys who didn't know how to handle this stuff. One chap called Christy tried to get in on the act. We'd seen him watching us searching and digging, and after we'd left he looked around at our diggings and by luck found a big stash of gun cotton that we overlooked. Noticing that the cotton was damp, he decided to take it home and dry it in his Mam's oven. If I'd been worried about John's method of drying gun cotton, I nearly had hysterics when I discovered Christy's method.

The inevitable happened. The gun cotton blew up in the oven as he was checking on it with an explosion that threw him backwards and dazed him. The others in the house called a doctor and ambulance. It wasn't long before the whole Lower Main Street was crawling with fire brigades, ambulances and Gardai cars. There was great commotion for a few hours.

Christy recovered. Rumour had it that he'd blown off his kneecap that day, which is something I never fully understood. He walked with a slight limp after the accident.

The *Wicklow People* got hold of the story and ran some articles about the history of Kynoch's in the town. Among our families, there was an immediate clampdown on the activities of the gun cotton club, but of course as other things happened throughout the summer, our parents soon forgot this incident.

As for the gun cotton itself, it eventually became so scarce that its existence became like folklore passed on from older boys to disbelieving younger ones. Peace once again settled on the town.

As I made my way through this golden childhood, I recognised I was lucky to have cousins. They say cousins are friends who will love you forever. If you were lucky enough to have cousins, life was grand. They were a part of a childhood that I never lost or forgot. The first things that I can remember I did in their company. Growing apart over the ensuing years didn't change the fact that we grew up side by side sharing clothes, food, mischief and contagious diseases. They were always around, always present. I couldn't remember a time that they weren't... until now, when they aren't.

12

'A world where I could go'

As I meandered through my time in Carysfort, each year got a little more interesting and learning a little more important. In junior school, learning seemed to consist of constant times-tables. Every day I learned new words in both English and Gaeilge, with occasional spelling tests.

Making the giant leap to senior school brought new adventures and new challenges. School became like a holy place, with desk after desk of children, heads down and tongues out in studious contemplation. I remember being introduced to the concepts of simple interest. Various sums at various rates for various periods of time became our bread and butter. We lived with simple interest for months.

When we knew everything there was to know about simple interest, we moved on to compound interest. I suddenly saw the patterns and progressions in the calculations; the repetitive sequences. Overnight I became very good at sums. Mr Smythe was delighted. He called me professor and I was equally delighted. I wore the name like a badge. Dad's constant explanation of fractions and measurements seemed to have rubbed off. I was happy and content at school. I took to wearing a fountain pen in my top pocket, casually hiding it when approached by bigger boys of dubious intent. I preened myself daily with this grand and golden pen. I discovered I was a natural school-goer.

Despite the monotony and routine of this learning, Mr Smythe occasionally rose unexpectedly from his chair, peered out the window, and said, 'Come on children, it's a pity to waste this sunshine. Let's get some fresh air.'

So we all trooped out, never really knowing what to expect. Mr Smythe had a fondness for rugby. He referred to it in a familiar way as 'rugger'. Down the Fishery, no one played or talked about rugger. All I understood was that there were moves peculiar to the game, and on sunny days, he often got the bigger boys out in the playground to practise them. He kept a ball on a shelf behind his desk especially for these events. During these playground episodes, he paid particular attention to those kids that everyone knew were going to boarding school, kids who seemed to already understand the importance of rugger and the further mysteries of rucks and scrums. Occasionally they shouted things like 'Up school, up school, up school.'

On another occasion, Mr Smythe tried to instil in us the connection between the sun in the sky and the passing of time. He made a huge circle of kids in the playground, all standing around a pole that he fixed in the ground. He had a big hourglass on his desk and every hour we went back to the pole in the playground to see the progression of its shadow. He made the connection between the falling sand in the hourglass and the passing of time so forcibly that for a while I thought all clocks contained sand.

One hot sunny day he marched the top classes to the large redundant water tank that inexplicably remained a feature of the playground. 'Notice how hot it becomes under the glare of the sun,' he commanded. Fortuitously a large cloud blocked out the sun for a while. This gave him the opportunity to explain how the metal did not hold the heat very well, but went significantly cooler in a matter of minutes, thus saving our hands from further sharp shocks. You never forget these lessons.

On another occasion, he showed us a large lump of glass which he called a prism. He angled the glass towards the sun and we were suitably amazed to see different colours coming from it. 'Refraction,' he explained, and gave the colours names that nobody knew. It took awhile to make the connection with a rainbow.

We struggled with the cardinal points on his large compass and learned where north-by-northwest was situated. Collectively we became obsessed with learning to tell the time, spurred on with the possibility of getting a watermelon watch for Christmas. Without a doubt Sammy Smythe lifted us into the air and helped us fly to rainbows.

Occasionally very pleasant things happened to me in Carysfort, usually completely out of the blue; unpredictable and unscripted. A few days before summer holidays, he dramatically called the whole school together. He had an announcement to make. Both sides of the room went immediately quiet.

'Today I was given an unexpected donation of five shillings from a past pupil. This past pupil,' he continued, 'asked me to give this five shillings to the student I feel deserved it most this year.'

The speech was now entering familiar territory. I was losing interest rapidly. I thought to myself, 'That'll be five shillings for some farmer's son or daughter who is doing extra study for a boarding school scholarship, or someone whose father donated a Christmas tree or wood for the fire.'

Mr Smythe looked pleased with himself. He was like the cat that got the cream. 'Well let's get it over with,' I thought.

'For this one I needed to put my thinking hat on,' he said. That was a great phrase of his. You either had your thinking hat on or you hadn't. Similarly if caught daydreaming you were 'in the doldrums'. Thankfully he explained what the doldrums were.

'Who deserved it most this year?' he repeated. 'I thought of giving it to the student who got the best marks in Primary Cert Examination, but that might not be entirely fair on those who haven't done the examination yet. So then I said myself what about attendance; school attendance and absence. That includes everyone and gives everyone a chance.'

He paused and looked up at the ceiling. 'So I decided to give it to the student with the least absence since last September.' He droned on, but in all fairness he did have everyone's attention. Five shillings was a lot of money.

'I checked everyone's absence in the roll book and in fact there is one clear winner. One student has got through the entire year with no sick days, no absence of any kind. His name is' – a lengthy pause – 'Richard Ruxton.'

I nearly fell out of my seat. True, I didn't remember having any sickness that year. Mam sometimes took me to Dublin in September to get school clothes but not that year, it appeared.

True to the rugger culture Mr Smythe hoped to promote in our sport-free school, he whipped the assembled throng into a rousing three cheers. I almost expected a rendition of 'For he's a jolly good fellow' but gratefully it didn't get that far.

He handed me the five shillings amid cheering and hand clapping. I eagerly deposited the money in my pocket. Mam and Dad were very proud. It was reported in the parish gazette and Mam bragged about it to the neighbours for months after. Where would you get it?

But school still had the capacity to suck you in and then slap you in the face. I lived with this paradox. On one occasion we were talking with Mr Smythe about the English queen, when he asked the question, 'Now then, who is heir to the throne after Queen Elizabeth?' I knew the answer and blurted it out. 'Prince Charlie,' I said with a little smugness. Mr Smythe scowled and said, 'Well I think we should call the future king by his correct name.'

'Prince Charles,' I said.

'That's better,' he replied. I realised from that moment that questions were often harmless but answers were potentially dangerous. I desisted from the occasional habit of sticking my arm in the air and shouting, 'Sir, Sir, Sir!'

With my new-found expertise in sums and my award for best attendance, I was in danger of becoming the class smart alec. Other depredations ensued, however, which prevented this from happening.

Sometimes Mr Smythe joined Mr Poyntz during religious class. This happened when they were most concerned for the spiritual welfare of some of us. It became a familiar and dreaded double act.

Mr Smythe spoke to the entire assembled school. 'It has come to my attention,' Mr Smythe informed everyone, 'that certain pupils have not attended church service for some time.' On cue, Mr Poyntz chirped in that he was most concerned for the souls of these absconders, these reprobates.

Sally and I knew he was referring to us. What's more, he knew that we knew. He looked directly at the townies in the school. Our eyes incriminated us, but he smiled; the smile never left his face. It was a permanent fixture.

'Certain pupils,' he reminded the school, 'have been seen going to the cinema – the Sunday matinee, in fact. So they have time to go to the pictures, but not to go to church...'

We fidgeted in our seats. Most of the kids in school lived on farms and were almost all Methodists, Presbyterians and Baptists. We suspected these religions might not allow them to do anything on Sunday other than go to church and do other holy stuff so it was obvious they just didn't have the same opportunities to sin as we had. I think we were the only kids in the school who went to the matinees, but it was part of town life.

On previous occasions when Mr Smythe found out we'd been to the matinees, he questioned us in front of the whole school. It was embarrassing, a dreadful experience and we had no defence.

We were often beckoned to stand before Mr Smythe's desk – the ultimate sanction. You were in deep trouble if you stood before the desk.

Mr Poyntz would take over the inquisition. He had the full attention of Mr Smythe, who perhaps hoped to learn something from the minister, some improvement in his own technique which often involved fiddling about with lists of letters.

As for the rest of us, of course we weren't listening. The words faded in and out like a boring radio programme playing at full volume but between stations. We looked at the floor – it seemed expected of us. I remember the minister's supremely polished shoes and the reflection of the window on both toecaps.

And I remember the sun suddenly breaking through the clouds, simultaneously bathing us in celestial light and our tormentors in a sombre shadow. I never knew Mr Poyntz to hit any of us, but when he made a sudden movement, it seemed best to flinch.

Eventually Mr Poyntz found it in his heart to end the proceeding and dismiss us so we could have our lunch break. Perhaps he and Mr Smythe had food on their minds as well.

Our souls were surely damned, but we took precautions. For a typical visit to the matinee, we would bypass the main street altogether using the river walk. Unfortunately this detour wasn't foolproof. To get to the cinema we still had to emerge onto the main street at the Hoyne's Hotel and continue up the street in full view for about a hundred yards.

Once, when using this route, we had just about got to the Ormonde steps when Mr Smythe came walking down Marlborough Terrace. He and his wife were out for their Sunday walk and he spotted us on the cinema steps. To add to the danger, two Protestant families lived in the main street. We knew if they saw us going past they'd assume we were going to the matinee. These kids always ratted to Mr Smythe. Someone always saw us. Someone always reported us.

Eventually we became emboldened as only hardened criminals do. We just didn't care. We walked directly up the main street to the cinema and suffered the consequences.

So Sunday afternoons during term time included a trip to the cinema. It was sixpence for downstairs, a shilling for the balcony. When John was with us, we went downstairs, but if he wasn't we'd try for the balcony. It was safer there.

The posters on the windows advertised the evening programme and gave an indication what might be shown in the matinee, but you never could be sure. The posters were always grand colourful affairs; most movies however were in black and white. Eventually people got fed up with being conned by posters printed in colour to fool the customers. We lived a monochrome existence and wanted colour in our lives.

Sometimes they'd stick on any old film. We were familiar with Edward G Robinson and James Cagney; I'm convinced John Garfield made a million films and that I saw them all in the Ormonde cinema on a Sunday afternoon.

John normally bought the tickets and we all bundled up to the ticket collector who tore the tickets with a look of disdain. Opening the door, we were hit by the usual wall of sound. In the half-darkness, you could see what only could be described as a madhouse. Kids were running up and down the aisle screaming their heads off. Others jumped from one seat to another, screaming of course. The continuous noise of the seats banging down on the supports added a certain beat to the proceedings. Others walked down the cinema on the backs of the seats. Nearly everyone in the cinema was on their feet and of course screaming.

Kids were hell-bent on acting out the last film they had seen. Everyone wanted to be the good guy because the good guy lasted till the end of the film. Nobody wanted to be the bad guy or an Indian. The boys pretended to shoot six-guns and rifles and raced around the aisles slapping their backsides pretending they were on horseback.

Occasionally you could hear toy cap guns being fired off. For some reason, the cinema ushers drew the line of tolerance at guns. If you were caught shooting anyone with a noisy cap gun, you'd get thrown out without getting your money back.

The girls were just as noisy and rowdy. Sometimes they brought skipping ropes and played games in the aisles.

Bigger boys and girls, John's age, huddled in the darker areas and smoked cigarettes. John had been smoking for years. He took after Aunt Connie in that respect.

In spite of the confusion and darkness, John picked out his friends and headed straight for them. Without being told, we moved into the row in front of them. I recognised most of them. They neither looked at us nor commented on us in any way. Younger kids just don't exist in older kids eyes.

The noise, the chaos, the bedlam... we sunk down in our seats and munched our sweets. It could be dangerous out there for a proddy. We always arrived early to get a good seat. If you arrived late, you could be sitting beside any lunatic; or you might not get in at all. With so many people out of their seats and running around, the ushers might call a full house to make things easier for themselves.

When the lights began to dim the screaming and cheering were overtaken in volume by the noise of everyone stamping their feet on the floor in approval. The ushers didn't like the floor stamping either. They rushed about with their flashlights shouting at us to stop, but it was a futile exercise. They invariably gave up after they'd evicted a few of the usual culprits and when the stamping died down.

The programme followed the usual pattern: advertisements, cartoons and then the main film. Cartoons which were a big favourite. We all imitated the noises and dialogue. 'Kahbong!' everyone shouted together. 'What's up doc?' we implored.

The din dropped a little when the main film came on. Most of us wanted to follow the story line and dialogue. Everyone laughed at the funny lines, so amid all the noise and bad behaviour, it was obvious that the audience were still paying attention.

After the main feature it was the serial. They showed *Green Arrow* for several months, sometimes the same episode repeatedly. Sometimes the film quality was so poor that it skipped badly from scene to scene. We usually watched it standing up and backing toward the exit. We didn't want to waste any time getting out of the cinema and avoiding the national anthem.

As soon as the doors were thrown open, everyone piled out. It was down hill all the way home and we ran most of it. In winter it was dark when we emerged so we didn't worry too much about being spotted by Mr Smythe's spies.

If we had been spotted, it was usually Tuesday when Sally, John and I were called up to the top of the class for the inquisition. Mr Smythe pushed his glasses further down his nose and spoke to us looking over the rims. We stood and waited. Looking around, we could see some of the class giggling, others looked worried for us; most ignored what was going on.

Mr Poyntz didn't say much, but you could see in his face that the next time he spoke to god he was going to mark our cards for us. We suffered the usual chastisement and humiliations, which lasted until the business of lunch took over.

We realised Mr Smythe or Mr Poyntz couldn't stop us from going to the matinees. I think we were used us as an example to deter other potential reprobates from following our sinning ways. We felt hard done by of course, but relieved there was no caning involved. Either way I always felt I had fallen from professor to condemned prisoner during these interrogations. If I prayed for anything at all on Sunday, I still prayed that I wouldn't be spotted going to the matinee.

13

'Lord don't stop the carnival'

In my child's life, the school terms changed without fanfare. Year after year I went up a year, a process that introduced me to new experiences, challenges and skills, and almost rid me of the worry of 'being kept back.' Life in the Fishery, however, changed at a much slower pace and generally not at all.

Although there was always the temptation to roam far and wide about the town, the handiest and nearest place to play over the years had always been the South Green. This wild, square, open space of common ground was bounded on one side by the high stout wall of the Shipyard. On another side, it was hemmed in by the narrow back gardens of twenty or more cottages and houses. At the end of this terrace, a rough track formed a route from the Dainty Bakery to the river. From anywhere in the Green you could see and smell the river and get to it through gaps between houses built along its bank.

In summer, beds of nettles and golden rag weeds, laden with insects, competed for space on the grass where we played cowboys and Indians, built tents and lit fires. Through this lush growth meandered tracks, hiding secret places where gangs of friends could disappear from the scrutiny of mothers and other adults.

On clear windy days the back gardens were ablaze with lines laden with washing. Brightly coloured garments licked at the wind and then simultaneously disappeared from sight. Occasionally; a mother's or a grandmother's head appeared over a back wall to check all was well in the Green.

In winter it was a desolate spot, given over to solitary males who trapped birds among the remaining dried thistles and nettles. They were members of the Cage Birds Society; they preyed on goldfinches, bullfinches, linnets and peewees. We would see their catch on display at exhibitions, and of course they sold them on when the occasion arose.

On bitter days, we'd catch sight of them brooding in the snow, noses red and raw. Even those occasions when icicles hung from the eaves, they were out there, stamping their feet and blowing into their cupped hands. I remember they were supremely protective of their chosen patch – woe betide any child that sauntered by with swinging arms and skipping gait.

Summer and winter the Green was an occasional home to tinkers and their caravans. You rarely saw them arriving, but when you did eventually notice them, they were sitting around a fire on car seats waiting for a kettle to boil. It was as if this Green had been their ultimate destination all along. Just as the Green gave us space to make our own fun, the Tinkers seemed to treat this area as a sort of refuge. They arrived in caravans like the ones Dad made. Occasionally they had a van or a lorry. Out of nowhere came tents and cooking fires. Soon men in groups were standing around smoking and talking while the women nursed babies and watched pots over the fire.

Around the Green, their distinctive piebald horses sampled the vegetation that the season provided, each one tethered by a lengthy rope anchored to a rock or other available heavy weight.

The Green was prone to flooding in wet weather so these visitors camped on the slightly raised patch of ground that served as our arena when dark pools of stagnant water dominated the area. When the tinkers were in residence we usually gave the Green a wide berth.

More interesting and more welcome were the summer visits of McFadden's Road Show. This travelling playhouse with its accompanying carnival arrived with enormous fanfare. Days before it arrived, posters appeared on shop windows and a car with a loudspeaker toured town advised us of the coming delights, with the kind of lavish, gushing descriptions that always turn out to be so much hot air.

The show usually arrived before a Bank Holiday week in the summer when people were sure to be looking for entertainment and had the time and money to enjoy it. Caravans pulled by cars and huge trailers pulled by old lorries attracted boys from all over the neighbourhood. The caravans were arranged in a neat circle away from the carnival stalls and show tent. Soon after they arrived, the roustabouts set about erecting the big tent which nightly would become our theatre of dreams. One huge pantechnicon parked snug against one end of the tent transformed into a stage. Gradually the attractions took shape: the chair-o-planes, the swinging boats, the rifle range, the bumping cars and of course the candy floss booth. We knew it was all good to go when the man who looked like the boss turned on the illuminated sign over the entrance. 'Showtime – 8 PM – Drama and Variety', it shouted. That usually marked the opening of the carnival and stalls. Everyone had to wait till the evening for showtime.

Suddenly the area was full of activity. The carnival folk had somehow changed into clowns and cowboys to encourage us to try the entertainment on offer. A loudspeaker boomed out 'circusy' music and a woman dressed like Calamity Jane handed out free lollipops and led children around the stands where everything was 'wonderful' and 'amazing'. The boss had changed into a suit and top-hat and was selling tickets for the night's performance. A clown walked around juggling balls, routinely dropping them to howls of laughter. The spectacle reminded me of a scene from the film *The Greatest Show on Earth*. The only things missing were the acrobats and the elephants, but there was certainly music in the air when the carnival came to town.

From about 7.30, an impatient and expectant queue had already formed. As night fell the coloured lights were like a flying carpet above us. The performers seemed to sense the excitement and raised their game in a programme that was a mixture of short plays, musical numbers, comedic turns and a lot of audience participation. I became familiar with plays like *Noreen Bawn* and *Pal of My Cradle Days*. The White Sisters, the Cormack Brothers and Tara Players were familiar show stars. These strolling actors laboured through tangled scripts, sang familiar songs and told hilarious jokes; sometimes the same ones as the previous year. They incorporated a talent competition into the proceedings each night with a grand finale during the last night's performance. Talented – and untalented – locals embraced the opportunity to strut their stuff. How we howled in delight.

The five or six days a year when the road show graced our lives was enough for them to become friendly with locals residents, shop owners and dignitaries. When they pulled away from the Green on that final morning, there were emotional goodbyes. 'See you next year!' was the enthusiastic shout. It served to confirm that the show would indeed return the following year; and it surely did, for many an encore.

With so many of life's simple delights, you have to enjoy it while it lasts. There comes a time when decisions taken elsewhere have a profound affect on people's lives. To me it seemed to begin when the council began constructing a road across the Green. This narrow track ran from the South Quay across the Green to the Dainty Bakery. 'Why do they need to do that?' we wondered.

'It's relief work,' said Mam. 'For men who are our of work.' I didn't think too much of it.

The work on the road progressed sporadically all through summer and into the autumn. On harsh icy days, the workers stood around fires blowing on their hands and smoking incessantly while a big mixing machine prepared cement for the next segment. On other days, no one appeared at all, and their equipment was left to the ravages of the weather. They finally finished coming up to Christmas.

Around this time, the outside world made its first impact on my young life. It came via the words 'Katanga', 'massacre', ' peace-keeping' and 'Baloobas'. The radio, TV and papers were full of it; the President and Taoiseach were constantly on Radio Eireann. The details, as much as I was allowed to see, were appalling. The country seemed in a state of shock and everyone suddenly appeared to know someone in the army.

Mam and Dad, not usually great fans of Irish radio, were constantly tuned in to Athlone, mesmerised. The local papers were full of pictures of solemn-faced priests and politicians of every stripe and level reassuring the population.

Somehow the road across the Green, though not officially named, in our house became the Katanga Road. Mam took her inspiration from the fact that in Arklow we already had a Burma Road, near the entertainment centre. 'It's good to remember those poor innocent soldiers that were massacred out in Africa keeping the peace amongst the savages,' she said.

It was a good idea but the name never stuck. My parents were the only ones who called it that. In our family you could always be sure they knew where you were playing if you said the Katanga. Dad said that the amount of time he saw the workers standing around smoking, it should have been named Tobacco Road.

Once the road was completed, it gradually dawned on us there were bigger plans for this piece of waste ground. By this time, our games of cowboys and Indians had given way to soccer. Where we were once the Lone Ranger or Tonto, now we played for Arsenal or Manchester United.

One day as we were making our way to the Green with a football, someone shouted, 'Hey, they built us a goal!'

Certainly from a distance the thing he was pointing at looked like a set of goalposts. As we got closer, we could see that it was an advertisement board, which read:

A New Scheme of Homes.

Move in by June 1962

£50 Deposit secures.

'They're going to build houses here,' someone said.

'Fifty pounds deposit! No one will ever be able to afford that.'

Mam begged to differ. I think she felt these new houses would give newly married couples the opportunity to buy a decent place. It was something that she could identify with.

As spring gave way to summer, work on the new houses began. The Green was always damp underfoot, so the builders put in the huge drainage pipes to remedy that problem. Nevertheless the estate was promptly nicknamed 'The Everglades' after the television programme of the same name.

In our house, changes were also occurring. For one thing, I found that my parents accompanied me to church less often. It was almost as if I was finally trusted to get there alone. I usually met Sally and Bobby on the way and sometimes Algy and Betty, who were still watching out for us. Both of them were into their teens and were working in the Pottery after a brief stint in a small crisp factory in Hudson's Square.

Algy often bought a paper in Curran's newsagents on the way up, and instead of continuing up the main street we turned onto the river walk. This route took us to the church back entrance, avoiding the main street. We never said it but I think we all preferred to go this way because we avoided walking by the Catholic church, and of course we met no one.

It goes without saying that using this route also allowed us to make the choice of whether we actually went into the service or not. The weather was a big factor. Sometimes if it was dry and fine we walked past the church completely and continued on the river walk out towards Glenart Castle. If the weather was really nice, we stayed in the church grounds and read papers or fooled around until the service was over.

Being one of the youngest of the group, I just went along with whatever happened. Anything was better than sitting through the minister's boring sermon. We all had reached the stage where going to church on a Sunday was complete torture.

One fine day in June, we arrived in the church grounds, having dawdled just enough to miss the beginning of the service. John crept up to the church door and whispered, 'I think the service has started.'

Algy quickly added, 'Feck it, I'm not going in if it's started. The minister will give us one of his looks and tell Mam.'

I sort of knew what was going to happen next. We'd all wait outside in the grounds until the service ended. Then before the congregation came out, we'd all nip down through the back gate and down to the river walk and no one would be any the wiser.

We walked around to the front of the church to check if the minister was in the vestry. It was empty, so we reckoned he was out doing his stuff.

'Where will we go?' Sally said.

Quickly Algy replied, 'Down behind the rhododendron bushes looks nice. We can escape through the gate and down the back lane before anyone comes out after it's over.'

Very few people other than us used the back entrance. A lot of country people usually came in cars and parked out front. We sauntered down to the bushes and settled for the long wait. Algy sat down and laid out her paper. We weren't great paper readers in our house. Mam definitely didn't like the English Sunday papers Dad bought. Algy had bought the *News of the World* on the way to church. In it was an article about the possibility of a Catholic president of America. I'd heard Mam talking about this as well. 'If they elect him,' she said, 'he'll be killed.'

Inevitably someone always bought the *Wicklow People*. As I got older and bolder in my reading habits, I often turned to the local court section in the *Wicklow People* for entertainment. Some of the court cases were hilarious and the excuses for traffic violations bizarre. One man who featured frequently before a particular justice defended his action of turning left across oncoming traffic without indicating with the statement, 'Why should I? Everyone knows I live there.'

'Indeed, everyone except the person you ran into, it seems,' the justice replied.

Other cases read like the script from a comedy film. Two regulars to these pages broke into a public bar not so much to steal anything but to help themselves to a night of drinking. All went well for the first few rounds but then they had an argument about whose round it was. They came to the conclusion what they really needed was a barman to keep tabs on things. The solution was to phone a friend, an erstwhile accomplice who had the necessary experience to serve them drinks. Soon they had a friend standing behind the bar doing the business for them. Apparently his performance was much appreciated and he was regularly including in the round. Next morning they were discovered asleep in the bar by the owner who called the police. It was the stuff of legend.

Time drifted on. We seemed to be lounging there forever. Occasionally Algy laughed at something she was reading.

'Ha ha, Lady Chatterley's in the news again.'

I was a bit mystified by Lady Chatterley. I'd seen both Mam and Dad reading a book called *Lady Chatterley's Lover* and wondered if it could be connected. Suddenly we heard a crunch on the gravel path quite near us.

'Mothera Jesus,' Algy cried, 'it's over, someone's coming.'

We all jumped up and dashed to the gate. I didn't look back, hoping that whoever it was didn't actually see my face. We ran through the gate and across the road laughing hysterically and screaming. The lane down to the river walk was very steep and somehow it helped if you screamed while you ran.

Amid the uproar someone said, 'Who was it?'

'Did he see us?'

'Keep going,' Betty said, 'maybe no one saw us.'

'Maybe we got away with it.'

'The eejit on the path probably thought we'd just come out of service as well.'

'Who was it?'

Nobody knew and we never found out, but the delicious feeling of having gotten away with something is not soon forgotten.

Gradually the houses on the Green were built and the estate was given the boring name South Green, so neither the Everglades or the Katanga Road ever achieving the fame they deserved for their inventiveness alone. To my knowledge, the Road Show never returned. Many of the actors who performed under the canvas went on to appear in *Tolka Row* and *The Riordans* weekly series on TV sets not a million miles from where they once performed their routines on the back of a McFadden's lorry.

14

'No more working for a week or two'

We never went anywhere on holidays. It didn't matter, nobody else did either. Holidays were not going to school or work. Going somewhere else to take advantage of this precious time didn't appear to be necessary. So it came as a big surprise to me when Mam announced in the spring of 1962 that she and I would travel to Swansea to visit Uncle Jack and Uncle Dick. As an afterthought, she said, 'Your Dad is coming as well.'

She had threatened for years to go over and visit them, but something always got her off the hook at the last minute. My delight was a little dented when I discovered that Connie was also coming, with Sally and Bobby. I had waited for years to go to Swansea, and Bobby and Sally got to go when they were much younger than me. Not fair!

The brothers lived in opposite ends of Swansea, and Mam arranged for us to stay with Uncle Dick while Connie, Sally and Bobby stayed with Uncle Jack. Connie was then going to travel down to London to visit some of her husband's cousins, and then on her way back to Ireland to call in on Uncle Dick. This annoyed me even more. They were going to be away longer than me, and get to visit London as well. Oh well.

We spent what seemed to be a couple of weeks packing, and panicking about sailing tickets, boarding tickets, rail tickets and train times. I didn't get new clothes for the trip. 'They're cheaper in England,' Mam said.

Dad as usual was relaxed about the trip. I knew he'd have a good time no matter what happened. He was already in a good mood because this year he'd not be required to work his way through the list of jobs that Mam always concocted to be done during his summer holidays.

Dad kept asking questions about when exactly we were going and when we were coming back. He had a bit of a bad memory with things like this.

'Where are you going from?' he'd ask Mam.

'Dun Laoghaire,' Mam replied with a hint of impatience.

'I suppose it'll be the train then from Holyhead.'

'Unless we decide to hitch down to Swansea,' Mam replied. And so it'd go on.

One evening Billy Martin from next door dropped in, having heard that we were going on a trip to England.

'I just dropped in Sally,' he said, 'to see if you needed a lift up to Dun Laoghaire, or even up to the railway station. I'd be glad to help.'

Billy and Marion were from Dublin and still had family in the city. Billy thought nothing of driving up to Dublin. For us, a drive to Dublin was a big thing. Mam was delighted with the offer. You could see it in her face, but she refused.

'No, thanks very much Billy,' she beamed. 'Connie and her two are coming as well and we've all bought the tickets all the way to Swansea. But thank you all the same.'

Not to be outdone, Billy replied, 'Well I could give you, Connie, and your luggage a lift up to Arklow station. The youngsters could make their own way up.'

Mam jumped at this offer. 'It's not too much trouble for you?' she asked, smiling.

'Not at all, not at all,' Billy said. 'I'll come in closer to the day and make sure I have the time right.'

Dad shuffled his paper.

'So you're all looking forward to the trip. I've never been across the water myself,' Billy said to more or less to everyone in the room.

Mam jumped in first. 'Yes, it's been ages since we've seen my brothers. When they were over here last, you weren't even living in the town.'

It had indeed been years since they'd visited. I could remember well. They weren't here very long before Mam couldn't wait to see the back of them. Dick and Jack usually wore out their welcome fast with their constant drinking, sleeping late, getting sick, smoking all the time and her waiting hand and foot on two big lazy men. They were always short of money and always on the 'Bill Hammy', as Mam called looking for money. Bill Hammy was an old Arklow down-and-out, who spent his time in the Main Street holding his hand out, begging.

'We're looking forward to visiting England,' she added.

Dad spoke up. 'England used to be a grand place thirty or forty years ago, before the war, but not now. What with the divorces and the scandals and the blacks. And what do you make of that Christine Keeler?'

I'd heard Mam and Dad talking about her after dinner on a Sunday evening after they'd read the *News of the World*. It was all spoken about in lowered voices like the discussions they had about Lady Chatterley.

Billy replied, 'I don't know much about the whole thing Ned. I think it's all to do with politics.'

'Politics and women,' Dad said, shaking his paper once again. That appeared to be his final word on the subject. Billy took this as his signal to leave.

The big day eventually came. As planned Billy Martin drove Mam and Connie up to the station with the bags. Sally, Bobby and I made our own way up. We were sent off early in case anything distracted us.

Inexplicably, Dad was also allowed to make his own way to the station. 'I have someone to meet up the street,' he explained mysteriously. Mam was indifferent; she had our tickets, papers and spending money. 'The train goes at 3.30,' she said to no one in particular. 'It won't wait for anyone...'

Contrary to everyone's expectation of us, we made it to the station early, so much so that by the time the train came in we were bored to tears. Dad arrived at almost the same time as Mam and Connie. Whatever bit of business he had, he seemed none the worse for wear as a result.

At Dun Laoghaire, it was just a short walk to the boat. We boarded almost immediately.

We'd booked a couple of bunks in what was called steerage. Mam had packed sandwiches and drinks, so we didn't need to wander far to get something to eat.

It soon became obvious that we were very inexperienced travellers. We got lost trying to get to the bunks and we couldn't find the toilets. We dragged our cases to the bunks when we should have left them in a little room by the door. Mam and I shared one bunk, with the three Sherwoods on the other. I was amazed to see our bunks were in a large open cabin with lots of other bunks. These were gradually filling up with passengers like ourselves who all seemed to be noisy and smoking. Each bed had several brown paper bags attached to the side. I asked Mam what they were for. 'They're for when you get sick.' She didn't say, 'If you get sick.' I hadn't much experience of boats except the odd trip over the bar at the Blessing of the Boats.

The smell of cigarettes was becoming unbearable. Underneath this familiar smell however there was a sort of bitter smell that you just couldn't put your finger on. I asked Mam what it was. 'It's the smell of all the sick from the previous sailing.' She was not happy.

The only word to describe the journey across to Holyhead was 'nightmare'. It had all those things that you associated with a bad boat trip. The sea was rough and that gave all us bad sailors the opportunity to behave accordingly. I was very sick, but I wasn't the only one. At one stage a queue formed of people trying to get into the toilets to be sick. Eventually people resorted to those bloody bags beside the bunk. By the time we docked in Holyhead, I didn't know whether I was alive or dead.

Going through customs was our next worry. Mam and Connie were sure we wouldn't be stopped. 'They won't stop women with children,' Mam said trying to reassure herself. I'm not sure what they were worried about. It wasn't as if we were smuggling anything. The Customs and Excise men seemed friendly. They were addressing most of the men going through by their first names. I heard several of them say, 'Hey Paddy', or 'Hey Mick, can you open this bag for me?' But they weren't that clever: they got Dad's name wrong. Somehow they also thought his name was Mick.

The train trip down to Swansea was terrible too; we couldn't find seats and had to stand most of the way. It was still dark when we arrived in Swansea. After about an hour, Jack and Dick arrived to pick us up. Mam and Connie hugged them like the long lost relatives they were. Mam had a little cry. We went with Dick to his house, which was in the dockland area. Connie and her two caught a bus to Penlan where Jack lived.

Waiting to greet us at Dick's house were his wife, Beattie, and my teenage cousin Maureen, their daughter. I looked at Beattie carefully and a little suspiciously. In our family, she was always spoken of – in hushed tones – as 'the divorced woman'. Dick was her second husband. She had a daughter called Elisabeth, who lived close by with her husband and baby boy.

After travelling all night, we had no trouble falling asleep. They left us for a few hours before Beattie called us for something to eat.

Their house wasn't all that big. It was in a terrace of about fifty houses, all painted the same dark green. Uncle Dick said it because the corporation owned them all.

The outside toilet was a novelty to me, and there was no bathroom in the house. There was a bath, but it was hidden under the kitchen table. You lifted up the top of the table and there underneath was a secret bath. All this was a bit disappointing. I thought that everyone in England was better off than us. If Uncle Dick's was anything to go by, the English actually lived in really small houses, with pokey little rooms. It had one advantage over ours, however: they had two television sets, one in the kitchen and one in the sitting room which was turned into a bedroom for Mam and Dad. It appeared that I was sleeping in the same room in a small fold-up camp bed. 'This is going to be cosy,' Dad said. Not half.

The whole neighbourhood where they lived was dreary. There were a few shops and pubs, but the area was made up of hundreds of terraced houses, row upon row. To get into town to visit the main shopping area, you needed to catch two buses.

I soon discovered there wasn't much to do in Swansea except go shopping, which bored me stiff. Beattie noticed and asked, 'What can we do with a boy?'

'He likes making Airfix models,' Mam said.

The next day Beattie came back with a present for me – a model of the Queen's coronation carriage. So I spent most of my time in Swansea putting it together and returned the thoughtfulness by leaving it behind when we went home.

Maureen was about the same age as Algy back home. She got up to the same things: reading magazines, smoking on the sly, always doing her hair and listening to pop on the radio. She was fascinated by film and pop stars and the walls in her bedroom were covered with pictures cut from magazines and newspapers. Also like Algy and Betty, she just couldn't wait for the time to quit school and find work.

She told us she'd been to see a great movie called *Play it Cool*, singing the title song to us to stress how good it was. 'Play it cool, baby. Play it cool.' She wasn't a great singer, a trait that ran through our family, it seemed, with a couple of notable exceptions.

She also showed us a magazine advertisement for the film which was reminiscent of the posters in the Ormonde cinema in Arklow. She read out loud, 'The screen sizzles when Billy Fury, Helen Shapiro and Bobby Vee play it cool.' Then she added with growing excitement, 'Loads of people were thrown out of the cinema for dancing in the aisles and on the seats!'

That was a familiar story. I began to wonder what frenzy drove these teenagers to violent behaviour, all because of a movie about music. It seemed I had a lot to learn about teenagers, music and movies.

Our holiday in Swansea was brief and somehow also terribly long. Mam, I knew, was fed up with the endless drinking in Uncle Jack's Working Mens' Club, and her immediate verdict was 'Never again.'

Dad's impression was probably a bit different. It seems that on one of his nights out with the boys, he had taken to the stage at the club and belted out a couple of tunes from his extensive repertoire. 'The first one went down so well they called for an encore,' Uncle Dick admitted. He couldn't remember what songs Dad had sung, and with Mum looking none too pleased, Dad just kept quiet.

For myself, I just about remember the unfaltering monotony of the area we stayed in, the rows and rows of deserted streets with their myriad small houses, without children playing outside, and the only living soul an occasional flat-capped old man with a dog.

Dad was amazed that with several minor repairs needed on Uncle Dick's house, the solution was to report the problem to the Council and wait for them to arrive to fix it. There seemed to be an utter dependency on social welfare and the Council was there to solve all ills. Post-war gloom seemingly was alive and kicking in Swansea.

The journey home I remember being equally horrendous, through a largely overcast and smog-ridden country. When we finally arrived by train at Arklow, the smiling sunlit face of Billy Martin, who was there to welcome us back, banished all the trials we'd endured on the journey.

Back home, relaxing in my own comfortable environment, the first song I remember hearing on the radio was some Irish guy singing 'I never will be a wild rover no more', which just about summed up my feelings on the adventure I had just experienced.

I settled back into my daily life faster than I expected and although it might not have been a concept I fully understood, I knew I would never visit Swansea or its like ever again.

15

'Too much sun will burn'

As the gloom and half-light of our long winter gave way to a bright and chilly spring, summer still always felt far away – until it suddenly arrived and that only really happened when it was warm enough to go to the beach.

Preparation for this great event began with a hurried search for last year's togs. If I was lucky, Mam spotted togs going cheap in George O'Toole's shop and bought some for me as a surprise. Failing that, I made do with last year's model.

Going to the beach was popular all over the Fishery. It was a way of life in the summer. When the weather was good, entire families traipsed around the dock to the beach behind the pottery, or the long way over McCarthy's hill, through the golf links and out to the Rock. It wasn't unusual to see people boiling kettles on fires of driftwood or on Primus stoves. The more adventurous caught mackerel and fried them up on the spot.

As if we didn't have enough water to swim in all around Arklow, the council decided to build a swimming pool in Ferrybank, with an attached dance hall, café, mini golf course and tennis courts. That changed the focus from the lovely unspoilt south beach, to this lido type of unheated, unsheltered outdoor pool. Rumours started in the town that you could catch all sorts of unmentionable diseases like diphtheria and scarlet fever from the pool, but stubbornly the young people kept going all summer long. The crowd that hung around the pool were a little cliquey, but you still could make your own fun.

The pool provided swimming lessons all summer, which was a

good thing. Over the years, many a youngster had got a job aboard a fishing boat without being able to swim a stroke. Now everyone could learn to swim in wonderful modern surroundings.

The swimming pool epitomised the changes that were happening in Arklow. We were being offered alternatives and choices almost without us realising or being ready for them.

Summer brought the Sea Breezes. These were special trains from Dublin to Arklow for a cheap day's outing at the seaside. I'm sure whoever started them envisaged an opportunity for city folk to have a day of fresh air and paddling. The reality was nothing like that.

Many Dubliners arrived at Arklow railway station already tanked up and with only one intention: to go to the nearest pub and get more drink. Conveniently most of the pubs were just a short walk from the station. So they drank in all the pubs down one side of the main street and drank their way back up the other side. By the time they were halfway back, they were beyond caring. Fights broke out. They sang. They keeled over and passed out senseless on the footpath. Women got on tables, raised their skirts and danced. It was wonderful. I learned and understood the phrase 'beautifully drunk'.

It was such a laugh on a Sunday evening to see them all tottering up St Mary's Terrace, making what speed they could to catch the last train home. Occasionally, to add to the spectacle, the Sea Breezers passed the chapel just as hundreds of worshippers were exiting evening mass. You needed to see it to believe it. It was like something from *The Quiet Man*. Locals were simultaneously outraged by their antics of kissing each other on the Main Street and entertained by their comical behaviour.

'Hurry up Danno,' a Breezer would shout with a broad Dublin accent, 'for Jasus sake, we're going to miss the effin' train.'

'You go ahead then Eammo, and lie down in front of the engine. They won't run over you.'

Mam called them 'sea boozers'. She along with many other locals were perplexed by the outlandish carry-on of the Breezers. But they truly enlivened our summers. For many days after, they were the topics in pubs, houses and where housewives tended to queue. Whatever your opinion, the visitors certainly spiced up our small town lives, if only momentarily.

During those summers, many things impacted on my life, and strange to say the issue of a local chip shop left a lasting impression. Chips seemed to be something we ate a lot of during the summer. For a long time, Arklow only had one chip shop. It was quite a distance from the Fishery and traded under the enigmatic name of Bumptas. Above it was a snooker hall. To buy chips in Bumptas was a little inconvenient. It took ages to get up the town and by the time you were back home, the chips were all eaten or they were stone cold. We couldn't believe our luck when a chip shop opened a couple of hundred yards from our house.

One summer, a small grocery shop in Old Chapel ground began selling chips. This was great, like a gift from the gods. We became regular visitors during the long summer nights. It seemed for a while that we were having chips with everything.

All went well with the new chip shop through the summer. Mam made the tea and then at the last minute sent me to run up for the chips to go with whatever she'd made.

Eventually someone started taking an interest in just how his man was cooking his chips. He didn't seem to have a big fryer like Bumptas. It transpired that he was cooking the chips in a top-loading washing machine. People were mystified and then incensed. The fact that the owner of the shop had three small children, two of them still in nappies, led to a quick bit of speculation and a very unsavoury picture indeed. His chip custom gradually fell away to almost nothing and within a week the delights of this chippy became just another summer memory.

Every summer brought new fads along with the regular toys. Spinning tops were popular one year. Every kid in the neighbourhood was out on the street every minute of every day throughout the summer. Then everyone simultaneously switched to yoyos and you wouldn't be seen dead with a spinning top. Some years everyone had soapboxes, giving rise to a summer epidemic of broken legs and arms. Next year everyone had roller-skates, or it might be skipping or footballs or kites. There was always something that everyone would latch onto all at the same time, and then almost as abruptly drop like it was the most boring thing in the world, and switch to something different.

One year we all became infatuated with something seen as particularly American. Hula hoops appeared in the shops in early June. I didn't know what they were at first but within a week everyone in the town owned one, adults included. When the shops sold out, local plastic factories tried to cash in on the fad, but theirs weren't as good as the real thing.

I first saw them as I walked up the Harbour Road towards the Toker. I could see Algy and Betty walking towards me near Mrs Myler's sweetshop. They both looked peculiar. Something seemed to be spinning around their waists and they were walking strangely. The things at their waists seemed to have a mind of their own. Algy's was bright yellow and Betty's was lime. They were going very fast, whatever they were. When I got up to Algy I could see she was gyrating and making a plastic hoop go round and round her body. Algy seemed to be better at it than Betty.

'What's that?' I said to Algy.

'Ah Rucky,' she replied – Rucky was my nickname – 'you'll have to get yourself one of these. They're called hula hoops and they're great for the figure.'

'Hula hoops,' I thought to myself. 'I don't think so.' They looked a bit girly to me.

So that summer every girl in the Fishery gave up skipping, hopscotch and playing happy clappy rolly polly balls against the gable ends of houses and took up full-time hula hooping.

A rumour went around the town, probably perpetrated by my mother, that you could loose a dangerous amount of weight if you did too much hula hoping, but it didn't stop many people from enjoying themselves.

There was great demand for them throughout the summer. They came in all shapes sizes and colours and everyone tried to outdo each other. Someone got a fluorescent one sent home from England. Gangs of women used them in the parish hall as aides to slimming. They made their way into dances to help people do the twist. Inevitably the shops sold out, and would put a little notice in the window telling customers when they expected the next delivery. When they arrived, they were always a little more expensive than the previous ones.

By September, when the schools reopened, the fad was wearing off, but it was still common to see girls going to school with their hoops spinning about them. It took until the end of the year for them to become just another distant summer memory. After that you'd see discarded hoops lying dejectedly on roofs of garden sheds or snagged around the tops of telegraph poles. Occasionally a shopkeeper with leftover stock tried a re-launch, but the fad never again regained such dizzy heights of popularity.

In those long days of summer, when the heat lay over us like a blanket, sometimes we escaped to the shady solitude of the Brow. High up in a vantage point, we could see everything below. The silvered links floated away to the seashore. People stretched out below us, like wind-flattened brightly coloured flowers. Patches of Hessian-coloured fairway were testimony to the summer's extremes and contrasted to the almost blue lush grass of the well-watered greens looking cool and soft for bare feet.

The sky remained truly cloudless: it seemed the heavens lost the art of providing shade during these torrid weeks. It was truly the time of summer skies and dragonflies. The blue canopy above us was almost devoid of vapour trails and planes, but when occasionally a jet did appear, its tiny silver wake gave us pangs for faraway places we knew of only from television and the cinema. I often wondered what the world might look like from up there.

'Ah come on, let's head home,' Bobby wearily whinged. He went on like this for ages: it was a bad idea coming out here... we should have stayed at home... at least there we had comics and the radio to distract us...

'Shut-up,' was my reaction. 'Shut-up, I'm tired too. We'll go soon. I'll give you the skutch of my apple,' I said, hoping that might distract him.

I knew that might keep him quiet, but not for long. This outburst disturbed my dog, Pal, who somehow managed to give us an annoyed look before yawning and resuming his indifference. Pal went everywhere with me; he seemed genuinely perplexed when he wasn't allowed to come to school as well.

I peered over the ferns that hid us from the rest of the world. Below lay the town golf links on a scorched semicircle of land between the Harbour and the Quarry. A fine golden beach formed a diameter joining these two points. The circumference was a raised brow. On this brow, the golf clubhouse had a prominent position. It was made of corrugated iron and a sort of green that's only achieved by not being painted for many years. The original deep green had bleached to a watery lime colour that made it stand out even more from its surroundings The veranda in the front was usually full of club members drinking and smoking while watching the progress of golfers far out on the links.

Along the foot of this brow, there was a well-trodden footpath which was a popular if longer route to the beach. It was particularly favoured by dog owners. On a normal Saturday, lots of people were out and about: people with prams and kids, boys on bicycles, groups going swimming with their towels and togs rolled in that peculiar and uniform way and held under the arm like some sort of military thing. This was not a normal Saturday however.

This particular Saturday was the day before Corpus Christi, when the townsfolk, mostly Catholics, prepared for the Sunday procession, the big day of the year. The population busied itself with bunting and flag poles, disguising eyesores and generally painting and cleaning everything in sight.

All of Arklow's bands took part, marching with military precision, practising their moves as if preparing for an invasion or perhaps a crusade. Groups of children who lately had made their first holy communion were drilled to distraction. Tomorrow they would perform in their best suits and dresses. Every club from the Caged Birds Society to the Women's Sodality of Our Lady declared their fidelity by decorating the town with flowers, grottos and an array of strategically placed holy statues. You could feel the commitment and intent in the air. It was a wonderful endeavour. It was religion in action. God was on their side.

On days like this, we Protestants felt uncomfortable. The might of the Catholic church took over the town. We were surplus to requirements. We knew our place in the scheme of things.

Today was one of those days when you really noticed the difference; there were fewer people around, fewer kids to hang out with. Bobby and I were spending the day alone, loafing about on this brow, until hunger drove us home for our tea.

Bobby said in despair, 'Ah come on, Rucky, let's go home. I'm fed up. We could get some money back on bottles and buy sweets.'

'Maybe you're right,' I said. I had my doubts if Mr O'Reilley's shop was open on this dreadful day, but I hadn't the heart to tell him. Let him live in hope, I thought. Pal got up and shook himself slowly and lazily. He could sense he'd be on the move soon.

As we prepared to vacate our spot, movement below the golf clubhouse distracted me. Shading my eyes, I could see the distinctive figure of the harbour master walking along the path. Henry was very easy to spot. He always wore a captain's hat and a gleaming white shirt. He was a big man with a reputation for grumpiness and gruffness. We usually avoided him like the plague.

He went for a walk to the Quarry ever day, whatever the weather. The times of this walk varied with the tides in the dock and river, but he always took the same route, passing under our vantage point and finally stopping at the grotto near the Quarry for a moment's prayer or rest or a drink of cool water from the nearby spring. His two frisky spaniels ran ahead of him, always giving plenty of notice that he was on his way.

'We'll wait till old Henry passes by, and then we'll head home.'

His dogs were going crackers at this stage, dashing ahead and doubling back and completely engrossed in this daily pleasure. It was nice to see animals enjoying themselves. Henry joined in with the frolics: whistling them when they were out of sight and throwing bits of wood for them to chase and shouting their names. Pal obviously heard the commotion and I noticed him heading down to meet the spaniels. I sat back down. Bobby buried his white head in the grass in frustration.

After a while I said, 'Give it five minutes. He'll be well gone by then.'

'Those dogs are doing a lot of barking,' Bobby said.

'Pal went down; he might be having a go at them.'

Bobby stood up. 'Did you hear that? Sounded like a dog squealing.'

I had to admit I did hear something but what it was I couldn't be certain. It just might easily have been a hawk or other bird squealing a complaint about the heat.

'It's nothing. We'll go down the path soon.'

We left it a little longer but Bobby was first down. In the distance I could see Henry's hat bobbing through the trees and bushes.

Bobby was standing in a clearing on the path when I reached the bottom.

'Can you hear that? It sounds like a dog keening.'

I whistled and shouted. 'Pal, Pal! Come here!'

Bobby spotted it first, beneath a large sloe tree. It looked like a piece of old carpet or a coal sack, but shivering, moving.

'It's Pal! Look! He's hurt!'

Pal looked up and moaned for good effect. I scrambled down beside him. 'It's his leg. What the hell happened?'

'He's not bleeding. It wasn't the dogs. He was hit by something.'

Lying beside Pal was a large beach stone, a little bigger that a hurling ball.

'He must have been hit by that,' Bobby ventured.

'Bloody Henry,' I said. 'The dogs were fighting and Henry used the stone to break it up.' He could have killed my dog, I thought.

We stayed for what seemed ages but eventually got Pal back on his feet. He wasn't a small dog but I was able to carry him for short distances. After a couple of hundred yards of this carrying and resting, Pal started coming back to near his old self. Eventually he was able to limp along unaided, but in a sorrowful state.

Bobby said, 'We'll have to do something to get back at that bully; we can't let him get away with nearly killing Pal.' He added, 'You're the smart one; you'll have to think of something.'

I'd already come to that conclusion, and was working on something that had been in my mind all summer. We had already experienced a few skirmishes with Henry. We often shouted at him from hiding places as he walked by, sometimes calling him names – 'Hey Admiral! Hey Commodore!' – or shouting things at him in Long John Silver voices: 'Aarrgh Henry Lad, are ye going to the rock to pray for a woman?'

Sometimes he shouted back saying, 'I know who you are and I'll have a word with your father in John-Joe's pub tonight.'

This was a huge threat in our small community. The last thing you wanted is your father embarrassed by someone like Henry in front of all his drinking friends.

As summer passed and we got more and more bored with the long hot days, we got bolder in what we might say to him. Henry of course got a little angrier in what he shouted and a little more threatening in his replies.

Once when the comments were flying from the Brow down to Henry and from him back up to us, he had said, 'Is that you Sherwood? You and yours were never any good. Where are you living now, or have you all been thrown out of the house again?' Bobby found it hard to live with that taunt.

'Right,' I said. 'I'll come up with a plan. We'll have to do it tomorrow. I have something in mind.'

Bobby was excited. 'What is it? What is it?'

'I won't tell you till tomorrow. It'll be something great, something historic,' I said, but this only got him more excited

'We'll need a couple of knives and a small hatchet.' Bobby threw me a worried look. 'Don't worry, we're not going to kill him, but nobody must know about it. Trust me,' I said, 'this will be good.'

What I was about to do was dangerous if it got back to our parents so it was important that we weren't associated with what might happen. I harboured doubts and thought the whole thing might be too risky.

Next day we made our way out to our usual place on the Brow. An hour before Henry was expected, we moved down to the path, sneaking along like Indians in a movie. I carried the axe and Bobby had the knife. The plan was to dig a series of traps along the path and watch Henry stumble into them. It was darker down on the path than up the hill, and the air was cool. There was lush green all around with splashes of blue and yellow from flowers that found the shade preferable to the harsh summer sun.

At the first point of attack, we carefully removed the sod in the centre of the path, and dug a neat hole in the sandy soil. Using dead fern stems as supports we replaced the sod, carefully brushing away all signs of our activities. About twenty paces away we prepared another trap also in the middle of the path. Further along we came to a spot where the path widened. We pretended to dig a trap in the middle of the path making it look quite obvious. Cunningly we placed a trap on each side of this bogus trap.

Our work finished with two more traps in a narrow part of the path further along, both within a couple of paces of each other. This was all carried out in silence in the shaded quiet of the overgrown path, with both of us concentrating on getting even with this horrid man.

After checking the handiwork, we made our way back to the top of the Brow to wait for Henry. Both of us were in hysterics driven by nerves and devilment.

The anticipation of what might happen was almost too much to bear and distracting us sufficiently for Henry to get on the path along from the clubhouse without us noticing.

Catching sight of him and that white hat getting closer, the laughing and hysterics increased. As the dogs got nearer, they ran ahead of him, occasionally stopping and barking madly in the sun. They skirted over the first trap without falling in or causing any damage. We both went silent, holding our breath but savouring the moment.

Henry stepped on the first trap and lurched forward. The words 'bloody hell' reached us. Henry lay where he fell, but finally got up and dusted himself off. He picked up the hat that hurled forward some distance. Bobby let out a cry of delight. This attracted Henry's attention. He looked about and scanned the top of the Brow. The sun was behind us, so spotting anything was difficult.

Eventually he moved on and was caught again. The hat came off and his heavy body was thrown forward as his foot went under him. He again pulled himself up on his feet looking about for the culprits. Failing to see or hear anyone, he moved along the path.

As he approached the next area, he saw the sod disturbed in the middle of the path. He immediately moved to the side pressing up against the bushes to avoid what he thought was another trap.

We let out groans of delight. Once again he fell forward, quite heavily this time by the sound of it, as he was walking at an angle around the centre of the path and his body was twisted. Shaken, he stood up faster than the other occasions. He shook his fist in our general direction shouting, 'I'll find out who you are and you'll be sorry!'

He continued along the path at first watching carefully where he was walking. We placed the next two traps quite a distance away but quite near to each other. He must have thought that was the last of the traps and began looking up at the Brow while walking along, with just the occasional glance at the ground. When he fell into the second-last trap, I thought I was going to choke. It seemed the most spectacular dive of all. The string of curses that came up initially frightened me but eventually the laughing took over. He lay there for longer this time, which frightened me more.

He slowly pulled himself up with an almost resigned manner, but after just about one step promptly put his foot in the last trap. This time he stayed down a long time, and the worry and fear set in again. Henry got up and turned around, tottering off delicately in the direction he had come. His dogs seemed as confused as he was. The change of direction stopped them short and brought a bout of barking that seemed to reflect the confusion of their master. It was comical to see them reluctantly return in the same direction and retrace their steps.

We re-enacted the antics and revelled in the drama of it all until it wasn't funny anymore. The laughter gave way to hunger in the end, and without much more ado or any more discussion we set off home.

It occurred to me that Henry might be lying in wait for us. To get home safely and without being seen by him, we headed up to the top of the Brow and through the fields behind the clubhouse. We arrived home safely and split up.

I don't remember returning to the Brow that summer or ever again. By the time we thought it safe to go back, school was open again. I was coming up to thirteen and more interested in Radio Caroline and the Beatles than the Brow.

Years later, I was to return with my son. I told him the story of the harbour master and the summer ambush. Traces of the traps were still there.

16

'It's a rich man's game'

As much as activities like the Life Boys and Sunday school drew you closer to what was expected in the parish, eventually other incidents pushed you away and sowed the seeds of rebellion and discontent. These were, in retrospect, minor and sometimes petty occurrences, but coupled with the fact that I was getting older and getting a mind of my own, they were telling.

A Cheshire Home had opened just outside Arklow. I'm not sure if it was a home especially for English people or Protestant people but it was supported as usual by the great and good of St Saviour's. It was common knowledge that Leonard Cheshire, the founder, was a famous Spitfire pilot from the war. Dad's boss, Kevin, had some connection with the war as well, as did his brothers Reginald and Roy. He was heavily involved in the charity – it was his thing – and he tried to get everyone else on side as well.

One summer morning Kevin arrived at our house. Dad answered the door and after a few minutes I heard him calling me. I walked down the stairs to the door and Dad said, 'Kevin's got something to ask you.' Kevin was standing outside the door and held a couple of white caged-wire boxes in his hand. Inside these boxes were loads of pink feathers with safety pins attached. They looked like something a little girl might play with.

Dad continued, 'These are collection boxes for the Cheshire Home. Kevin was wondering if you'd take one around the town and sell them for the home.'

As usual Kevin was beaming with enthusiasm, almost hopping up and down. This enthusiasm usually involved roping in other people to take part in something he was interested in, but not necessarily doing it himself.

I had to think fast. He wanted me to walk around the town, go in and out of pubs selling pink Protestant feathers on a bank holiday weekend, at the same time as other kids would be collecting for the Lifeboat. I couldn't see that going very well at all for me. Dad and Kevin were waiting for a reply. I could feel the tension in the air. Things seemed to be moving in slow motion. Kevin was just about to hand one of the boxes over to Dad. It was now or never.

'Nope, I'm not doing it,' I blurted out. 'Sorry I just don't want to do it.'

I could see Dad smiling slightly. Kevin put the box back under his arm. Dad said, 'Well there you have it Kevin, you have your answer.'

Kevin was slightly taken aback. He hadn't expected this but said, 'I like a man who speaks up for himself.'

I was quite proud of this small display of independence. Dad seemed impressed as well. Mam, on the other hand, had she been present, would have been mortified. To her, all employers, especially Dad's had some sort of god-given hold on their employees and their families.

On the back of this experience, other opportunities for defiance arose which sometimes I failed to grasp and regretted later.

One day in school, we learned that the key to the belfry had been lost or stolen. Everyone was asked to look out for it and those present at its last sighting were questioned. After a couple of days, it remained missing and the parish was faced with the problem of a locked door and no way of getting into the belfry. Mr Poyntz was distressed that the bell ringers couldn't do their stuff before his service, and of course there was all that practicing that was so important. He enlisted the help of a retired sailor, Commodore Tyrrell, who funnily enough was a distant relative of Mam's. He appeared to have the necessary gumption to solve the problem.

The Commodore didn't make much headway, and eventually found his way to our front door to speak about it to Dad. I think Dad's nose was a bit out of joint, because he hadn't been asked to sort this out in the first place. He said he'd give any help he could, but as he needed to earn his living, he couldn't spend all day every day working on the lock.

They went up to St Saviour's so Dad could show the Commodore what he needed to do. Dad brought the toolbox in which he kept all his locksmith stuff: blank keys, spare keys, files, screw drivers and all sorts of tools that Dad had accumulated over the years, along with the knowledge of how to use them. I called it his 'criminal box' for picking locks. Gardai occasionally called on his skills and took Dad and his tools off in a squad car. We never knew until later whether it was because a lock couldn't be opened or had been illegally opened.

The door to the belfry had a big old lock and they were lucky to find a blank key that fitted it. All that was needed was to cut the blank to fit.

Dad showed the Commodore what to do: stain the blank key with the candle, insert the key and turn it as far as you could. This left an imprint on the blank and you then used the file to whittle down the blank to fit the lock. This was tedious and time-consuming. Each night the Commodore appeared at our house with the latest imprint and Dad did the filing. This went on for about a week with the key getting nearer and nearer to the required shape.

When the Commodore finally got the door open, he couldn't wait to tell Mr Poyntz. They met up in our school. Mr Smythe got in on the act and announced to the entire school, 'The belfry door is open! Three cheers for the Commodore!'

The whole school went mad except for me. Dad didn't get a mention. Even the Commodore didn't have the grace to mention his contribution. I knew Dad was the brains behind the operation and felt it needed to be said. I should have said something; I was going to say something; but I never did open my mouth. It left an anger and pain, carried for many years.

I was a bit fed up of the church and had begun to tire of the cult. For one thing, both the church and our school were constantly asking for donations; every spring they needed money for this or that. Inevitably I brought the bad news home to Mam. It came at first in the form of a note given to all students, but as the weeks went by and more and more parents paid up, there were verbal reminders for the tardy ones.

'Mam, Mr Smythe mentioned money for the upkeep of the school.'

'Oh he did, did he?'

'Well,' she harrumphed, 'Mr Smythe can whistle for his upkeep money for the next week or so.'

'Oh no,' I thought to myself. I'd have to give Sammy the usual excuses – I forgot it, or Mam forgot it, or I'll bring it in next week – while he did his best to embarrass me in front of the whole school.

I really believe that Mr Smythe never imagined anyone could possibly be short of money to pay for upkeep. Mam eventually paid it.

The parish distributed a magazine to promote activities and information pertaining to the parish. It also published all the yearly accounts listing donations to the school and church. All the families in the Fishery were at the bottom of the list with their ten bob or seven and six donations. Farmers and business men were inevitably at the top.

'The less you give, the further from heaven you are,' Dad used to say, worryingly.

The parish had other ways to bring in extra money. At certain times of the year we were encouraged to take part in what were called beetle drives. They drew in people from all over the parish that we hardly ever saw.

The Marlborough was the usual venue. To get in, there was an entrance fee. For this you got a cup of tea and some cakes at half time. You always got too much milk in the tea and not enough sugar. 'Farmers' tea,' Mam called it.

During these events, everybody seemed to maintain a churchly silence. It just added to the tension. The country people, who indeed were in the majority, seemed to get a great kick out of the evening. The townies, especially Sally and me, thought it was about the stupidest thing ever.

The farmers also turned out to be very good at the game. One of the few times I attended, I came last and got the booby prize. Even Sally did better than me but at least I got a prize. I realised I wasn't a great contestant.

As I got a little older, there were other activities in the parish and other opportunities to do something for the parish. One day after church service, sneaking out through the side door, I was collared by Roy Keegan and asked to join the bell ringers group. Roy possessed the same enthusiasm levels as Kevin Kearon, but on reflection it was almost inevitable that at some stage I'd be asked.

For some reason I said yes. Sally, who was with me, decided to come along as well. It was somewhat contrary to what my parents might have expected. Maybe it was to do with growing up. I was genuinely surprised that we decided to go.

On the way to the church on the first night, both of us talked like the venture was already doomed; it wasn't something we were going to brag about among our Catholic friends. Sally was singing, as usual. This time it was 'God gave this land to me', from the film Exodus. It was one of her favourites. She normally kept it for Sundays and church-related activities. This outing seemed to qualify.

We appeared at the appointed time and were shown the ropes, literally. We were the only young people there and were treated as I suppose all newcomers to a club are treated. The other ringers were genuinely delighted to see us. They were mostly young adults who had been to college and were now settling down to work for their parents and continue with an orderly life in the parish, to inevitably become the good and the great of the parish.

They proceeded to introduce us to the ropes – the bell pulls – and assorted paraphernalia. On one side of the room was a collection of hand bells. They hung neatly from the wall and looked like they were seldom if ever used.

The bell pulls were stout ropes that went high up to the ceiling and had a velvety red, white and blue part where your hands did all the work. I was interested to discover these colourful things were called 'Sallies.' In a room where varnished wood and church grey stone dominated, the Sallies were the only colour.

It quickly became apparent that bell ringing involved a lot of concentration. It was quite physical as well. I could see myself getting bored pretty fast.

After three of four visits, we were about to give up. On what we expected to be our last night, I took up the now familiar position. I pulled on the rope with as much strength as I could muster, trying valiantly to keep up and in time.

There was a point where, having let the rope go back up for a certain distance, you needed to grab it and pull back down. I grabbed on hard and pulled for all I was worth. All of a sudden I felt myself shooting upwards. It was if the rope had a mind of its own. I wasn't prepared for this and was expecting to return to the ground at any minute. But no, I kept going upwards being dragged inexorably towards that little hole way up in the ceiling.

I felt someone grabbing my knees and shouting, 'Let go, Richard, let go.' Seconds later, I was on the floor watching the decorated rope disappear through that small hole in the high ceiling.

Several people rushed over and asked if I was okay. Sally paled a little, and I'm sure I did also. My saviour, Roy Keegan, was non-plussed.

'This happens quite often. The beams break with the weight of the bell pulling against and whoosh, up the rope goes. You've got to be ready to let go or you could smash your skull against the ceiling if you weren't on your toes.'

While I was trying to understand the 'toes' bit, he continued. 'Can you let your dad know that we'll need a new beam as soon as he can do it.'

'Fine,' I said. 'I think I'll go home now, Roy.' Actually I was feeling a little sick.

Roy took this declaration in his stride. 'Okay, we were about to finish anyway.'

Sally and I stood looking at each other. The others had stopped. Some were sitting, others were leaning awkwardly against the walls. There were brief smiles of understanding. 'This happens a lot,' someone said. Someone else nonchalantly chipped in, 'It happened to me last Christmas.'

I followed Sally down the worn steps. At ground level, the door to the outside was reassuringly ajar. We made our way up the drive in silence except for the crunch of our footsteps in the gravel. The bells were silenced. As we reached the heavy gates and stepped out onto the busy road, the streetlights came on.

We didn't speak for awhile. Eventually I broke the silence.

'No feckin' way am I going back to that death trap.'

Sally agreed.

The journey home took forever. By the time I got there, I'd just about decided the parish could get by quite nicely without my involvement in its activities.

17

'Who shaves the barber?'

In September of 1962, a momentous year began for me. I returned after the summer holidays to Carysfort Primary School for my final year there: a year that ended with me sitting both for the Primary Certificate Examination and the Entrance examination for the Christian Brothers School that had opened the previous year. Before we broke for the summer holidays, Mrs Jacob, the teacher in the Infants school, went off on long-term sick, and subsequently retired.

In the intervening eight weeks, the Infant school had a succession of retired teachers, big girls, do-gooders and local eccentrics looking after them. Mercifully the new teacher was appointed before things got too much out of hand. Miss Maud Marshall was her name. She was young and pretty, and she had that beautiful name. Miss Marshall had prayer-book black hair, ruddy country girl cheeks and was given occasionally to wearing nail varnish and a hint of lipstick. Such occasional daring splashes of colour plus an exotic fragrance got the blood racing of her twelve and thirteen-year-old charges.

As with Mrs Jacob, Miss Marshall took the entire school for singing on Tuesdays and Thursdays. These affairs went from a cringingly boring experience with Mrs Jacob to one of participation and encouragement with Miss Marshall.

Mrs Jacob always had us singing hymns or psalms, or carols at Christmas. Miss Marshall introduced us to what she called 'pop songs'. *My Darling Clementine* and *She'll Be Coming Round the Mountain* weren't real pop as you'd expect in the hit parade, but still a long way from *Abide With Me* and *Shall We Gather at the River*.

She was very popular with the students in both schools, and in his way, I think Mr Smythe was quite fond of her also. Perhaps he saw her as his replacement when he retired. She had everyone eating out of her hand.

Very soon after we started back to school in September, Miss Marshall announced at one of her singing classes that Carysfort would be putting on a school concert at Christmas. 'There's a lot of work to do,' she warned, 'but I'm confident we'll come through.'

She was going to test everyone's singing in the next couple of lessons and pick the best for the solos. We all had to sell tickets to our families and friends to make it a success.

I didn't think much of it and completely forgot about it. Sally of course had a big part in both singing and acting capacity. Surprisingly I found myself also chosen for the double: to sing a solo and perform the part of Joseph in a short sketch. The son of a carpenter playing the part of the Nazarene carpenter was not lost on me. I approached both tasks with unusual energy, possibly to impress Miss Marshall. The show was of course held in the Marlborough Hall and was a typical example of the peculiar social activities and entertainment that the Protestant community produced.

Life continued as usual in our house. As you get older, it's funny how the normal and mundane become a little more interesting; even having a haircut. When I needed a haircut, Dad took me up the town on a Saturday afternoon to Wolohan's barbers at the Bridge. It was an old-fashioned men's hairdresser in the true sense of the description, and was rightly called barbers. It had a striped barber's pole on the wall outside. Inside the shop were several up and down chairs. In the corner Mr Wolohan kept a couple of wooden boxes for kids to sit on in these chairs. The leather belts for sharpening the cutthroat blades hung on the back of these chairs, glistened in the very bright lights, and ever ready for action. Dad never got a shave but it was common to see men lathered up with the barber wielding that blade skillfully on their cheeks and throats.

The shop was a bright, white, brilliantly lit room with painted floorboards and tall mirrors dotted about, giving customers a good view of progress of their haircuts.

I usually got my haircut from Mr Wolohan's apprentice. On this occasion a new boy was on the job.

'Where's Seamus gone?' Dad said to Mr Wolohan, referring to the previous apprentice.

'He's joined up in the 'Fert' last week. It's hard to keep good young lads nowadays. They don't want a trade anymore; just shift work and big money out in that god-forsaken place.' The Fert or NET factory (short for Nitrigen Eireann Teo) wasn't universally loved.

Dad agreed with a nod of his head as he settled down to the important business at hand. Dad had hair that needed and loved hair oil. He kept it short on the back and sides but quite long on top. It was light, flyaway hair so he needed to batten it down with lots of oil. I had quite similar hair to Dad's, but a lot thicker. I needed to have a crew cut for my hair because it was always standing on end. It stood up like a toilet brush all day, and when I got up in the morning, it was standing up again.

'That hair of yours son,' he'd say, 'it's because you have a double crown.' Then he'd joke, 'It gives you that unique stand-up shape.' Without a doubt it would pop up again today, leaving me somewhat self-conscious for awhile until I forgot about it. I observed other chaps to see if I could detect another double crown, but to no avail. I hoped I would grow out of it in time. Eventually I did. It took years.

The atmosphere inside the barbers was heavy with the smell of tobacco, hair oil, shampoo and cut hair. It was a great place for chat and gossip. Everyone seemed to be a comedian or joker. Dad fit right in. It was interesting to sit quietly and listen to it all. Mr Wolohan continually looked in the mirror in front and spoke to the waiting men behind him.

Out of the blue, Dad said, 'What do you think of those Beatle haircuts they're all talking about?'

'Ned, we've seen it all over the years. Styles come and styles go. I don't expect they'll catch on in this neck of the woods. Two young lads came in here ten days ago asking for a Beatles cut. I explained that my prices needed to be increased for such a specialty cut. That was the end of that for them.'

He lifted Dad's hair up with the comb and, standing back, said, 'You don't fancy one of them now yourself Ned?'

Dad sort of laughed. 'No, I don't think so, but I'm not too sure about Richard.'

Everyone seemed to have an opinion about the Beatles. Someone started whistling one of their tunes in the shop as if to confirm their popularity. Their pictures were on every paper and magazine cover in the newsagents. Owens shop had some of their records in the window.

Betty and Algy knew all about them. When I was last over in Sherwood's house, Algy showed me a cut-out paper Beatle wig that came with one of her pop magazines. She held it on my head and pointed me towards the mirror. I didn't think it looked too bad on me. The colour was a lot darker than mine, but the hair covered my ears, which I suppose, if you were unkind, could be said to be a godsend. I think I decided at that moment to give up the crew cuts as soon as I left primary school. The October after that, when I began in the Brothers, I would become a teenager. Long hair was tied up with my future; it would be my destiny.

The old guys in the shop clattered on for quite a while about the Beatles. The usual themes; they were girly-boys because of the long hair; they couldn't play guitars, couldn't write songs, and couldn't sing. They couldn't sing like Perry Como or John McCormack.

'John McCormack: now there's a man who could belt out a song.'

The new apprentice caught my eye. He was a few years older than me but the look he gave me confirmed that we were thinking along the same lines. After what seemed an age, the black cape was lifted from Dad's shoulders with a gallant flourish and he was brushed down and dusted off. He paid for the hairdos and we left.

Outside the barbers, we turned right up the main street. Dad had promised Mrs Kearon of Kylemore that he would pop up that afternoon to measure a new sash window for her kitchen. Mrs Kearon of Kylemore lived in Kylemore house next door to the grounds of Saint Saviour's church. Dad worked for and knew so many women called Mrs Kearon that he needed to add a sort of nickname to remind him who he was dealing with and where he needed to go to do the work.

Mrs Kearon of Kylemore lived beside the church. Mrs Kearon of Springfield lived in Springfield house, which was up the Coolgreaney Road near the cemetery. She was Roy Kearon's wife. Mrs Kearon of Beulah lived over Ferrybank near the swimming pool and was married to Dad's boss, Kevin Kearon. Mrs Skid Kearon was a widow who lived up near the railway station. Her husband had been known as 'Skid' by everyone.

I liked going with Dad when he went visiting these women. Mrs Kearon of Kylemore was an oldish Protestant lady who was a little bit posh and a lot old-fashioned. Her house had a grey stone dullness that changed entirely when the summer sun appeared. She was one of the few people who put out a spectacular coloured awning to protect the paintwork on the front door.

Mrs Kearon was like a walking antique. When I went to her house, she always produced a chocolate bar or an orange for me. Sometimes I'd get a homemade scone with butter and jam, all set out on a little plate with a napkin for the crumbs.

Dad muttered, 'Spinsters and widows, they've nothing else to be getting on with.'

Dad knocked on the door; howling dogs announced our presence and I jumped. Ever since the incident with Nugget in Granny's house, I was wary of strange dogs, especially significant ones.

Mrs Kearon opened the door. It looked like she was expecting us. The dogs were nowhere to be seen. She had a sheet of paper in her hand that she had folded and kept running her fingers over the crease. A small tray with what looked like doughnuts was on the small table in the room where the piano stood. Another thing about accompanying Dad on such visits was constantly being confronted by work he did over the years.

'Sit down there, Edward,' she said, 'while I get the tea and then I'll explain what I want.'

'How are you Richard?' she added as she went into the kitchen. I mumbled something that seemed to get me through the moment. I could hear her humming away while she made the tea. It reminded me of a tune I'd heard in church. I looked around.

The room we were in was full of dark furniture and you could float on the smell of mansion polish. The windows, which opened into a small garden, came right down to the floor like doors, and were slightly open. A breeze blew the floor-length curtains gently back into the room. The sunlight reflected on polished floor and tall bookshelves. Here and there were large conch shells.

On the walls were several paintings of men that appeared to be naval officers: Mrs Kearon was from a sea-faring family, so that was no surprise. The maritime theme continued on the mantlepiece with a small ship-in-a-bottle. There were also several vases of fresh flowers.

Dad noticed me looking at them and said, 'Mrs Kearon's a great one for the gardening as well.' I thought I noticed him raising his eyebrows but maybe he didn't.

Soon we were having our tea and then Mrs Kearon and Dad went through to the kitchen to survey the job. I could hear them talking in the distance. She certainly knew what she wanted from Dad. After a while she returned to the tea table and started talking to me.

'I haven't seen you in church lately, Richard. Have you been ill?' Mrs Kearon was always in church. It was like a job to her. She supplied the flowers for weddings, funerals, christenings and just about any celebration anywhere in the parish.

'I had a bad cold over the holidays and Mam kept me home,' I chanced, certain that it sounded as guilty as it felt.

'Are you still going to Sunday school and the Boys' Brigade'?

'I haven't been to Sunday school since I was confirmed, but I still go to the Boys' Brigade.'

Only old people called it the Boys' Brigade but I didn't try and correct her.

'And what class are you in now in Mr Smythe's?' she said, taking a sip of her tea.

'It's my last year. I'll be doing the Primary in May.'

'And then what's in store for you?'

'I'll be sitting the entrance exam for the Christian Brothers around the same time. I'll be starting in the Brothers in September.'

'And what do you think Mr Smythe thinks of that?'

I didn't repeat Mam's reply to that question: that it was none of his business. I said, 'I'm not sure if he knows if I'm going to the Brothers or not. Nobody has mentioned me going anywhere next year. I have to go somewhere. Maybe he thinks I'm going to the Tech.'

'I'm sure he doesn't think you're going to the Tech. Has anyone mentioned boarding school to you?'

'Jesus no!' I thought to myself, but I blurted out, 'I'm not that keen on going to a boarding school. All my friends and everyone I know will be going to the Brothers. I think Mam has mentioned it to the minister.'

'Surely your friends from Carysfort will be going to boarding school?'

I tried to let the conversation die off. The fact was Mam and Dad couldn't afford boarding school for me, and I was resigned to going to the Brothers. The conversation seemed to be over and Dad came back into the room. They went back into the kitchen to agree on the work and how much it was going to cost her. We left soon after.

On the way down the street, Dad said, 'You and Mrs Kearon were having a great cuffer. What was all that about?'

'Nothing,' I said, 'just school and church stuff.'

I began to realise that my going to the Brothers was attracting some attention in the parish and that maybe we hadn't heard the last of it.

The first school examination I ever took was the entrance examination to the Christian Brothers School in Arklow. It preceded the next examination, the National Primary Certificate examination, by only a couple of weeks. In some ways the entrance exam was like a trial run for the Primary Cert. Mam was in close contact with Mrs Condren over the previous couple of months, and found out what she needed to do and when to do it. The preparations happened all around me. All that I needed to do was turn up on the day and get all the answers right.

I was still not sure if Mr Smythe new that I was sitting the exam or even that I was intending going to the Brothers. All I know is that I didn't ask any advice from him in preparation for it.

On the day of the exam, which was Saturday, I was sent on my way with my ruler, pen, pencils and eraser, all kitted out for the job ahead. It was Maths and English in the morning and good old Irish in the afternoon. Mam arranged for me to call for Joe, Mrs Condren's youngest son, as he knew his way around the Brothers. Joe, I felt, was sympathetic to my situation of being a Protestant entering a Catholic school. He helped by acting normal when we got there. I wouldn't have been surprised if Mrs Condren had taken Joe aside and explained my predicament to him.

As well as the religious thing, the prospect of sitting an exam made me nervous, but looking around it was obvious that everyone was a little unsettled.

I noticed immediately that the school was bright and clean and as modern-looking as schools you'd see in American movies. The contrast with Carysfort was immense. All around were central-heating radiators: a long way from the single pot-bellied stove in Mr Smythe's. There was an incredible air of warmth and light.

Every room had its own holy statue up on a pedestal in the corner, covered by a glass cage. Over the door, a thorn-crowned Christ looked painfully down on us all.

The Brothers came in all sizes and ages. They dressed in long black robes with a wide belt around the middle and a lot of coattails flowing from the belt. They fidgeted quite a lot with these belts.

In charge of proceedings was Brother Loughnane, the head Brother. He gave us directions where we should go, first in Irish and then helpfully in English. The Irish he spoke was hard to understand. It seemed to have a harsher tone than what I was used to. He was a partially red-headed man and, as we eventually discovered, a red-faced man when riled. He had a habit of running his right hand over his balding head.

Two lay teachers accompanied him but neither spoke. A grave-looking priest with a book in his hand said a prayer and made a blessing sign at us all. It reminded me of the Blessing of the Boats. Maybe this was the Blessing of the Brains.

When we were all eventually sitting down, Brother Loughnane clapped his hands loudly to get our attention. Not everyone reacted so he banged the lid down on the desk nearest to him. Everyone went silent pretty fast. Tersely he told us how to fill in our exam papers, and without further ado, we started.

As I worked away on the English paper, the room seemed to be swarming with Brothers and priests. Two primary school teachers from the boys' school across the road were also present. Most of the places in the Brothers were taken by pupils from this school. During the course of the day, both these teachers walked around the room checking how everyone was doing. They eventually came up to me and of course not recognising me, asked me what school I was from.

'Carysfort,' I replied.

'I know Mr Smythe,' said one. 'He's a fine teacher.' He clapped me on the back and said, 'Well done.'

Numerous clocks seemed to toll each passing hour. The day flew by and suddenly once again the Brother's clapping hands brought us all to attention. 'Thank you all for attending,' he said. 'Your parents will have the results by the end of June. I hope to see all of you in September.'

We ended with a further prayer and within minutes we were filing out of the room, down the stairs and out into the fresh air.

Those I spoke thought the exam was a little like the Primary Cert, but perhaps a bit easier. When I got home, Mam was waiting nervously for me but by then I had almost completely forgotten the exam and could hardly add anything other than assuring her that I did okay. Dad was nowhere to be seen.

By the time I went back to school on Monday, my experience sitting the exam in the Brothers was an inconsequential memory. I told no one a that I was doing the exam. You learned in Carysfort that some things were best kept secret. I suppose as well as that I was a little bit embarrassed to admit to my friends in the school that I'd be going to a Catholic school next year.

We prepared for the Primary Certificate exam for quite a long time. These preparations seemed to have started just after Christmas. At first we concentrated on types of questions that regularly came up on the paper, and as we got nearer to the date we did entire exam papers under conditions that were similar to those on the big day. I usually did quite well in these trial exams and was regarded as being in the top two or three students in the class.

While this preparation was going on, a great sense of purpose and calm came over our class. We all seemed to be focused on what we needed to do, and Mr Smythe seemed to be focused on us.

If he knew I'd sat the entrance exam for the Brothers, he didn't let on. With those two Catholic primary teachers having mentioned that they knew Mr Smythe, I knew it wouldn't be long before one of them mentioned to him that they spoken to me in the Brothers. Things had a way of getting back to Mr Smythe, as I well knew.

But there was no time to worry about that as we practised our declensions, our spellings, our translations. We did our essays in English and Irish on such topics as 'What I did on my holidays' and 'A visit to a foreign country'. It was as if we were training for some Olympic event. Alongside all these preparations for the Primary exam, Mr Smythe regularly took a special group of our class aside for extra tuition for entrance and scholarship exams.

Eventually the big day came. The exam was held in the Marlborough Hall which was just next door but one to Carysfort school. The hall was the centre for all the other small Protestant schools in the parish, so there were quite a few strangers sitting the exam.

Mr Smythe got our attention not by clapping his hands but by slapping his cane down across the nearest table. It immediately produced the silence he wanted. He explained in a very loud voice what we needed to do and when we were to do it. I felt very experienced compared with my friends and was almost blasé about this exam.

'Anyone who needs to use the toilet should go now before we start,' he said. Nearly everyone took up the offer, surprising even Mr Smythe. I suppose it was nerves. As if in reaction to all this sudden activity, the door under the stage creaked slowly open like the page of a book, revealing a little of its contents, mysterious and magical.

Eventually we got started. The day wore on. It was strange trying to do school work in this huge church-like space. Every now and then, someone came back from the toilet and the noise from the cistern refilling seemed to go on forever.

In the weeks before the event, the exam had been a big topic in the playground. I heard wide-eyed stories of kids who'd written entire poems on their shirtsleeves, or arms or thighs. Someone swore blind that they knew of a boy who'd written an entire essay on his belly. It was hilarious. I couldn't wait for Mr Smythe to catch someone with a load of writing on his or her stomach. It would be priceless.

But of course it didn't happen. The only excitement was when a girl from another school felt faint. It was just before lunch. She probably hadn't eaten anything. She stood up at her desk and keeled over. There was a lot of confusion: girls screamed, boys shrieked. Mr Smythe picked her up and got her out into the fresh air. Miss Marshall followed him. They were both outside for quite a while. Inside all order broke down. Everyone was talking. A few girls cried. It was great.

All good things however come to an end. The girl was brought back in and she continued the exam. The afternoon droned on. Whenever I raised my eyes from the paper, I caught the eye of someone who was also looking up. In the warm afternoon, our endeavours were soon etched as condensation on the window panes. Eventually it came to an end.

Although it wasn't quite the end of the school year, we in the sixth class felt it was the end for us. On the Monday when we went back to school, Mr Smythe was already organising the seating for the next sixth class. 'Stay out in the playground until this is all over,' he commanded. It appeared we weren't needed anymore; there was some truth in that.

We went on a school trip to Dublin to fill in the time. The first stop was an ice-cream factory and we stuffed ourselves on Patsi Pops, Orange Splits and tubs of Raspberry Ripple. Our final stop was St Michan's Church which was famous for many things I'd never heard of.

'This very church, these surroundings, were the first to hear Handel's Messiah when Handel himself played it here,' Mr Smythe solemnly proclaimed to all. You could hear our yawns.

Unimpressed, we lined up instead to shake hands with a six-hundred-year-old crusader in the crypt. He had been tall for the times – an amazing six and a half feet, taller than most film stars. Round and about were numerous coffins falling apart, their inhabitants apparently eager to get in on the business of hand-shaking, no doubt. It was starting to feel a bit like Dracula in the movies, and someone helpfully told us that Bram Stoker, who wrote the novel, had also paid the crypt a visit. After that, I decided to give the four-hundred-year-old nun, who was also on view, a miss.

This last day of the year always ended in a school sports day up in Lamberton football field. The tradition was for both upper and lower schools to walk up in pairs, by class: the youngest first and sixth class bringing up the rear.

The end of term feeling continued up to this last day, and now we were part of the memory. We had joined the old boys club. No photographs were taken of the leaving class, which seemed a shame before we all broke up for good, so it was as if a little piece of the history was lost each year.

The day was a scorcher and dragged on and on. Instead of taking part in the races, this time our class helped run them. My job was to write down who came first, second and third in each race. Others helped start the race by dropping a hat and generally doing the teachers' jobs.

At lunch I remained cool and detached from the feeding frenzy, just eating the odd cake and sandwich. I felt somehow much older than the new sixth class.

I hadn't noticed it on previous sports days but loads of grown-ups from the parish were hanging around, leaning over the long metal fence that formed the boundary between the road and the pitch. As usual, a couple of past students from Carysfort turned up. Mr Smythe was all over them. He seemed to know a lot about the schools they were attending. 'Probably talking about rugger,' I thought.

This spectacle of the returning students somehow contradicted my opinion of the whole day. I felt that as soon as this sports day was finished, and I walked away from Lamberton, it was the last time I'd see most of the kids in my class. The past pupils returning threw me a little. It got me thinking that I'd actually never get away from these people and move on. I consoled myself that by going to a Catholic school, I was sort of removing myself from my past and looking forward to a bright but uncertain future.

As always, the day petered out quickly after the races finished. All that remained was the prize-giving for the scripture exam that was held earlier in the year. One by one we were called up and given our prizes. Mine was the *Observer Book of Birds*, which I'd chosen myself.

And that was that. We went our separate way without further ceremony. The townies faced a long walk home past the new Christian Brother school. The country kids were whisked away on the school bus although today a steady stream of cars also arrived to collect children.

I felt a little sick when I got home, which wasn't unusual after the sports day. I just wasn't used to all those home-baked cakes and buns, and drinking all that orange and lemonade. It wasn't long before Dad was home from work. 'I suppose it was lemonade and right gas all day at the sports,' he said as soon as he spotted me. I wasn't up to answering him.

'Did Mr Smythe mention that you're going to the Brothers?' Mam asked.

'No,' I said, 'I kept out of his way all day.'

Without looking up, Dad said, 'Oh, I was talking to Mr Smythe after church on Sunday and I told him what was happening.'

Mam was obviously surprised. 'You didn't mention this before. What did you say to him'?

'Oh he was singing Richard's praises, and he said that it was a pity he couldn't go somewhere better than the Christian Brothers. I got the impression that he wasn't too pleased about where he was going.'

Mam threw the tea-cloth on the table and said in exasperation, 'And what did he expect us to do with him, not send him anywhere? Well,' she added, 'it's all over now. He'll be in the Brothers in September and it won't cost Mr Smythe a thought.'

'We'll all want to keep out of his way for a while,' Dad suggested.

I think I made up my mind there and then that my church-going days were over. It was too tied up with school-going; it was part of what you did when you were in a Protestant school. When you moved on, all bets were off, it ended.

When the commotion died down, Dad said to me, 'I'm going

back to the yard to finish off a special job. It's something you might be interested in. Do you want to come down and give me a hand?'

When we got down to the workshop, Dad let us in with his own key. Although it was still quite early on a summer's evening, Dad needed to switch on all the lights. As they flickered on, I saw on the workbench four large wooden boxes. They were painted white; 'Tuck Box' was stencilled onto the lids and fronts. 'What are these for?' I said to Dad almost immediately.

'They're Tuck Boxes, of course.'

Well I could make that out myself. 'But what are they for?'

'Well that's the interesting part. You know who they're for?'

It didn't take a lot of figuring out but anyway I said, 'No I don't.'

'Well,' he said, 'they're all the same so it doesn't matter who gets what. They're for Roy and Jack and Alan and one for Jo Greene.'

These were my friends from Carysfort who were all off to boarding school. Dad continued, 'The boss got four enquiries about tuck boxes and hey presto, I knocked them up today. It was easy to make them all at the same time.'

I helped Dad put on the hinges and locks, but it was all a little unsettling. I really didn't know what to make of it all. He thought it was great making these tuck boxes for these lads going to the front. I felt like the one that didn't make the cut.

Midway through the summer, the results of both the Primary Certificate and the Brothers Entrance exam arrived. I did well in both of them and was quietly pleased with myself. Our neighbour Kitty's son, Michael, had also sat the exam in the Brothers and she was around to our house to see how I'd done.

'Did Richard get his results?'

'Yes,' Mam said, showing Kitty the letters. 'He did fine.'

Kitty read the letters and said to me, 'That candle I lit for you in the chapel seems to have worked wonders for you.'

I'd heard Mam asking Kitty to light a couple of candle for me before the exams, so I said, 'Thanks Kitty. I don't know what I'd have done without them.'

I left Mam and Kitty in the kitchen talking about the cost of books and the cost of all the new clothes we'd need.

When Dad came home for his dinner at midday, Mam presented him with both letters. 'He's done very well in all his exams,' she said as if I wasn't there.

'Well he gets the brains from my side of the family,' Dad replied with a smile as he read the letters. 'It's going to be all hard work from September, young man,' he added. 'He'll be well able for anything they throw at him,' Mam said. 'Mr Smythe said to me he was one of the best ever to go through Carysfort. He'll manage fine.'

It soon became obvious that the exam results were the topic of the day on the main street. I walked up the street with Mam to George O'Toole's shop, and nearly every woman we spoke to asked us about the exams. During our epic trip up the street, Mam dragged me round all the clothes shops in Arklow, checking the prices and sizes; and in spite of my fitting on numerous shirts, trousers, jackets and shoes in each shop, she bought nothing.

'We may have to make a trip to Dublin before September,' she said as we walked home. 'A lot of that stuff was expensive and old. You get the bargains in Dublin. We'll go up some Thursday on a cheap day excursion.'

After I left Carysfort, I tried to familiarise myself with Catholic things that were happening in the world. I thought that it might be good for me to understand them a little better as I was going to be spending the next five years in one of their schools.

I was a bit lucky the way things happened. First of all, the Pope died – Pope John XXIII, which is twenty-three in normal numbers. Apparently you could go the best part of your entire life without experiencing the death, burial and election of a pope. Here I was a just a couple of weeks finished in Carysfort and the entire kit and caboodle had happened.

The radio and the newspapers were full of it. The weeks after the new pope, who took the name John Paul II, was elected, the Pathe News in the cinemas ran and ran with newsreels of the funeral and the election. In the Fishery, people who owned televisions put them close to their windows so people in the street to see the sights. There were lots of Masses in the Catholic chapel and the cinemas closed down for the funeral. It was worse than Holy Week and Lent put together. When the election for the new pope was going on, everyone was excited. Dad explained to me about the white smoke and the black smoke. I was bemused. Everyone seemed to have their favourite. Everyone who came into the house gave an opinion on the good points and bad points of all the main contenders. It was as good as a heavyweight fight. I was glad to get to know about all these things. I didn't want anyone making an eejit out of me because I didn't know what was going on.

I also learned that President Kennedy was the first Catholic president of the United States. All the Catholics that I knew were proud of this fact. Dad said they all forgot that there were many Irish-born presidents before Kennedy who were all Protestant. Almost to support this pride and love of Kennedy, it was announced that he was going to visit Ireland in the summer.

It was all excitement through the summer and I was looking forward to my first day. I couldn't help feeling however that it was my first ending. Dad consoled me. 'The last day of anything is the first day of something,' he said. I began to realise life might be changing for me, but not quite ending. Freedom was just around the corner.

18

'Pretty soon you're going to get older'

I was anxious about my first day in the Christian Brothers school, and it truly did keep me awake at night. Where to go? What to do? I needn't have worried as, much to my relief on that crisp and fresh day, Brendan Coburn and his younger brother, Michael, called in for me on the way past our house. It was Michael's first day as well, so it was nice to tag along with another new boy. The brothers were both altar boys in the Catholic chapel, so I considered them experts on priests and Brothers and the Catholic religion in general. I was just about ready when they shouted for me through the open door. I grabbed my new school case and rushed out to meet them, before Mam got into her head to do something embarrassing like kiss me goodbye.

That year, I also graduated from a satchel to a small case, which looked a little like something you would take on holidays. They were popular with the older chaps I'd seen coming and going to the Brothers, so I went with the fashion. The case was quite empty; just a copybook and a pen and pencil inside. I realised it was lighter now than it would be for some time, as the list of books I'd need indicated that I soon was destined to carry a lot heavier weight indeed.

When I got out on the South Quay, it became obvious that the three of us were all wearing brand new clothes. I'm not sure if our short trousers were an indication of the warm weather or if we weren't grown up enough to warrant long trousers. We were like three chaps dressed up for first Holy Communion, or worryingly going to serve Mass. It all added to the suspicion that I was entering the realm of priests, popes and endless prayers.

The starched collar on my shirt was the most uncomfortable I'd ever had on, but I knew I had to put up with these little discomforts. I also wore a stripy tie. A tie was not specified in the notes we received about dress requirements but Mam said it might be best to wear one. I was relieved to see both Brendan and Michael were sporting school-type ties as well.

By now, Kitty and Mam were also on the road to see us off. I don't know if it was just a happy coincidence or because of all the commotion, but the rest of the neighbours, Mrs Heaney and Marion Martin, were outside viewing the spectacle. When we finally set off up the quay past the shipyard gates, they all waved us goodbye. It was if we were Sons of Leinster setting off for the trenches on the Western Front.

We were all jokes and laughing on the way up the quay. Until now, I had always gone up the Harbour Road to Carysfort. The River Avoca on that day was tranquil and serene, the water lapping gently onto the slipway to our right where until lately I skimmed stones.

Walking up by the river was certainly different. As we passed the shipyard, I could see the workers busy on the last stages of a fishing boat. The work had begun months ago on a cradle in their enormous workshop. How delighted the shipwrights must have been to finally work outside in the fresh air and the still warm late-summer sun. Soon the finished boat would be pushed onto the slip, where it waited for its inevitable release into the murky waters of the river, and the welcome arms of the owner. On both sides of our path, the honey-coloured grass of the long summer was still evident.

This river always held endless fascination for me. The hulks and ancient ship remains had all but disappeared, greatly encouraged by the constant use of a dredger which was finishing at a rate of knots the work started years ago by storm and tide. The cormorants had finally lost their familiar resting places, some now favouring the few remaining slime-covered rocks, and moored skiffs. Gulls hung in the air above and screamed as if to encourage them to move.

The river traffic also had changed considerably. The pit props with their dried bright orange bark had almost disappeared. The ore from Avoca mines had become a rarity – much to the delight of housewives who waged a constant war against the unwanted dust it brought – had given way to a steady stream of new products associated with the new NET factory situated upriver. Oil, ammonia, potash and lime were now familiar sights across from our house.

The old red brick Kynoch's buildings were finally demolished, making way for huge warehouses that became a holding area for the potash and lime. The area was now a constant hive of activity, giving unexpected employment to local dockers in the area, whether they wanted it or not.

Near the bridge, despite all the winter floods, the ancient sewage outlet survived, jutting out into the centre of the river, a precarious walkway that attracted the adventurous and foolhardy. On the bridge into town, an intermittent stream of cars and bicycles was already noticeable on this blue and warm morning.

During my primary school days, it was evident that girls rushing to work went toward the Main Street, for that is where the employment for office staff traditionally lay. We were passed this day by some mini-skirted girls who were employed in the many concerns that began trading around the dock area due to the NET factory.

Brendan was going into third year and told us about the Brothers and lay teachers in the school. He left me with the impression that everyone who taught in the school was either a raving lunatic or a bully. Brendan had a loud booming voice which added dramatically to his stories of caning and other forms of punishment. When he described the leather strap which the Brothers seemingly preferred, I found it difficult to visualise. However his facial expressions and grimaces and the accompanying sound affects filled me with dread.

He told us about how difficult Latin was and how, two years on, he couldn't make head nor tail of Spanish. 'Jesus, I hate Spanish,' he repeated several times, adding, 'and that feckin' Brother Doherty is a bollix.' He also warned that the Brothers were particularly hard on slackers in Irish language classes. I took some consolation in that at least I hadn't to contend with Spanish: it was French for me that year. But my vocabulary for describing teachers was expanding considerably with Brendan's help.

The town had changed quite a bit through my primary school days. A supermarket had opened in the Main Street across from Christy's bar and up from the bridge. Everyone was delighted with what this new shop had brought to the town. The modern world had slowly squeezed its way into our everyday life. Even the word 'supermarket' had all sorts of connotations. The fact that the town had this modern shop put us on a par with those towns we saw on television every night of the week. Soon we all experienced the pleasure of pushing a supermarket trolley, and were willingly introduced to the delights of Vesta Beef Curry and Sugar Pops cereal. Snap crackle and pop became the dominant sounds of breakfast.

There were more motor cars about, and more delivery vans. Even so, when a German-registered sports car stopped outside the Royal Hotel, it attracted the attention of every teenaged boy that passed by. When the blonde female owners rejoined the car, they attracted even more attention.

Opposite the hotel was a row of shops each with a brightly coloured canvas awning, protecting the precious wares from the impending September sun. There was briskness about this stretch of the street. Shops and banks were opening for the busy day ahead. It seemed that everyone going into the bank was male and wore a suit.

Footpaths were swept and signs indicating bargains were hung out in the breeze. Rabbits and game birds hung outside a butchers shop. Inside, the blood-spattered sawdust was already attracting numerous flies. Bicycles were balanced precariously on the kerb along the street. A TV rentals shop had recently opened as had several public bars. With the advent of the NET factory, all these shopkeepers were optimistic that some of this new money would find its way into their tills.

Up the street and on the left, Power's souvenir shop was open. Outside blowing in the wind were the remnants of the summer season items: beach balls, swimming rings, fish nets and the inevitable unseasonal hula hoops – all forlorn, forgotten and, for the foreseeable future, redundant.

Power's also specialised in religious pictures and statues. Row upon row of Virgin Mary statues and numerous Sacred Heart pictures were on display. Arklow people christened the owner 'Chalky Jesus' on account of these quality plaster statues. Walking by this shop was never comfortable for me. My strategy was to avert my eyes before the annunciations, creep by the crucifixions, and ignore the boxes of holy cards and tiny statues of St Patrick containing holy water to go. Across from this shop, in the park, pensioners sagged in seats contemplating this religious extravaganza.

Going up the street, past the turn for St Mary's Terrace, I saw some Carysfort pupils I recognised. Were they still being hassled along the way? Were they still serenaded by 'Proddy, Proddy on the wall'? Probably, I thought. It was their turn now and they were welcome to it. The statue of Father Murphy in front of the Catholic church seemed to point the way to the CBS school.

Around the church there was the usual activity. Numerous uniformed girls flitted up and down the steps, occasionally blessing themselves. The familiar groups of older men smoking and older ladies gossiping remained. Some things never change and that's just the way it was. The chapel seemed an unhappy place and still scowled and glowered at everyone within its precincts.

Groups of boys trudged their way to school and an almost equal number of uniformed girls went the opposite direction. Some of these girls were dressed in a green uniform; others had a blue and white version. They seemed to keep true to their colours, only mixing with similarly suited girls.

When we got to the school, Brendan went off to join his class. There was a steady stream of students arriving by bicycle, testimony to the distances many travelled to get there, and how glad they were to attend. The arrival of the Keenan boys on tandems from Aughrim became a familiar sight. Strong, handsome ruddy country chaps, their cycling to school in all weather became a sort of inspiration for me. I recognised lots of boys from Ferrybank arriving on new bright modern-styled bicycles that had exotic foreign names, making me feel a little apprehensive of my old bog-standard black model. I was glad I left it behind. Bicycles were wheeled straight into a spacious bicycle shed, out of which cigarette smoke was already billowing.

A brace of Brothers at the entrance directed new boys towards their appointed rooms. Brendan's earlier reference to the toughness of the Brothers and how they meted out punishment was foreboding, so I examined the ones standing before me. They were fresh-faced young men, and dressed in classical full-length Ignatius Rice robes. Their manner was terse and business-like. One had a beard trimmed close to his face and the other held a board which looked like an attendance sheet. His hands held the board very tightly, the bulging veins indicating some type of fervour. A bulletin board with a foolscap sheet of rules flapped and whipped in the breeze, heightening the intensity in the air. No mucking about here, I thought, with an optimistic hope that underneath the heavy dark tunic there maybe lurked a human.

I discovered first year was divided into two classes, 1A and 1B. This was bellowed out by a Brother several times in Irish and English. After somewhat nervously declaring my name, I was told to join 1B and pointed in that direction. When I reached my room, I recognised boys from different parts of the town. I sat down beside Joe Condren.

The first lesson was Latin, and began almost immediately, despite the fact that none of us had any Latin books. Our first Latin teacher, Mr McCarthy, was from Arklow. He had owned a private school in town before the Christian Brothers arrived. I occasionally played football with some of his sons. We jumped straight into Declining and Conjugating, without really knowing what it meant. Our starting point was '*mensa, mensa, mensam*'. I repeated these for days; eventually someone told us what it meant.

Mr McCarthy continually repeated what appeared to be an important message relating to this process. 'We decline the noun, we conjugate the verb' was his mantra. By the end of the first week, I think most of the class wished they could decline Latin entirely.

Mr McCarthy knew my Dad, and when he discovered who I was, he conveniently explained the non-denominational status of the school to the entire class, firmly putting the spotlight me as being a non-Catholic.

The Brother Superior came to our new class room. He made a speech about the education we were about to receive, and what a start in life it would give us. Flanking him were two Brothers and two lay teachers who over the next few weeks took to wearing graduation gowns occasionally, which seemed terribly flamboyant.

They advised us of the repercussions of misbehaving or not doing our best. The lay teachers were sporting canes, much the way Mr Smythe had done on my first day in Carysfort; almost like an educational prop. One of the Brothers introduced us to the strap. It was surprisingly rigid and hard, about eighteen inches in length and had the appearance of two leather belts sown together with rounded ends. It looked like it could do serious damage, maybe even break bones. Brendan conveniently let us know that the Brothers were in the habit of hiding the strap up their sleeves, so students didn't realise the extent of the trouble that was imminent.

It turned out to be a morning of timetables and book lists, of introductions and rules. Seemingly endless hours of queuing to purchase books from the school shop, hours spent marking time and kicking heels in boisterous giddiness outside this small room.

Every hour on the hour, every class stopped for prayers. Led by a favoured student, these prayers involved numerous responses of 'Pray for us' to myriad names for the Virgin Mary. It seemed that Catholics were big fans of the Virgin Mary. Sadly she didn't figure very much in the religious classes in my Sunday school. I couldn't concentrate like the rest of the class; I didn't really have any idea what to do during these prayers, so I just behaved like everyone else in the room: that is to say I stood up, looked at the ground and acted solemn. It was like I had stumbled into an alien world.

I had no lines in this drama but accepted somehow that perhaps God kept his eye on us all. To confirm this, the Virgin Mary smiled benignly from high up in the corner of every room, each one housed in a circular glass case. Respectful crosses were dotted about the entire school. Chalky Jesus had definitely done some good business here.

During my years in Carysfort I was always Richard Ruxton. It was the name I answered to during roll call, in class and outside. I was comfortable with the name. From day one in the Brothers, I was given a new name. Now I was Risteard Mac Riochtain. It was a totally fabricated name, but I accepted it was the new me for the coming years.

Class 1B had one other Protestant, and I was delighted to see he adopted the same prayer strategy as me. His name was Tim Cox. He was English and his father worked in NET. Tim became the envy of everyone in the class when we discovered that during Irish language class, he was allowed to go home. No Gaeilge for Tim, it seemed.

The really good news for all of us non-Catholics was the extra quarter of an hour we got every day for lunch, a precious fifteen minutes when everyone else in the school had religious classes.

On the way out of the school early on that first day, I met all the other Protestants and discovered that there were six of us. Tim Cox and I were in 1B. My friend Bongo was in 1A, another was in second year and two were in third year. It did not dawn on any of us, as we dashed away from the school, that our souls might be in peril by this cessation of our religious instruction. We had other things on our minds.

It was midday on the Main Street and the town was brimming with people. Women were everywhere with shopping baskets, heading home to make dinners for husbands and families. Here and there I spotted some uniformed girls, seemingly like me, prematurely released from school because of our religion.

Having spent the last nine years having midday lunch out of a plastic lunch box, washed down with a cup of Oxo or Bovril in winter and lukewarm milk in the summer, it was a welcome treat to have a hot dinner for midday lunch.

Dad joined us for dinner soon after I got home. He interrogated me about the new subjects and was particularly interested in geometry and algebra. He said that he had touched on them during his apprenticeship and asked me whether I had learned about the 'value of the squaw on the hippopotamus'. I was again mystified and vowed to keep this to myself. When I thought he was finished, he questioned me further about the 'humble pie'.

His work jacket was hanging on the back of his chair. From the inside pocket he took out a small black case that vaguely looked like one you might see in a jeweller's window. 'Here,' he said. 'I came across this a while back and thought you might like it.'

I opened the box. Inside lying on what looked like velvet was a very stylish and fine geometry set: a protractor, dividers and all the other bits and bobs that a student might need. I have to admit I was surprised. To this day I'm not sure where he got it from. I immediately decided it was too nice to take to school. It was reserved for homework. Mam was also delighted with this gift, so perhaps she had a hand in it.

The unusual heavy midday lunch had a drowsy effect on me, but Dad assured me the long walk to the CBS would brighten me up. One final time he said, 'Don't get any slaps.'

The school was organised with first year on the ground floor and all other years above us. Occasionally we heard shouts from the floor above us. Sometimes these shouts were threatening, sometimes in exasperation. Some implored improvement, some recalled seemingly old transgressions. We heard desks being pushed about as if some horseplay was taking place. It was all very sobering. Occasionally we heard doors slamming and hard metal heels ringing out on marble floors. We could only guess what drama was involved.

We were introduced to our Irish teacher, a young-looking but experienced Brother named Brother Miniter, who we also had for mathematics, the two subjects that made up the majority of periods. He was almost playfully threatening in his teaching style. He seemed to know one of our classmates well; this boy was the son of the head teacher in the primary school across from the CBS. It gave me some hope that the Brother could be friends with everyone.

Our day ended with a bell at four o'clock. We soon learned it was often late. The Brother frequently left before it rang; perhaps to ring the bell for us. When he had gone, the room almost sighed in relief and excitement spread among my fellow students like a warm breeze.

There was one final thing: the four o'clock prayers. It seemed that even if the Brother or teacher left the room, the prayers had to be recited. They were destined alas to become very rushed affairs indeed.

When I got home after my first day, I climbed the stairs to deposit my new books in my bedroom. I was surprised by a makeshift desk in the corner. Dad, always good at re-inventing and re-using things, had made me a desk from an old chest of drawers.

It was a stroke of genius. He removed the bottom two drawers of a three drawer unit, together with their supports, put some panelling on the sides, and came up with a passable desk with one nice big drawer for my pens and geometry set. He covered the top neatly with a sheet of Fablon, to give it a pine look.

As I sat down at my desk, in my room, placed my new books in a neat pile, it dawned on me that I had reached a new stage in life.

19

'Keep still and draw another breath'

As weeks lurched forward, the days gradually went from summer to winter. Boys who were full of ears and shorn bare heads in September went to knitted balaclavas and tartan hats, with great flaps like wings in flight.

If anything was the same as when I attended Carysfort, it was the solid daily routine for my journey to the Brothers. Each morning I meet the Coburns and started the brisk walk up the South Quay, struggling with my surprisingly full school case. Predictably, with up to six different lessons each day, the number of text books and associated copybooks had increased uncomfortably. As Michael and I were in different first year classes, naturally we compared teachers, homework and our treatment in the classroom. If we'd been keeping score, it would have worked about even-steven.

On the daily journey, we were often distracted – delightfully, achingly so – by two girls hurrying the other direction. One dressed in bright flowery clothes like she was going to a party, and walked with a bouncy gait. She had a confidence that made me think she owned the world. As she walked along, she swung her hand bag inches from the ground.

The other girl was taller and dressed more as you might associate with an office worker or a secretary. She walked very straight as if her head were a ball she was balancing on her shoulders. When they passed, we occasionally caught a whiff of perfume or hairspray. Strangely, our tongues seemed to be tied until we'd extracted every bit of scent hanging in the air.

These girls became a focus of heated discussion and, frankly, of major disappointment when occasionally they didn't appear. We savoured their diminishing perfumed presence at least until we rounded the corner into the main street.

Life in secondary school settled into a tense normality. Pragmatism and survival were uppermost in my mind. I realised very early that it was better not to loiter or dawdle anywhere in the school or school grounds. Loiterers were fair game to receive a cuff on the back of the neck from one of the enthusiastic young Brothers. In class, failure to have a correct answer at the ready when a Brother was explaining something at the blackboard often resulted in the unfortunate student being dragged out of his seat by the ear, to be interrogated in more detail at the board, so concentration was imperative.

Not all the Brothers behaved so, it must be said. There were several older ones who were mellower in their behaviour, the passing years presumably having knocked the edges off their teaching techniques and their ambitions.

So each day we went through the school's solid doors and experienced some meaningful and valuable education that possibly might help us cope in the altering world we were being prepared for.

As well as our Latin teacher, Mr McCarthy, there were several other lay teachers. Usually young and fresh from university, favouring dusty tweed jackets with seemingly obligatory leather patches on the elbows, they inadvertently became sounding boards for examples of life beyond secondary school. We quizzed them on politics, scandals, movies and books where they were most helpful. However, try them on controversial subjects or on anything even slightly racy and they stonewalled with a skill borne, like ours, of survival.

In a strange way, we were impressed by their experience and behaviours. One teacher constantly pulled at his ear and neck as he pondered a reply. He had a habit of flicking and turning pages without reading them, concentrating on what was going on in front of him, watching everybody – in my mind, the height of maturity and sophistication.

The Brothers moved around the school, up and down the corridors, with confidence and enthusiasm. Initially this was a bit of a shock to me. After all, I'd seen *The Nun's Story* with the young Audrey Hepburn, who while being inducted into the Order, was told to walk close to the walls to demonstrate humility.

Our Brothers certainly didn't subscribe to this. They ran around the place like they were the cat's pyjamas, shouting at loitering boys and issuing threats. Some were occasionally seen smoking while simultaneously trying to dissuade their students from picking up the habit. The Brothers strode through life as though they were on their way to some kind of heaven while making life hell for those around them. It was all very confusing.

Occasionally something happened which made me re-think my opinion of what kind of lives these men of cloth and prayer led. One older Brother in geography class tried to explain about natural deposits of manures and chemicals that could be used in agriculture. To help reinforce the point, he told us that in the book *Dr No*, the bad guy lived on an island of naturally occurring phosphate called guano. This really worried me. Dad had a copy of *Dr No*, and I'd read it unbeknownst to him. What I had read didn't seem appropriate reading for a Brother.

Surrounded by new people, and immersed in new subjects and new knowledge, I felt that as well as being a student at the school, I was also an observer, almost standing on the sidelines while things went on. I could see everything but the volume was turned down. Take the recurrent prayers: no one ever explained to me why they needed to say so many and what it was all about. No one ever said that maybe you should get a prayer of your own and say it to yourself while everyone else chanted away. No one told me to stand up or sit down. It just happened around me. Nobody asked me how I felt about it, if it embarrassed me. It just went on as if I weren't there. For a couple of minutes every hour, it was as if I didn't exist. It was as if I had been plucked out of my own life.

The prayers were so regular they became almost like a religious advertisement break. I eventually found myself muttering during these peaceful moments:

'Pray for me in Irish.'

'Pray for me in Latin.'

'Pray for me in Maths.'

'Sin A Sin B Sin C.'

It was like being caught up in some indoctrination programme. I was determined that it wouldn't be successful but in the process I feared becoming a stranger everywhere.

Several weeks into my first year in secondary school, I turned thirteen. Everyone in the class seemed to be having a birthday around the same time. Thirteen in Arklow was a long way from the confident, sassy teenagers I saw frequently on TV or at the movies. I seem to remember I was still wearing short trousers, as were most of the class. Although I technically became a teenager on my birthday, I felt I had become one in spirit well before that. And what contributed to this big change?

Across the road from Curran's newsagents at the Bridge, there was an ice-cream parlour called Tracy's. Mrs Tracy, the owner, opened a small café at the back of the shop. It was a place where families often went for an ice-cream or a soft drink on the way back from their Sunday afternoon walk.

It was a nice respectable place with wooden tables and matching benches, all painted in bright blue. It stayed like that for a couple of years, serving ice creams and cream buns to families, and would probably have remained like that forever had Mrs Tracy not put in a jukebox one summer.

Everything changed. Overnight the jukebox began to attract most of the working teenagers in the town. Families gradually lost interest as Tracy's developed into the most popular hang-out for teenagers in Arklow. It did attract a certain type though as most of those who frequented the cafe were working and earning money. School-going teenagers didn't seem to fit into the scene.

I didn't either, but often when I was passing by on a Saturday or Sunday, above the sound of the latest hits I'd hear a familiar voice shouting, 'Rucky! Rucky!' My cousin Algy was a regular in Tracy's and wanted me to come in too and listen to a new record or a good B-side that you wouldn't hear on the Radio Eireann or the Light programme. During rainy summer days, I spent a lot of time in there, especially when I discovered that the jukebox accepted American five-cent pieces. Thanks to the travels of Uncle Ronnie, I had tons of them.

During those dull grey days, the music spoke to my poor deprived senses. I discovered that this jukebox had a soul. In this dark smoke-filled room, where every square inch of the tables, benches and floor was covered in the scorch marks of careless cigarettes, the jukebox was almost like a religious object on some altar; golden and metallic with bleeding-heart-coloured lights beckoning to the converted. When music you liked emanated from this glorious machine, it was if someone walked up behind you and put their arm around you while simultaneously pounding your chest. I became convinced every young person should have to stand in front of a jukebox early in life and if necessary be compelled to listen to loud pop music.

In the middle of the café was a little dance area and Algy tried frequently to get me to dance with her. Algy was as outgoing and confident as I was shy. I suspect she did it to embarrass me; if so, she succeeded. When she got me up, the other dancers invariably retreated to the edges of the dance area where they did their best to unsettle me. Pointing and laughing did nothing for my dancing confidence. I did my best to avoid these situations and consequently never did master the jive.

Courting couples loved the place. You could vaguely make them out cuddling in the darker kissing corners. Everyone seemed to know everyone else, and the couples seemed to switch around. Sometimes when I went in, I'd notice a girl with one particular fellow. The next time she was all over someone else.

It's no wonder then that Tracy's had a bad reputation among parents. There was talk in the town that the parish priest had warned Catholic girls about the temptations to be found in places like Tracy's. With a bit of luck, they discovered them all on their own.

Connie always complained about Algy and Betty spending so much time in the café. Both were especially forbidden to go there 'if your father comes home.' This always seemed to be Connie's biggest fear. Jack wasn't known for tolerance.

Thinking back, I blame it on Cliff Richard. His film *Expresso Bongo* was shown for several nights in the local cinema. Everyone who went to see that movie came away with the impression that every town needed a jukebox café and of course teenagers needed espresso coffee.

'It's just a dive,' Mam could be counted on to remark, despite her never having set foot in it since the jukebox arrived.

So inadvertently this jukebox introduced me to the new sounds at a time when pop music was barely tolerated on radio stations in Britain or the republic. People older than me all had their particular music. Dad liked Frank Sinatra; Freddy liked Elvis and country and western music. I came to realise that their music was not my music.

All in all, it seemed as if life for me was just beginning and random things continually reinforced this teenager feeling. One day as I was going up the main street, a sign in Ralph O'Connell's shoe shop caught my eye. 'Get Your Beatle Boots Here,' it said. I stood outside the shop mesmerised by the boot display. I knew I just had to get a pair and almost went crazy thinking about them.

I spent the next three months trying to cajole Mam into buying me a pair, but with no success. I even tried to get her to buy them for me as a Christmas treat. It was a pattern repeated over the years for various items. To be fair, I'm not completely sure I had the neck to wear them. They were so flash and mod and I gave up looking for a pair after about a year. By then, they'd gone out of fashion. I never did get my Beatle boots.

That was the one thing I began to accept about being a teenager: yearning for stuff and never getting it. It was about eternally making wish lists for records and clothes and books and never getting the chance to put a line through anything on the list. This seemed to sum up my existence as a teenager.

I was outside this same shoe shop several weeks later when a girl by the name of Bernie English shouted across to me that President Kennedy had been shot. I didn't really believe her. 'Shot dead,' Mam confirmed when I got home. To me, that's what 1963 was about: the Beatles and the assassination of J F Kennedy. Mam wasn't far wrong about a Catholic President. It seemed like only yesterday that he had been laughing and joking with locals down the road in Wexford and having a pint in a pub.

Some weeks after my birthday, the Beatles arrived in Dublin to play two concerts. Up to this, they were just something that I heard on the radio, read about in the newspapers and heard grown-ups discussing in mainly disparaging terms. Coming to Dublin made them real and alive. For a couple of days that November, the country embraced Beatlemania. Their every move was reported. The evening newspapers from Dublin covered every aspect of their lives, their families, their music, their hobbies and desires.

Just as President Kennedy had done when he visited nearby Wexford, the Beatles were keen to highlight their Irish family connections. They seemed genuinely proud of these often tenuous links.

We discovered that Ringo had a family line going back to County Mayo. John had recently had a press shot taken in front of a tea warehouse in Liverpool which was the exact spot where his ancestors from Ireland first arrived during the Great Famine. Paul's ancestors had likewise arrived in Liverpool via Scotland from Ireland. George, who apparently was notoriously secretive about his Irish roots, because contrary to the Irish Catholic norm, his grandparents had never married. He met them secretly, to avoid this fact attracting too much attention from nosy neighbours.

We further learned that the first Beatle fan, an Irish girl from Liverpool called Pat Moran sent food parcels, gave money and even paid for a holiday for the struggling musicians.

The entire nation was proud of this Irish connection. Mammies and older folk were won over. Suddenly the Beatles were grand chaps. And there were all those lovely ballads to listen to. It seemed to satisfy a longing of ours as a nation for Irish success at any level, in any field. We yearned for success. Anything would do.

Just as Joyce had invented his Dublin, just as Toulouse-Lautrec had invented his Paris, just as Dickens had invented his London, the Beatles had surely invented their Liverpool. We however knew that the Irish had invented the Beatles.

I saw the affects of Beatlemania on the news when they appeared in cities in England, and so I didn't expect their visit to Dublin to be any different. I also saw the effects pop music had on teenagers in Arklow and Swansea, so I was prepared for anything. Before their visit, there were outbreaks of Beatle haircuts in Arklow. Owens's record shop displayed a few of their records in the window, and some of the local teenage characters took to wearing those Beatle boots I coveted.

On the day the Beatles arrived, hundreds of teenagers met them at Dublin airport and everyone, the great and the good of Irish broadcasting, interviewed them. Frank Hall, Gay Byrne and Larry Gogan all got in on the act. Not that you could hear much with all the screaming...

Naturally politicians and bishops were asked for their opinions of the Liverpool lads, and of course they deplored the effects they might have on the holy Catholic children of Ireland. 'We have to protect our young people from outside influences that might dilute our Gaelic culture,' said various worthies with their pious straight-faces. We had our own music which was the best music in the world and didn't need electric guitar music from across the Irish Sea. The last thing we needed was young British lads telling us about music.

As usual nobody paid any attention to either the clergy or the politicians. They were supporting acts to the main attraction, a side show. They somehow forgot that the Beatles had Irish connections.

The Irish radio station RTE was full of information about their two concerts in the Adelphi Cinema. Of the songs they sang, I recognised *She Loves You, All My Loving* and *From Me to You*. You couldn't help but know these tunes. Everyone but the dogs in the streets were whistling or humming them.

The lyrics described a world that I barely understood. I read somewhere that if you break your leg you turn to a doctor, if you break you heart you turn to music. That sort of ended up an unforgettable statement for me. I was truly ready for heartbreak when it came.

RTE also informed us with undisguised delight us that some youths caused trouble in the streets of Dublin before and after each concert. Some of the fans tried to overturn cars in Abbey Street. It was all very exciting and not at all like Ireland – more like Memphis or New York. It was a long way from dancing in the aisles in the Ormonde Cinema to fighting in the street. Some fans were arrested and others taken away in ambulances. 'It's the modern world and we'd better get used to it,' Dad observed ominously.

As the last show ended, fans besieged the cinema. It looked as if the Fab Four might have to spend the night inside until an enterprising *Evening Herald* delivery van driver managed to smuggle them out of the cinema in the back of his van. When I heard this, it captured my imagination. I could picture it clearly because every evening on my way home, I passed an *Evening Herald* delivery van outside Gallagher's Newsagents in the Main Street. This van delivered the Dublin evening edition of the papers to the shops between Dublin and Wexford each day. Maybe it was the same one that rescued the Beatles and spirited them back to the Gresham Hotel.

The next time I passed the van, I had a good look inside. The driver had conveniently left the back door open for easy scrutiny. I was dumbfounded. Written on the inside of the van in black marker was 'Ringo woz 'ere'.

Feckin' great! The van that came to Arklow was the one that the Beatles had used to escape. I was excited but I never told anyone about this. It was the first of my little secrets about the Beatles and pop music that I kept to myself. By this time, I had realised the world was changeable and people are changeable, especially your parents with their moods and regrets. You needed your secrets if you were to remain sane.

20

'One mad dog and
his master watched'

It became increasingly obvious even to the non-committed that Gaelic football and hurling were important to the Brothers. They considered themselves the Guardians of the National Game, in capital letters, never mind the Gaelic Athletic Association, or GAA. And they took the role seriously. Country chaps universally followed the National Game, whereas townies like me tended to be soccer fans. That's where my interest lay. I was always playing on the nearby south Green. I even picked up a few medals along the way

Gaelic football to me was all tied up with Irish history and Catholic culture. Every aspect of it was overseen by the parish priest. Whenever Dad dragged me to a match, invariably on a wet Sunday, he handed over our ticket money to a grumpy little man crouched over a small table with a cash box. 'I'll bet that never makes it to the GAA coffers,' he'd mutter surreptitiously, perpetuating the common rumour of the time.

I knew nothing about Gaelic games. I didn't even know the rules. It didn't appear to be a very welcoming environment. I noticed that for big games in Croke Park, the advertisements in newspapers itemised the prices for adults and boys. Girls weren't mentioned. Perhaps they simply weren't welcome.

It seemed to me if you lived in the Fishery, you were reared on soccer. The game featured in the mostly English comics I bought. This indoctrination began subtly in *The Beano* and *Dandy* and as I got older, continued with *The Hotspur* and *Victor*. They had their own fictional heroes, but I soon became aware of those real-life stars who featured in both English and Irish newspapers. My passion for the English leagues was on a par with my obsession with the progress of the Beatles in the charts: I was as interested in Liverpool FC as I was in Liverpool's Fab 4.

Around that time, sports coverage on television was exploding, with occasional live broadcasts and weekly roundups. Add in the qualifying matches for the 1966 World Cup and I was hooked. Ireland almost inevitably were pipped at the post by the USSR after a respectable run. Compared with these showpieces, the dour attritional games from Dalymount Park on dark, cold winter nights held little interest for me.

We knew Ireland would never qualify for the World Cup. The romance for us was in teams from West Germany, Spain. Portugal and yes, even England. They had the superstars who played the exciting football we were familiar with. Bobby Charlton and Geoff Hurst were our new gods. Mam even sang along when the 'E for B and Georgie Best' egg advertisement came on the TV. For kids living on the east coast, the GAA didn't stand a chance in the face of the glamorous soccer culture.

Since the inception of the state, the GAA struggled to raise the profile of their games among the youth of country. The revival of the Irish language was helped by making it a mandatory subject in schools, but the GAA couldn't really pull the same stunt. Initially along the east coast and in large urban areas, the GAA's battle against the increasingly advertised and publicised foreign games seemed old-fashioned and out of step with the burgeoning youthful population. Fighting against the tide seemed to suit the Brothers to the ground. It was their aim in life to counter foreign culture by any means. They picked up the baton, so to speak, and wielded it like a cudgel.

Every Wednesday, games were scheduled. On our first day we got a lecture on the importance of GAA to the nation. 'Gaelic football is our game,' the Brother said in a loud and serious voice. Hurling wasn't mentioned. I remember someone telling me, 'Wicklow isn't a great hurling county.' I'm not sure it was a great football county either.

So the whole school togged out for games. New boots, new shirts – the enthusiasm was genuine. It was part of secondary school education. Up school and all that. I was surprised the Brother in charge similarly hadn't stripped into football kit. Instead he did something peculiar with his cassock, tucking it into his wide belt to free his trousered legs. It didn't look very athletic but he got full marks for ingenuity. As for the new lay teachers, I don't remember any being involved.

After the first week or so, the Brothers identified those who were good at it and formed teams with them. The lads who were uninterested, disabled or just plan unable to play any type of sport were simply ignored. I was one of the ignored ones and happy at that. After a while, I didn't even have to pretend to go to the fields, I just went straight home every Wednesday afternoon. It was as if the National Game was only for those who were good enough to get on the school team. Playing for pleasure? What an odd idea.

As with many activities in life, when those in command notice you're not interested in a particular endeavour, they find you something else to do. As the year progressed the ones who didn't, couldn't or wouldn't play football were put on a rota for floor duties in their classroom every other week .A pair of us had to remain behind to clean the floor with an electric polisher, all because we didn't play the National Game. I think I remember the Brother Superior saying something to the effect that 'It'll be character forming.' Today it would probably contravene child labour laws.

Saturday mornings, I often went to Lamberton for a kick-around. It was at best a continuation of kicking the ball around randomly on the South Green. We had to pass the Brothers school to get to the soccer pitch. Occasionally we were spotted and the following Monday interrogated by the more fanatical GAA-loving Brothers. It was a familiar problem, so to get around it, we dodged up the riverbank and then cut across country, emerging at the tennis club, which was well out of sight of the Brothers. The irony didn't escape me. I seemed to have spent most of my life sneaking up back alleys so as not to offend or anger someone in authority.

We were able to avoid walking past the Brothers easily enough, but as time went on and we got a little older and a little bolder, we elected to openly and shamelessly walk past the school. When we spotted a Brother in the school grounds, we got some gratification by waving to him and shouting 'Good morning!' and them brazenly continuing up to the soccer pitch.

Eventually I figured out that as well as being the invisible man when it came to religion, the Brothers didn't actually care if I played soccer. I also concluded that they weren't really upset that I didn't play Gaelic games. It was almost as if they expected it. So much for my moment of rebellion.

In late October we all were looking forward to a soccer match that was to be shown live on television. It was billed as England versus the Rest of the World with kick-off at 2.45pm. True to form, we were all rooting for the Rest of the World, even though the English team comprised First Division footballers who everybody supported on Saturdays. Somehow the Brothers got wind of this and organised a school game to clash with it. Their game was at one of the local pitches away from the school. Attendance was obligatory.

That Wednesday, we plodded down to the playing field and stood around plotting when and how to sneak off. The GAA match kicked of at 2pm before a decidedly restless crowd. By 2.15, the number of onlookers was diminishing rapidly. By 2.30, half the school had absconded. By 2.45, there were probably more people on the pitch than on the sidelines. The rest were already occupying front-row seats in front of TV sets.

It was a wonderful game but I remember being somewhat dismayed when England won. It sometimes happens.

However rebellion was in the air and manifested itself in other ways. Everything was being pushed to the limits by each year's new intake. Hair length, smoking within sight of the school, hanging out in the slot machine hall, wearing blue jeans: all these became passions among the students and of course issues with those in authority.

The Brothers' reactions were sometimes brutal, sometimes comical, sometimes both. The mid-Sixties brought an epidemic of longish hair: you wore it as long as you thought you might get away with. When someone pushed it too far, the Brothers' at first sent the offender home. Often this produced no result. The student didn't go home, or didn't tell his parents, and his hair stayed defiantly longish.

So the Brothers changed tack. If the Brother Superior identified a boy with hair that was deemed too long, he was given a half a crown, sent to the barbers in school hours and told to report back within the hour with his hair cut. This usually did the trick. Over the years however the interpretation of what was and what was not 'long hair' changed to such an extent that when I was finally leaving the Brothers, students wore pretty much any hairstyle they wished.

Sometimes, in spite of all their control and dominance, the Brothers became unstuck. Events happened that brought their whole establishment into disrepute. One that haunted them for years happened during my last year.

That year, the school football team reached the county final in some cup competition or other. It caused a great buzz around the school. To the Brothers, it was like the heavens had opened in vindication of their hard work. Inevitably we were all press-ganged into attending the final in Baltinglass, about thirty miles from Arklow.

So on the appointed day, the entire school piled into a fleet of buses for an uneventful journey to the match. Most of us were wondering why the hell we were going to see this game. Few among us even touched a Gaelic football in our entire time at the Brothers. Any loyalty to school teams was irrelevant compared with our interest in pop music, soccer and girls.

The game was bleak. A light drizzle settled over the pitch and drove us all back to seek shelter under trees a good distance from the action. This of course didn't impress the Brothers but they and some stalwart students, the manly Christians, remained on the touch lines. Other stoic spectators stood still like works in a museum. Far away, on the other side of the field, whatever drama there was played out in silence. People gesticulated and waved their arms about as if trying to scare off demons. Occasionally on the breeze you heard the shouts and shrieks like gulls against a gathering storm. They looked like dancers without music. Eventually the drama concluded. Arklow CBS won.

With the final whistle, we rushed back to the buses and eventually set off for home. It had been a long day and someone somewhere decided that it might be a good idea to stop at a shop so that we might get something to eat and drink. Outside Baltinglass, we pulled over at a Spar supermarket and about a hundred and fifty hungry and thirsty boys crammed into the relatively small shop. The owner and his staff didn't know what had hit them.

A couple of days later, the shit hit the fan. It transpired that not as much money went across the counter that day in Baltinglass as should have. In fact, the owner claimed that Arklow CBS students had stolen everything off his shelves.

To be fair to the Brothers, they acted decisively. They didn't try to cover it up. They marched everyone who attended the match into the science room. The Brother Superior had put some thought into his approach to discover the guilty ones. He told us to get two pieces of paper each. 'Write your name on both pieces of paper,' he said. Then came the killer bit: 'I want you to answer two questions on these pieces of paper: did you see anyone steal anything and did you steal anything yourself?'

A nervous hush came over the room; it was the sound of soul-searching. The process completed, the papers were gathered up and we were told to remain in the science room until we were set free. The next few hours proceeded with an inquisitional fervour. All our answers were cross-referenced. There was nowhere to hide. If you lied to protect your friends, you weren't sure they would reciprocate.

All through the morning and afternoon, the door to the science room opened and closed. All day it seemed, students were called out to answer what they'd written on the pieces of paper. The day wore until all the confessions had been checked. About a dozen students were left in the room when the Brother Superior burst open the door and said that those remained could go home. 'It has indeed been a bad day for the school,' he told us somewhat emotionally, 'but that at least there were a few honest boys in the school.'

For the next few days the school was rife with rumours of court cases and Gardaí involvement. Neither happened, but the ridicule in the community that the school had to endure for some time was arguably a worse outcome.

21

'I wish today could be tomorrow'

As far back as I can remember, every summer one all-consuming fad or craze emerged among the young people in the town. Where these originated was always something of mystery. We graduated from spinning tops to hopscotch to hula hoops. Some years we went mad on swapping comics. Other years we built tents all summer long. We played rounders until we never wanted to play again. Occasionally we were distracted by bicycles or roller skates

Each fad was totally engrossing. When hopscotch was the thing, every bit of flat concrete in the neighbourhood was covered in chalk patterns. Everyone had an arsenal of slippy stones to perform that practised ritual of hopping, skipping, jumping.

In early 1965 and then through the whole summer, a new type of madness took over. This was a particular craze and to be quite honest, I think it was mostly confined to the Fishery, leaving the rest of the town scratching their heads in bafflement.

We'd all seen the movies where the rich American college kids said, 'See you later, alligator', to which the chirpy reply was, 'In a while, crocodile.'

What we saw and heard in the movies, and of course now on television, made a big impact. *Batman* gave us 'Back to the Bat cave!' and 'Suffering cowpats, Robin!' From the *Battler Britain* comics, 'Sacre bleu!', 'Gott in Himmel!' and 'Englander Schweinhund!' became part of our day-to-day language. John, my cousin, had his own collection from his love of Kenneth Williams and Leslie Phillips on BBC radio. 'Oh Matron!' and 'Ding dong!' were two of his favourites.

We latched onto anything that was catchy whether it made sense or not. One saying in particular caught on. No one was sure where it came from, but it took a grip on our lives and language for an entire summer.

The catchphrase in itself meant nothing. But then did any of them? Having said that, it was a loaded collection of words, this phrase. The first time I heard it was one evening as I was walking down the Harbour Road with Mam. She stopped to talk to Bernie English. I naturally moved on. Their conversation didn't last long, so I hadn't gone on too far. When they parted, Bernie shouted back at Mam, 'Bye now Sally,' and added with some volume, 'Get them off ya!'

Mam looked surprised. I thought I'd misheard Bernie. Bernie herself continued up the road and let out a long dirty laugh, followed by another loud 'Get them off ya!'

The phrase quickly found its way into everyday speech to such an extent that you had to constantly remind yourself not to say it when in a particular situations The idea that you might tag it onto an answer about Latin declensions in the Brothers was too much to think about. It was like swearing. We all did it, but you didn't want to be caught doing it in front of your parents or teachers.

The phrase appeared on walls, written in chalk and paint, or in the dirt and dust on vans and cars. In school you saw it on the backs of copy books and on the insides of satchels. It was everywhere. A rumour that a fisherman renamed his boat 'The Get Them Off Ya' for luck unfortunately proved to be just a yarn.

Mam and Dad weren't impressed. I think Mam put it on the same level as swearing. 'It's just plain common,' I heard her say once.

They used to speculate about where the phrase came from. Dad came up with a choice explanation that really got my eyes going for the heavens. Dad told everyone that the 'get them off ya' craze started on *Dr Kildare*, one of the most popular programmes on the television..

'On one programme,' Dad said with authority, 'Dr Kildare turned to one of his nurses and said, "Get the morphia."'

Dad was convincing and it seemed reasonable enough... but no, not really. It was rubbish. I knew Dad. He'd made it up and repeated it until he believed it himself and hoped everyone else did too.

I knew it didn't start with any of these crazy explanations, because I knew without a doubt where it had really started. Little old me had sussed it out. I didn't tell anyone, even Algy, because no one would have believed me. What did I care? As long as I knew the truth. Knowledge was smugness.

If others paid as much attention as I did to the lyrics of pop songs, they might have figured it out too. Around Christmas, the Kinks had released a single called *All Day and All of the Night*. About two minutes into it, they utter the immortal line, 'Oh get them off.' I reckoned this is where it all began, without a doubt. The phrase on the record wormed its way into our subconscious: subliminally like. I never knew if anyone else had picked up on this.

Of course the 'Get them off ya' craze grew and grew until it became just plain silly. It littered every conversation and what had been edgy and dodgy became boring. Towards the end of the summer it all but petered out. Funnily, it was replaced by a similarly bizarre catchphrase.

'Get them off ya' was limited in conversation. Its main use seemed to be if you were denying or challenging something. If someone said to you, 'Did I see you falling home last night, and you with not a leg to stand on?' you could reply, 'Get them off ya!' in disbelief, in much the same way as you could use 'Feck off' or be very up to date with 'No way man.'

The new fad phrase, 'Razz goo man', was more useful. You could use it as a comment and as an encouragement, depending on the situation. It was handy as a sort of universal reply to anything you weren't quite sure of. If someone asked, 'How's she cuttin?' you could reply 'Razz goo man' without giving much away. At football, if you got bored shouting 'Come on!', you could intersperse it with a few 'Razz goo mans' and be the epitome of cool.

Television, the pictures and music had a lot to answer for. By the mid-sixties, everyone young finished each sentence with 'Cool man.'

At the bottom of the town where I lived, young people were called Fishhawks. Fishhawks lived anywhere around the Fishery, up to the Dainty Bakery and across the Green to the river. This meant that even though I lived on the Quay which was not generally regarded as part of the Fishery, I was a Fishhawk through and through. Membership came with where you lived. Loyalty was expected.

Past the Dainty, and up around Abbey Street and Connolly Street was the Starlights' territory. They were our sworn enemies; you had to be very careful if you drifted into their area. This territorial thing caused the Sherwoods and me some problems. One of the ways up to Carysfort school cut right through Starlight country. On our way up the Ditch, we sometimes bumped into Starlights and ended up having our schoolbags emptied out on the ground or our hats taken. It was a tough life.

Through the year, the tension between Fishhawks and Starlights was hardly noticeable. It might boil over at a football match with kids' parents arguing over a goal or a bad tackle. So for most of the year, we carried the heavy burden of the membership of our gangs pretty lightly.

Around May Day and for the couple of weeks building up to it, the allegiance were more marked. May Day was a great day in Arklow. Each neighbourhood had its bonfire and was proud of it. Each tried to outdo the other in size. The bonfires consisted of May bushes and as many old tyres as you could get. Pit props from the dock went onto the pile, but of course they needed to be stolen. There were raids on building sites to pilfer anything that burned.

We'd start collecting fuel for the fire in February, gathering and hiding every tyre, or 'bowlies' as we called them, that we came across. It was a great coup if you came across some hidden by the Starlights and took them; not so good if they found your stash. As soon as the flowers appeared on the May bushes, we started gathering them in and stacking them in our gardens for the big day.

From the morning on the first of May, as you walked around the streets, you'd notice people were still putting out newly plucked flowers on their doorsteps to welcome in the summer. Starting early, everyone hauled to the South Green what they had collected over the weeks. The bigger boys added it all to the pile until it was as high as a house. Then it was guarded until set alight at the official time. At that moment, the Green was usually black with people. Everyone, it seemed, liked to take part in these celebrations. In the evening the pipe band took to the streets doing its stuff, making occasional detours to get close to any bonfire activities.

The bonfire itself eventually attracted almost everyone. It was a health and safety nightmare. The Gardai in their police car roamed all over the town from one fire to another to make sure everything was above board and that everybody was behaving themselves. The Civil Defence people also got in on the act, reminding everyone not to get too near the fire.

In spite of all these people getting involved, nearly every year someone got badly burned. The fire brigade was always called out as each year's fire was bigger – and in our eyes better – than the previous one.

Down our way, the evening occasionally culminated with a pitched battle between factions. We threw stones or anything that came to hand at the Starlights and they obligingly threw them back at us. The standoff usually took place on either side of a stream that formed a border between us and them that ran down Gussets Lane. Despite the potential for injury, it was a tame affair. Nobody was killed.

Days later, when the smouldering remains of the fire finally went cold, you could see the devastation left behind. The black scar left on the grass covered with rolls of wire from the numerous tyres remained for months and months. Many a mother cursed the May celebrations when their child arrived home as black as sin, having tumbled into the dried ashes of last year's fire.

Our back garden was shaped like the bow of a boat, with a gate leading onto a back lane which brought you out on the Harbour Road, beside Reilly's shop. We used this back entrance all the time. It was a bit shorter than going through the front door which faced towards the river.

The Harbour Road stretched right down from the Toker corner to the river side. Terraced houses lined both sides of the road. The houses were similar, but a variety of colourful doors and brightly painted walls stamped an individuality of sorts on them.

The Harbour Road was kinder than it looked; kinder than you expected. When the sun shone, it swarmed with children playing all the games: hopscotch, porridge, skipping and ball, which required space but not necessarily grass. Mothers sat in their hallways watching and knitting, ever ready to sort out arguments or to doctor some scraped knee. Everyone played there after tea and into the long evenings until nightfall. Adults left us pretty much alone.

This road could always be depended on to provide inadvertent entertainment. There were two families living in the Harbour Road. The father of one sold vegetables and the other father worked away from home, somewhere like New York. The mothers seemed to get on well. The kids played football together on the road year in year out without a problem. Everything was normally peaceful and calm.

Occasionally though, and always it seemed in the summer, the absent father came home to spend time with his family, and old grievances and arguments resurfaced. Emotions spilled over, resulting in a big punch-up on the Harbour Road. It could go on for hours. Up and down the road they'd beat each other. The wives screamed. The rest of the road just looked on. These weren't young men, nor were they particularly fit. Had they been either, it might have ended sooner and with more damage than wounded pride. Occasionally, a neighbour tried to talk some sense into them. It was difficult to get them to stop and, to be honest, nobody wished that. It was a tradition.

Someone, out of pure boredom, eventually might call the police. When the Gardai discovered who was involved, they actually didn't bother turning up. 'Not worth the effort,' they would explain. The neighbours loved it of course. Harmless entertainment but the wives were mortified.

I remember playing football with a couple of the boys. There was a convenient telegraph pole outside their gate that we used as a goal. Sometime during a lengthy session one of the boys announced that their Mam had just had a baby, a sister for them who was to be called Melissa. I remember thinking that it was the most beautiful name I had ever heard.

Summer could be hard work for an only child. It never lived up to expectations of that final day of school. I met older people up the town who always said, 'So you're on your holidays now, isn't that wonderful.

They're the best days of your life.' Little did they know. The boredom and loneliness were something that grown-ups didn't seem to notice.

One such evening, I decided I was going to my bedroom early to catch up on reading. It had gone really quiet. In the distance occasionally I could hear girls on the Harbour Road singing skipping songs. Behind me I could hear that *The Archers* had finished (dump de dump de dump de dump, dump de dump de dump dump).

Pal, dozing away at my feet , suddenly woke up and barked loudly towards the lane. 'Someone's coming,' I thought.

After a while, a hand came through the hole in the gate and opened the bolt. It swung open, scraping loudly across the gravel. Algy stumbled into the garden. She began walking up the concrete path to where I was sitting. Walking wasn't really the right description: it was more like staggering.

She was holding a man's white handkerchief to her eye. Quite close behind Algy, I now could see Auntie Connie. It was obvious from the way she was walking that something was up.

I jumped up and put my head around the door.

'Mam,' I shouted, 'it's the Sherwoods.'

Before Algy or Connie reached the house, Mam had appeared in the door. I heard her say, 'Oh god no, ah no ah no ah no. God, Connie, what has he done?'

Before Connie could reply, Algy said, 'I did feckin' nothin', I just want a fucking normal life.'

Algy's words hung in the air. A screaming silence reigned for a few moments. Connie, with a desperate air of resignation, took the time to light a cigarette.

Algy always behaved like she hadn't got a care in the world, always giggling at something. She dressed so colourfully and had boy-like short hair. She looked as if she just arrived from Carnaby Street. I'd seen the word androgynous used to describe girls like Algy.

I was surprised that neither Mam nor Connie checked her about her language. This as much as anything else convinced me that what was going on was serious.

Algy continued, 'I was just getting ready to go to the dance in the

Centre and he came up to me and called me a name and hit me in the face.' Algy was wearing a mini-dress. Her hair done up like a singer I'd seen on the television. The remains of her make-up were all over her hands and the hanky. The side of her face was swollen and there was blood around her eye.

She looked over at me. She must have noticed something in my face, shock or worry. 'Ah Rucky,' she said as she came over to me, 'I'm all right, don't look so serious.'

I felt like saying to her that she didn't have to look after me: someone needed to look after her. Although I was six or seven years younger than her, I was just about her height. She put her arm around my shoulder. She usually teased me this way when I was over at her house. I was a bit shy around her, and she played on this, embarrassing the hell out of me. She often tried to kiss me, much to my discomfort. On this occasion, she did kiss me but it seemed the right thing to do. I felt I was going to cry but Mam came to my rescue.

'Was it the drink,' she said. 'Was he out drinking?'

'Of course he was – all day up in John-Joes,' said Connie. To Algy, she said, 'You should be more careful what you say to him and not be so feckin' sarcastic when he has drink in him.'

Uncle Jack had been home for a few weeks now and the novelty was wearing off. Algy and Betty were constantly singing 'Hit the road Jack' while he was eating his dinner, and having a great laugh over it. It seemed that after the excitement of his arriving and the money and the presents, Jack had outstayed his welcome.

Mam said, 'Where's the rest of them?' meaning Betty, Sally John and Bobby.

'None of them were in the house when it happened.'

'We'll have to tell them where we are though,' Mam said. 'Is her eye all right. Will I send for Dr Costello?'

'No,' Connie said quickly, 'we'll clean off the blood. There's no need for the doctor. It's bad enough without getting the doctor involved.'

Cups of tea appeared and everything seemed to go quiet. 'What are you going to do?' Mam said.

'Well we can't go back there tonight' Connie replied.

'I'm never feckin' going back,' Algy added.

'We can't go back. As sure as hell he'll kill her if he sees her tonight.'

'You all better stay the night then,' Mam said

I felt Mam wanted to say 'tonight at least,' but it was left hanging, unsaid.

Pal was couched down beside me, seemingly taking everything in. I thought to myself, 'Isn't it strange that in spite of dogs being stupid and crazy, they seem to know when things are serious?' In spite of all the commotion going down, he didn't make a sound.

I sat down on the back step. Mam caught sight of me and seemed to think clearly all of a sudden.

'I'll get the camp beds down, and put them up in the front room.' She always had the camp beds ready for emergencies. She looked at me and said, 'Can you go down to the yard and tell your father.'

Connie said, 'I don't know what Ned Ruxton's going to say this time.'

I knew Dad wasn't going to be too pleased at having his house overrun by our cousins once again. I left Mam and Connie in the living room.

The Sherwoods 'landing in on us', as Mam used to describe it, was happening more and more. Several times in the last few years we'd had them as 'visitors'; sometimes for a night or two; once for almost two weeks. It coincided with Jack's getting a job that took him on shorter trips, with the result that he got home more often.

Dad was getting a bit weary of it all. I'd heard women talking to Mam about it up the street. 'Oh,' they'd say, 'Ned must be some sort of angel or a very quiet man.'

Of course Dad was neither of these. They had constant rows over these visits. 'What could I do?' she'd say to him. 'What could I do but take them in?'

Dad was working inside the yard with the gates locked because his workplace shut down during August and he was officially on holiday. Knowing that he couldn't hear me with the machinery on, I climbed quickly over the gate and ran to where he worked. In case he was using an electric saw or plane, I shouted ahead so as not to startle him. The workshop was a solitary place and Dad often got lost in his thoughts, but having heard my shout, he was looking out for me when I arrived.

'Jack Sherwood has kicked them all out again,' I blurted out.

Dad swore under his breath. 'I was just about finished anyway.' He spent a minute or two tightening a clamp around a new sash. He was making windows and there was a heady smell of wood glue.

When we got up the house, things had quietened down a bit. I was surprised to see Mam and Connie both sitting on the sofa and silently weeping. The Martins, who obviously heard the commotion, were there too.

When Dad come into the room, the talking stopped and Mam began explaining what had happened. Billy Martin waited until Dad had heard the whole story before he stood up and said, 'I'd better be getting back inside. We'll be heading off down the country in a while.'

Connie jumped up and grabbed his hand. 'Thanks very much Billy, I don't know what to say.'

Billy looked embarrassed. He fiddled with the keys in his hand and said, 'I'll drop these into Sally before we go.' It appeared that when Billy had heard Connie's story, he'd offered them their empty house for the next two weeks.

When he had gone Connie said, 'You're so lucky to live beside someone like that. He's an angel. The whole family is. Our own wouldn't treat us that well.'

By 'our own', she meant Protestants in the parish. The Martins were Catholics. And sadly that's how things turned out.

Eventually Bobby, Sally, John and Betty arrived at our house. They had come home to find their house bolted up, back and front. It hadn't taken them long to figure out something was wrong and that our house was the best place to come to; they certainly knew their way, as Dad always said.

The whole family seemed to cling together for a while. Algy had calmed down and soon seemed oblivious to what had happened. She asked John for a cigarette and was puffing away as if nothing had happened.

'Rucky,' she said to me, 'be a sweetheart and put on Radio Luxembourg.'

I was just beginning to get into pop music and listening to the radio on summer evenings with the windows all open was something I enjoyed, especially when Mam and Dad were out of the house.

When the wireless warmed up, the first record to come on was *I Remember You* by Frank Ifield. Everyone knew the words. At the end of every line I expected even Pal to join in with an 'Oooo'.

Algy was a great one for the pop music. She seemed to know all the words of all the records and sang along with them. She was always asking me if I knew this or that song by this or that group. I could hardly keep up with it.

I heard the front door opening and thought, 'I bet that'll be Uncle Billy.'

'Has Sherwood done it again?' he said on seeing the state of Algy's face. Mam nodded but no one really answered. Connie told him about moving in to the Martins' house. He seemed relieved as well.

We sat for quite a while with Radio Luxembourg providing the background entertainment. Algy sang along to her favourite songs while puffing on the odd cigarette. Occasionally she rolled her eyes and said, 'Oh he really sends me,' meaning the singer.

My cousins were excited about spending two weeks next door to us. It seemed to me as if they were treating it like a holiday. The Martins had a huge new television. Billy had erected a tall aerial that could pick up the BBC and ITV when the weather was good. Like our house, Martins' also had a bathroom and an indoor toilet, which was a novelty for them.

As soon as Mam got the keys from the Martins and we waved them on their way, the Sherwoods piled into the house and had a good look around. The Martins had loads of modern things like a toaster, a shower and a fridge. I was a bit jealous of them. Upstairs in the bedrooms, Marion had left out clean sheets and blankets.

'Oh, it's going to be great here,' Betty said. I must confess I was delighted with the prospect of more company in the house.

Connie realised that she needed to find somewhere permanent before the Martins came back from their holidays, as they surely would. She looked into flats and houses. At one stage, she approached the parish to see if she could rent Mrs Jacobs old house, which had been lying vacant since her retirement. They refused. Sure they must have had their reasons, but the fact was that in her hour of need, 'her own' turned her down.

After that, Connie was never interested in church life or church activities. Without a doubt that experience left her embittered. She felt that our religion was run by rich people for rich people. She had a point.

22

'We gotta get out of this place'

When I started back to the Brothers for my second year, it was immediately evident that during the summer months we had all grown up a little and were edging towards those teenage years. To my great relief, we were now wearing long trousers too.

Some classmates from my first year hadn't returned, but it was obvious that many more from Class 1A were missing. Our two starter classes were amalgamated into one second-year class, and as if to complete this great change, our new classroom was upstairs.

Tales abounded of former students getting jobs in local factories, some on fishing boats and some moving to the technical school. We could see that this would be the last year for many more of our classmates as well. Some just weren't interested in the subjects and almost certainly would leave as soon as an opportunity arose. The journey to this inevitability was often a violent one.

The Brothers continually stressed that we were preparing for the Intermediate Certificate in two years time, one of two main big exams we would sit before we left this place. We were shown the course topics; what books we needed to read, what poems we needed to study and told that our Shakespeare play was to be *The Tempest*. Our school was judged on how well we all did in these. It became obvious during this year the Brothers were going to do whatever it took to make sure everyone did very well indeed. A new school needed to be successful.

So this new academic year began with an increased intensity of ambition. Borderline students had until the end of second year to shape up. Woe betide any trouble-makers on the way to that point.

The violence level was ratcheted up gradually as the late summer stretched into a chilly autumn. Some students from Class 1A seemed to attract particular attention. Two boys named Noel and Liam seemed to be a thorn in the Brothers' sides each day that passed.

This year we had the Brother Superior for mathematics. Long afternoons were set aside for the different aspects of the subject: geometry, algebra and calculus. Sometimes it felt the air that we breathed and the lives we led were filled with equations. I hadn't realised the lowly letters X and Y could have so many meanings. Maths classes were particularly tense. You could have nightmares about mathematics.

Some days we had maths and Gaeilge. These were traumatic afternoons; a tedium matched by a certain terror. Life could be a little like *Tir na nOg* in reverse. I quickly learned to loathe the Gross God of Gaeilge.

My experience in the hourly prayers confirmed the suspicion that in this school I was definitely an outsider, an observer, an inhabitant of one. Protestants in the class were, as my new-found mathematics knowledge indicated, a subset of two: or of one when we had Gaeilge. It became obvious that Tim Cox and I, merely by being Protestant, weren't going to be exposed to the level of punishment our Catholic classmates were experiencing, with a result we were marginalised by all, with no real sense of belonging here. School was a bubble and our place was somewhere in the membrane sliding about and looking in.

I lived through this predicament with a sense of awkwardness. Life in the Brothers was tough and violent and the violence happened around me. Saying it happened around me was no exaggeration. I just wasn't involved. Often doing work at my desk, the systematic boxing and thumping took place as if I weren't present. When it happened at the rear of the class, I knew better than to turn around and look. You certainly lost any happy glow during these classes. It was as if a troubled maniac was running amok in the class. Whatever colour there was in life was quickly sucked out and eliminated.

What happened around me was desperate. Watching this on a daily basis, my relief at being exempt from it sometimes brought on nervous hysterics.

Often the violence grew from insignificant incidents. One sunny languid afternoon everything began well with the Brother explaining a complex geometric theory regarding angles in a triangle. He did this in his own inimitable style, rushing through it and assuming that all the class was following him. The Brother then started on one side of the class asking questions about the proposition in question. Some stumbled through the interrogation. Some didn't and got a few thumps around the head. Others missed the cut altogether and escaped for another day.

This time he picked on Noel. Maths wasn't his strong point. Interrogated up at the blackboard, he answered the question regarding a particular angle as 'The angle ABC,' but unfortunately it came out as 'Dangle ABC'. An opportunity to be human beckoned for the Brother, but he scorned it. Of course the rest of us at this stage saw a comic side to the drama. Somehow we knew the laughing wouldn't last, but it was funny, even when you repeated it, silently. Laughing or smiling might attract unwanted attention from the Brother. This of course represented a new complicity that implicated me as much as anyone.

The Brother squared up to Noel. His face was like a corpse, Noel's was no better. You just knew that the next syllable from Noel was going to dictate what happened for the rest of the lesson. Noel changed his mind about the angle in question and chanced 'The angle BAD,' but again it came out as 'Dangle BAD'. It was rumoured the girls St Mary's College received elocution lessons; perhaps we should have had them as well.

In times of stress, everyone tended to pronounce words poorly, but the Brother was going to make a point this time. He cranked the drama up a notch by repositioning the wide black belt around his midriff, a kind of athletic preparation for what was going to happen. The Brother then brayed, alternately chortling and scolding Noel. Shifting from one foot to another, he said with an edge to his voice, 'What did you say?' Now Noel reconsidered his answer and ventured another angle.

Thump, thump, thump. A few fists were aimed at Noel's head with unexpected ferocity. Then he was asked the same question. Noel held himself erect and seemed to accept this unhappy fate with teenage stoicism. He twitched, a reaction to a perceived movement by the Brother. His eyes looked furtively to the floor, his chin sunk into his polo neck shirt. Whatever he did he further entrenched himself in his predicament. It was not possible to walk backwards from this situation. This continued for an awful long time until it was just silly. The whole class was reeling.

At this stage everyone just wished for it to be over, longing to be somewhere else. I stared at my watch, willing the time to pass faster only to see, as often happened in Disney cartoons, the second hand seemingly move backwards. If time indeed slowed down, the metronome of the heart gathered pace.

Even if you weren't the religious type, you knew everyone said a prayer and held their breath, but it didn't matter because their prayers only said, 'Get me out of here and make it stop.' I adopted the habit of cursing silently to myself.

This random brutality was occasionally and comically interrupted by the hourly prayers, when the entire class seemingly forgot what was occurring, and stood up and faced the statue of the Virgin Mary. 'Bless me Holy Mother for I have sinned.' We had a momentary parole from the guilt, but with a sure acceptance that God wasn't here all the time. They say violence is death at work when all reason is lost, and this recurring drama was truly an example of this.

Often we went through a terrified giggling stage until we realised that something was badly wrong here. Eventually the drama finished and we awaited the next entertainment. With lessons constantly whirring in our brains, it was easy to distract ourselves from this predicament. The desire to swallow and sometimes not being able to was normal. We overcame our fear and emotions. Silence beckoned.

This silence after the assaults was formidable. It was like the silence of an empty house. What black dog mist propels people to commit this violence? How did the Brother reconcile his rage with Christian mercy? We never spoke about these outrages. Somehow this cruelty was matched by our indifference to one another. I was grateful for the fact that others got treated worse than I did and I felt like I was in another world. They say other people's happiness does not happen to you. I realised this also applies to other peoples' miseries and their misfortunes.

As we progressed in Latin, the Brothers regularly introduced phrases into the conversation to further motivate us. We were familiar with *misericordia bellum* and there was always a *post mortem* about something on the horizon.

One of their favourites was *Carpe diem*. 'Seize the day,' they declared. After violent episodes, the feeling was that it ought to be *Carpe puerem* – seize the boy.

Of course the Brothers didn't always come out winners in this violence. There was this one time in our English class when Liam, a lanky awkward boy who always sat at the back of the class, was called on to recite a passage from *The Tempest*. He stood up and mumbled his way through the lines. The Brother, obviously in a bit of mood, stopped him and shouted at him, 'I can't hear you! Speak up!' Liam tried but it was obvious his heart wasn't in it: passing his hand continuously across his mouth didn't exactly help either. I remember he had a a pencil in his other hand. He turned the pencil over and over, as if that would help him understand what he was reading.

Reading Shakespeare demanded concentration, and perhaps due to that concentration, Liam forgot to turn up the volume on his voice. Perhaps he was embarrassed reading the pretentious words, but the Brother wanted volume. 'I can't hear you!' he shouted louder. What happened next took us a little by surprise. He screamed at Liam, 'Get down to the playground and read it!'

Liam slowly left the room, in what to me seemed quite a mature manner. After an eternity, he appeared in the playground under the second storey window with his book at the ready. He spoke the lines again. The rest of the class were all watching him from the windows.

It has to be said that you could not hear what he was saying. The inevitable happened. The Brother shouted, 'I still can't hear you! Get out in the middle of the football pitch and read it again!' Liam now seemed quite at ease. Perhaps it was the cool air, perhaps it was just the increase in the distance between them. He walked calmly out into the middle of the playing field. We were trying to guess what great woe was going to befall this poor fellow when he came back into class. He seemed to be on a hiding to nothing here.

'Read it again!' the Brother roared. Revulsion on our part gave way to a sort of furtive enjoyment and curiosity. Liam looked up at us. A wit asked if anyone had any popcorn.

The Brother's face had turned red; he looked like he was going to have a coronary. I briefly entertained a hope that the whole thing was a dream but something reminded me that I knew the difference between dreaming and the harsh reality facing us. My body felt like it was somehow melting into what we were seeing.

Down on the field, Liam hesitated. A dramatic pause you might say. The Brother obligingly added to the moment by shouting, 'Come on! Come on! We haven't got all day.' Liam still hesitated. In hindsight, he had perfect timing.

There followed a profound silence. I think the birds in the hedgerow stopped singing in admiration of the drama unfolding. Liam looked up and this time shouted loudly enough that we could all hear him perfectly. He said, 'Fuck off you old queer bollocks,' and threw the red book he was holding into the air as a university student might do with his mortar board on graduation day.

It was fantastic. The Brother, after a moment's disbelief, ran to the door and down the stairs, presumably to administer the now very familiar beating to the miscreant. As we watched though, our hero walked slowly across the playing field to the far side and disappeared through the hedge into St Peter's Place, never to be seen again in the school. The class had collective hysterics. We were rolling around on the floor with our knees up.

For the next few days, the Brothers were harsher than ever, but they couldn't stop the elation among students around the school. There were huddled whispering conversations in every corner of the playground. Everyone was smiling the same knowing smile. For awhile, Liam achieved folk hero status, but the memory of his magnificent insubordination was soon overtaken by the importance of that next essay, that next poem or that next test.

The horror of this random violence in class was writ large in our lives. It assaulted our senses. We tried to ignore it but events always took control. You looked up, you thought you had stopped reading, but you had stopped long ago. You did not move. Your twin or your double was perhaps there instead of you. You did not stir, you closed your eyes. You were not there. It was morning or afternoon still and it had been for a long time. I thought about the fact that I hated it and thought that everyone else probably hated it too, but no one was prepared to say so. I can't pretend that I wasn't glad somebody was being picked on instead of me but I understood nothing other than realising I could do nothing. I was marked for life.

I'd seen movies and read books where schools were depicted as being the safest places on earth. The Brothers seemed to wield extraordinary powers over the children in their care which was completely at odds with these perceptions. It is the memory of the thumpings and lashings with the strap that will stay with me the longest. The Christian Brothers are remembered nationally on the one hand for educating the men who founded the Republic, and on the other as those for tarnishing many lives. Prior to 1968, they provided cheap education when there was little of it about and contributed to the social mobility of a nation. They were somehow victims of a society with ambitions that said, 'Do anything you like as long as you get him through his examinations.'

23

'Life was Medium Cool'

Life at the Christian Brothers School was like being in another dimension, where things were definitely familiar, but ever so slightly strange – strangely strange but oddly normal. I enjoyed the multitude of subjects, in particular mathematics. I soon weaned myself off writing the word 'Sums' on my copy books; it was Mathematics all the way now. I was naïve enough to mention maths when I once visited Algy, but I learned my lesson. 'Maths,' she cried out. 'Mathematics, mathematics, how posh Rucky! Sums were good enough for the rest of us.' She laughed her trademark laugh.

I realised that Class 1B was largely the top end of the Entrance Examination results and everyone in it was coping well with the new subjects. Occasionally someone didn't produce the homework and the room resounded to an instantaneous six of the best administered by the cane or the strap, whichever was conveniently at hand for the Brother.

Not so for our sister Class 1A. Through the thin walls of the dividing partitions, we could hear continually what Dad used to call 'blue murder'. It seemed the teachers were struggling to convince some boys to complete their homework. Their hands took some punishment.

Two or three weeks into the academic year, we had all our text books, and life in the CBS began to take on a reassuring routine. We were starting to feel at home with our new subjects and regular progress exams every few weeks kept us on our toes. Spoken Irish featured heavily in the curriculum and it certainly seemed that despite my worries I was at least as good or as bad at speaking Irish as the rest of the class.

Frequently we were tested in the conjugation of verbs. We of course got advance notice of these tests and their format, which made us all the more anxious. The Brother took us into groups of five or six students in a circle at the top of the classroom. He stood in the middle of the circle and quick-fired questions on the conjugation of verbs in the range of tenses. If you were slow, or got it wrong, whump! He punched you in the chest, sending you flying backwards.

'I *will* go to heaven,' the Brother asked. Slight hesitation from the student, a mumble. 'Wrong!' Thump.

(Pray for us.)

'I *might* go to heaven,' the Brother enquired. 'What?' Another thump for another student.

(Pray for us.)

'I *should* go to heaven.' Silence. 'Ha ha ha,' the Brother squealed triumphantly. Another thump.

(Pray for us.)

Sacred mother tongue, we have suffered for you.

The thing was the Brother administered his punches in a light-hearted manner, smiling and maintaining a demeanour that suggested it was all a big joke. Those on the receiving end had a somewhat different opinion.

Everyone hated this process. It was like some sort of blood sport where we were forced to play the part of the trapped animal. I was growing accustomed to this place being full of threatening noises, but I wasn't expecting to get hurt in it.

When these tests were imminent, I began to know what to look for when the Brother entered the room, and over the years I became very good at it. You had to look for tell-tale signs of how he had got on with his previous class. If he was riled or annoyed, you could see thunder in his face and knew it would be brutal. If however he was carrying an armful of test papers, he might just go through them with each individual, while the rest of the class got on with revision or some other worthwhile endeavour. Your safety in this case depended on how you had scored in the test.

The Brothers was an expensive school. There were fees to pay and books to buy; all possibly incentives not to send your child there. Notwithstanding this cost and the violence meted out on their sons, parents were keen to send them to the CBS. Maybe they thought the beatings contributed to their betterment.

We had to dip into Mam's contribution to Miss Murphy's Ladies Christmas Savings Club frequently. I think even the inscrutable Miss Murphy began to realise that school fees and books in some quarters were as important as Christmas. Whenever it happened, you could tell she wasn't entirely pleased.

Being able to pay our way put something of a gloss on the whole endeavour for Mam. I think even Dad was proud of his involvement. To Mam, the plethora of books arriving in the house was daunting, but Dad found them interesting and occasionally downright marvellous. I think at times he was jealous of what he might have missed growing up.

Occasionally I noticed him flipping through the maths-related books, especially algebra and geometry. He also showed more than a passing interest in the Latin books of Ovid and Livy and liked to read the English translation of the Gallic wars.

Others did not have the same good luck. As certain as it was that I would attend Arklow CBS, Connie had made it plain that Sally would not be following a similar route to St Mary's Girls School. Recently separated and living alone with her children, she simply didn't have enough money to cope. For once Mam was not asked to contribute. It was just too much to ask.

Just as John had gradually disappeared from our lives when he went to the Tech, so I was cast adrift (or so it felt) to follow my new direction. It was inevitable that I wouldn't meet my classmates from Carysfort on a daily basis any more; similarly Sally and Bobby faded from my life. We suddenly had nothing in common. No shared enemy. No shared obligations. Nothing. I was on my own again.

As I was edging my way to the final year in secondary school, a change for the better occurred in Irish education. Some people said they were long, long overdue and, fifty years after the Easter Rising, I suppose they had a point. There was a definite thirst for education among those who couldn't afford it in the country. Major changes to the system were announced. After Mam and Dad has scrimped and saved for books and fees for several years, a very decent Minister of Education introduced free secondary education in the Republic. A year before, he introduced free school transport. Parents throughout the nation considered the man, even though he was a politician, to be a bit of a saint.

Telefis Eireann, or RTE as we now knew it, got in on the education act as well. They introduced a series of programmes under the banner of Telefis Scoile, planning to broadcast science programmes during school hours. It was all terribly modern, and seemed to be an indication of the optimism and hunger for change gripping the country.

The lovely Minister of Education's budget didn't however stretch to providing a TV set for each school. That needed to be funded locally. At our school, to call went out to parents to contribute £5 toward the purchase of a television. I'm not sure every school opted for this solution, but ours did. The TV set was duly bought and installed on a sturdy shelf in the science room. Months after it has been installed, I hadn't heard anyone from any class mention that they'd seen any science on it.

However, this posh, extravagant television didn't remain totally redundant. One day I was on my way home for dinner while the rest of them were having religious classes when the Brother Superior caught up with me at the door and handed me a sealed envelope. He was a red-haired man with a soft pink glow.

'A Risteárd, a buachaill,' he said. They always tried to use a bit of Irish every time they spoke. I was going to reply, 'Shea, shea, shea,' but quickly thought the better of it.

'Yes Brother,' I answered with the appropriate humility.

'Can you give this message to your Mother or Father? I'll need a reply this afternoon.'

'Okay, Brother,' I said with some relief. I was obviously intrigued but eventually reasoned that it was probably another begging letter for something or other. I gave the letter to Mam who opened it. She smiled as she read it to herself.

'Here,' she said 'have a look at it yourself.' The note mentioned that the Pope was visiting the Holy Land and that the visit was being shown on the television. Brother Loughnane wanted to know if my parents objected to my watching the Pope on telly, and if they did, he'd let me off school. I must say I didn't object to being let off school, but I was going through a stage where I watched absolutely anything on the box. Sitting down with fifty or sixty other boys to watch telly had its attraction, for a while at least if only to avoid real school work.

Mam scribbled on the note that she had no objections and I passed it back to the Brother, who seemed relieved when he read it. As it happened, the programmes showing the Pope in the Holy Land were on about the same time as religious study, so I never did get to see the great man in the science room.

In all my time in the Brothers, I got to watch that telly only twice. Once was when the race horse Arkle was at the height of its fame. The Brothers took a keen interest in many things unrelated to their chosen way of life; things which interested normal Irish men. This included horse racing. I'm not sure if the Brothers put bets on horses, or indeed how they put bets on, but they certainly showed a greater interest in the outcome of this race than perhaps they should have.

As television edged its way more and more into our lives, it exerted a subtle but pervasive effect on our lives. Programmes like *The Monkees* and *Top of the Pops* helped and coached us on how to be teenagers. Without realising it, I did a lot of preparation and personal preening before these programmes; checking my hair in the mirror, making sure that it looked as close to my heroes' hair as possible. I assumed that these preparations were going unnoticed, but one day when Mam and Dad had a laugh at my expense, and I realised that nothing goes unnoticed in the family home and those you loved could hurt you.

Discussion programmes exposed us to topics that previously were the domain of grown-ups. I took the assertion that there wasn't any sex in Ireland before the Late Late Show with a pinch of salt, but sometimes I heard stuff that hurt and wounded me.

One week *The Late Late Show* featured a discussion on how

Protestants had fared in Ireland since Ireland became a republic. One side of the argument, presumably made by a Protestant, was that we had come out of it rather badly, and were not fully accepted by the Catholic majority. The actor John Crowley, who played Tom Riordan in the Irish soap opera *The Riordans*, joined in the discussion. He added, 'Protestants have only themselves to blame You even hung onto the Union Jacks in your cathedrals after we got independence. What did you expect?'

Listening to this, late at night, I was overcome with embarrassment. I thought it just about summed up the predicament that I was beginning to find myself in. It was difficult to accept that I might be considered an outsider by my own religion, but the realisation that I was an outsider to everyone was a heavy burden to bear.

One morning there was a great buzz going around when I arrived in school. The Brothers in particular were excited: cock a hoop was the best way to describe it.

'Have you heard the news?' someone said in class. 'They've blown up Nelson's Pillar.'

'Who has?' I said, genuinely mystified. 'Who blew it up?' Ever since I'd first seen it on a trip to Dublin, I'd wanted to climb to the top but never got the chance. 'Who blew it up?' I said again.

'The IRA, of course.'

'The IRA?' I thought. The IRA to me were a bunch of old guys who wore black berets and black gloves and medals on their chests. They were always marching somewhere or following a coffin with a black beret and black gloves on top of it to the cemetery.

That day continued to be memorable. The Brothers were behaving like giddy school girls. I was beginning to expect that we might get a half day off in celebration, but it wasn't to be. The normal business of the school gradually took over, only to be disrupted again a week or so later when an Irish folk group released a record celebrating the great deed.

That evening, the television programmes told us every aspect, every detail of Nelson's Column. We learned who had built it and who was suspected of destroying it. Frank Hall, on his magazine programme, *Newsbeat*, even interviewed a man who had worked at the column all his life. This man, from his early teens, had sold entrance tickets to tourists and visitors for the long journey to the viewing platform.

'I keep the place clean,' he said. 'I lock up every evening and open up again every morning. It's been my life's work, it has.' He was a small man, not unlike Dad, and appeared utterly flabbergasted to suddenly – through no fault of his own – be out of a job.

I always remember his parting comment: 'At least I wasn't up there when the lads blew it up.'

24

'Fed up? Turn the Beatles up instead'

I think I liked the Beatles as soon as I heard them; in 1962, they were difficult to miss. When their records came on the radio, it seemed like I was listening to the future. Visiting Connie's house had an added attraction for me at that time. Betty, Algy and John were all bona fide teenagers and I liked to hang about their house and watch the antics of these crazy creatures. Betty and Algy shared a transistor that was constantly tuned into pop programmes, mainly Radio Luxembourg.

'They're the Transister Sisters,' Mam said, which impressed me, but I knew they preferred the name they concocted for themselves: the Sizzle Sisters.

I also had a Bush transistor radio, as well as a big old valve radio. Whenever possible, I sneaked the tranny up to my room in the evening to listen to the pop programmes. I learned the words of all the songs and joined in. As the night wore on and the AM reception faded in and out and the sound rose and fell. It wasn't great but it was better than nothing. During the daytime, there were very few radio programmes dedicated to popular music for teenagers. It would take a revolution spearheaded by a young Irishman in the coming years to change all that. When the Beatles or any of the other famous acts were played on 'normal' radio, it was as if they were a phenomenon to be studied; something to be deciphered to understand what the attraction was. Of course older people just didn't get the fact that pop music was forever young, forever aimed at and understood by the youth of the time. Ever it were thus.

Request shows became my essential listening during the day.

With the increasing popularity of this new music, requests for Beatles records enlivened dull old shows like *Two Way Family Favourites*. It was simply the best way to hear them, the utter randomness of their possible selection adding to the delight. On British radio at the time, you were more likely to hear the likes of Frank Sinatra, Perry Como or Andy Williams and comedy records such as *Right Said Fred* any time of the day.

For teenagers, the highlight of the week was the BBC Light Programme's *Pick of the Pops* which gave you a weekly countdown of the British Top Twenty best-selling records all crammed into one blissful hour.

Irish national radio had nothing for teenagers. It seemed to cater for lovers of GAA and celidh music. Broadcasted ominously from Dublin GPO, it would many years before it moved to Donnybrook and, with the addition of RTE television, became better accepted.

For my parent's generation, the Ormonde ballroom had been the venue to hear music and dance to it; they were a clientele that revelled in the big band sound and enjoyed the waltz and the quickstep. In the late 1950s, the Entertainment Centre in Ferrybank offered a modern alternative to this. The Centre, as it was known, had weekly Saturday night dances, attracting the biggest names on the showband scene and occasionally a big star from Britain whose popularity was on the wane. The bands faithfully reproducing all the current hits were popular up to a point but they were still mired in the past. The one breath of fresh air came with the introduction of a record hop on Sunday afternoon.

All this dullness changed with the Beatles. I became a big fan, maybe an obsessive. Probably an obsessive. I liked them better than any other artist or group around. I defended them and loved when they won awards. I was delighted when their latest single went straight to No 1. They appeared almost at the same time in Arklow's one record shop, such was their popularity and selling power. I joined the Beatles Fan Club and read everything about them that I could get my hands on. I revelled in their Christmas fan club records. I suppose I loved them, but then I'd just become a teenager, so somehow all this infatuation and obsession was acceptable and normal.

My parents, like most, were still stuck firmly in the Frank Sinatra, Bing Crosby era. Their taste even went as far as the newer singers of recent years like Cliff Richard and Elvis and all their shoddy look-alikes from England. This made them feel even more old-fashioned. When they swooned over records by Ken Dodd, I knew it was time to move on.

They had such crazy opinions about some of the groups and the records that very soon I wasn't even able to listen to the radio in the same room as them. It was impossible to be neutral about the new culture; battle lines were drawn. Depending on your age group, it was a time of ecstatic liberation or blatant irresponsibility. The pairing of the words 'juvenile' and 'delinquent' crept into parents' conversations. Everywhere teenagers were emerging from the chrysalis of childhood as the colourful butterflies that identified the period.

The world seemed full of singers and groups performing fantastic songs. Each record sounded like a minor masterpiece. Most of these artists were having what appeared to be their fifteen minutes of fame. Groups like the Applejacks and the Moody Blues with songs like *Have I the Right* and *Go Now* made a lasting impression on me. While they were in the charts and getting airplay, they took over my daily life. I jumped when they came on the radio. Seeing them performing on TV added to the sense of involvement. The clothes, the fashions, the language of the DJs, the formats of the shows were all part of the attraction. Let the stars express their opinions about anything under the sun and I was all ears.

When the music wasn't on the radio or telly, reading about them filled the gaps. That wasn't as easy at it's become in the Internet age. There wasn't any publication in Ireland that covered the teenage music scene. Occasionally the Irish Sunday papers carried articles about personalities in the news, but in general all views and debates that interested me came from the BBC Light programme and English pop magazines.

The big change came when the *New Musical Express* – the *NME* – became available in the town. One day I noticed Algy with what appeared to be a newspaper. She was sitting on the sofa with her knees tucked up under her, smoking a cigarette with an intensity that I had rarely seen.

'How are you honey,' she said as I walked into the room.

'Grand,' I replied and sat down opposite. 'What's that you're reading?'

'That's the *New Musical Express,*' she said emphatically. 'They've started getting it again in Gallagher's. You should order it. It's full of good stuff, couldn't be without it.' She tossed it across to me. 'Have a look,' she said, lighting up another cigarette.

'Do you want one,' she said mischievously, knowing full well that Mam would go spare if I started smoking. Embarrassed, I said, 'Not just now' and picked up the paper. My refusal brought on one of her raucous laughs.

Nearly everyone I knew smoked. All of Algy's family smoked. Even Bobby, who was only twelve, had the occasional pull when he could. Dad was a heavy smoker but Mam hated it. I had a touch of asthma and the smoke made it flare up. Dad smoked everywhere in the house. It was dire going into the bathroom or toilet after him in the morning. Although I hated it, nearly all my school friends smoked and sometimes I felt a little left out.

As for the *NME*, I hadn't see it before, but even skimming through the pages, it was a million times more interesting than anything I had read. It reviewed the new singles and albums released in England. It contained articles about forthcoming records and concerts. At the back, there was a page of rumours and scandals portrayed in a jokey sarcastic sort of way. I made my mind up immediately to get this every week myself.

Algy was reading my mind. 'You can have it when I'm finished with it,' Algy said as she took another long drag.

'Wow, thanks,' I said, but I knew I couldn't depend on her buying it every week.

As Algy had confirmed, the only place in Arklow that you could buy the NME was in Gallagher's newsagents. As well as selling newspapers, books and magazines it also stocked a big range of model cars and Airfix models. They also sold pipes and tobacco. At Christmas, it was a great shop for presents. Gallagher's was owned, unsurprisingly, by Mrs Gallagher who in my opinion was at least a hundred and fifty years old. She had a moustache and worrying hairs growing out of her nose, the type you always wanted to give a good tug to see if they were attached. She knew my father quite well. He'd worked on her shop over the years, so I needed to be very mannerly towards her all the time, which occasionally was a bit of a challenge. If anyone ever had any suspicions that Auntie Moll was a witch, they never had encountered Mrs Gallagher

'Can I have the *New Musical Express*, please?' I said.

'We don't stock that trash,' she replied, and then inexplicably added: 'What's that you said?'

I repeated, 'Can I have the *New Musical Express*?'

'Why didn't you say that first,' she boomed.

This was the way our weekly encounter went. It was a bit cat-and-mouse but I could get her going without being nasty.

'How's the schooling going?' she asked suddenly as I handed her the money.

'Fine,' I replied and added, 'I have the week off.'

'Good,' she said, 'get as much as you can off those Brothers. Their education will set you up for life.'

I picked up the change and escaped from the shop without further interrogation.

When I got home from collecting my *NME*, I went straight up the stairs to my room. I shouted out, 'I'm home' but there was no answer. Before settling down to my weekly ritual I put on a record to get me through the moment: today it was *All Summer Long*.

The end of the year was always a great time for music. The *NME* published its New Year edition the first week after Christmas and in it listed their awards for best single, best group, best LP, best newcomer. It was interesting stuff, especially if your favourite group got an award.

The *NME* also did something that I'd never noticed before. They compiled a list covering every chart entry for the past year and allocated points to each artist for each week they spent at a particular number.

For No 1, the artist got thirty points, for No 2, twenty nine points and so on down to one point for No 30.

In the January 1964 edition, the official Top Ten – according to the *NME* – for the whole of 1963 was:

Position	Artist	Points
1	The Beatles	1331
2	Cliff Richard	1150
3	Gerry and the Pacemakers	929
4	The Shadows	919
5	Frank Ifield	903
6	Roy Orbison	781
7	Billy J Kramer and The Dakotas	657
8	Jet Harris	645
9	Billy Fury	636
10	Freddy and the Dreamers	580

I noted that I disliked nine out of ten of the artists of the year, but was pleased that my favourite music had got the top position. Being a Beatles fan, I was desperately interested in how they were doing as the year progressed. Unfortunately the *NME* didn't provide regular updates, just the year-end figures and positions in January. I couldn't wait that long, so I bought a notebook and completed the figures week by week, allocating points, adding up the totals and listing the Top Ten. It became a bit of an obsessive ritual, on a par with train-spotting. Had they known, the *NME* might even have commissioned me.

It was interesting to see that even after just three months, the Shadows, Cliff and Elvis were way outside the list's top thirty. All the acts that in 1963 looked like rivals to the Beatles were nowhere to be seen. Groups like the Applejacks, Jan and Dean, the Nashville Teens, the Searchers had come and gone. Each had their moment in the sun, produced at least one memorable single, and then sunk into relative obscurity.

But these flash-in-the pan acts produced the real soundtrack, the real musical score for life in the Sixties. Their quirky hits were plugged incessantly on the radio. Some lyrics you just knew you were going to remember for the rest of your life.

The Beatles eventually won top spot easily in 1964, and I could see them winning it every year forever. Up to the end of March 1964, the unofficial Top Ten – according to R Ruxton – were:

Position	Artist	Points
1	The Beatles	328
2	Engelbert Humperdinck	243
3	Solomon King	243
4	The Love Affair	236
5	Tom Jones	231
6	The Bee Gees	225
7	Manfred Mann	220
8	Amen Corner	215
9	Georgie Fame	191
10	John Fred and the Playboys	180

It was strange that in spite of this preoccupation with pop, not many of the lads I hung around with learned how to play musical instruments. Those who did were quite well off or just a little bit odd. Nearly all the rich town Proddies that went to primary school with me learned the piano. This was one of the fundamental distinctions between the poor and rich Prods in the town. The rich ones could spare the money for the non-essentials while the poor ones didn't have anything to spare.

To be fair, my mother wanted me to take up the piano. I knew a boy who was learning music and was picked on and bullied for it. 'Liberace,' they called him. And of course he was a bit odd as well. I didn't want that happening to me. Other people who played instruments seemed to come from Catholic families who earned money playing in celidh bands. In these musical families, every member seemed to play a bodhran, a flute or a fiddle.

Nobody, in either my father's or mother's family, could play anything, my cousin Freddy being the one exception. He worked in a local print shop and played in a band at night. He had learned the guitar from a Bert Weedon home study course. By all accounts, he was pretty good. He started off playing in concerts in the local parish hall and eventually played in a series of groups, notably The Red Seven, The Colombia Showband, The Family and Sheilanagig. He became quite famous in the county and the local scene.

Locally and nationally, we were always hoping and searching for some Irish success in the charts, and by chart success it had to be success in the English charts. When the Irishman Val Doonican had a big hit in England with *Walk Tall*, he was immediately adopted by the Irish music industry as the breakthrough artist that might pave the way for other Irish successes. He was something of a local hero in Arklow as he once played a summer season in Courtown Harbour, a nearby seaside resort. People said they remembered him singing and performing a sort of vaudeville act before films in the Ormonde cinema. He was also remembered for living in a small caravan in a nearby car park. Such was the life of a journeyman musician.

25

'East Coast girls are hip'

If people thought that an only child like me, living alone with his parents, would automatically have an orderly and uneventful existence, they were entirely wrong. The frequent comings and goings of two uncles, the lengthy visits of Sally and the occasional appearance of her entire family – together with holiday visits from our relatives in Dublin and Swansea – pleasantly upset any home routine that I might have wanted or expected.

As for me, it's possible at some stage I thought any further disruption to this strange existence was impossible. Also wrong, entirely wrong.

Annie came into our lives after Kevin Kearon Ltd decided they needed a secretary in the office. It seemed inevitable, what with an increasing workforce both in the yard and on their burgeoning fleet. They found a young Protestant girl with secretarial skills and hired her. The problem was that Annie was a country girl and lived far enough away that she couldn't travel to Arklow each day. So Kevin Kearon asked Mam and Dad to provide accommodation with full board for her.

The plan was for Annie to stay with us Monday to Friday. It wasn't an unusual arrangement: many country girls worked in shops or offices for Protestant companies in the town. I overheard a short conversation between Mam and Dad. It was obvious they were in favour of the arrangement, but I think initially Dad thought there might be additional work involved for him.

'We'll need to decorate the room and get a new mattress for the bed,' said Mam. 'We'll probably need a dressing table as well. I'll get Connie to do the painting and decorating.'

I thought I saw Dad breathing a sigh of relief. Thankfully he said nothing. There the conversation ended and I heard no more about it until the day I moved from my increasingly congested small room to the larger back bedroom. To Dad, this was a blessing in disguise. That vacant backroom had provided too easy a solution to any of his in-laws who needed emergency accommodation.

A week later, Mam and Auntie Connie re-papered the room, putting in a new dressing table and wardrobe. Connie was great at the papering and painting, working and smoking and getting everything done. Somehow the room was completed just in time.

Annie arrived at our house on Sunday evening. Her parents delivered her to our front door and almost immediately headed off with a promise to collect her from work on Friday. She was friendly, rosy-cheeked, with tousled blonde hair. I liked her immediately.

To tell the truth, I was in awe of her, as I was of all the young women who passed through our house.

Mam and Dad were keen to make her feel at home and made quite a fuss of her. On Monday morning, Dad accompanied her to work that first morning, walking the short distance from our house down to her new workplace.

Over the coming months, Annie settled into the house and became a part of the family. In spite of being from the country, she was pretty normal. The day she arrived, I noticed a badminton racket among her baggage. Within a week or two, she had joined the parish club and played either in the Marlborough Hall or an other parish hall three or four times a month. It wasn't long before she had boy friends calling at our door. Dad got all strict with her telling her to be in by a certain time. He was getting things mixed up again.

Annie ended up staying with us for a few years, and left to get married to a Protestant farmer who lived out towards Avoca. Their wedding was the first one I'd ever attended.

I remember the house being dead without her. Over the years she had become much more than a lodger. She brought friends home for tea and almost became an accepted part of the household. Dad really didn't like people staying with us, despite all the lodgers of one sort and another. He could be a bit jealous and sulky if he thought he was playing second fiddle to somebody in his own house.

After Annie got married, she held on to her job for a few months, her husband driving her to work each day from his farm. It soon became obvious there was a lot of work Annie could do on the farm, so she left Kearon's to become a full-time housewife and farm office worker.

With a vacancy in both the office and our house, and it wasn't long before history repeated itself and Isabelle, another Protestant country girl, arrived. Despite having cousins living near the dog track, she decided to lodge with us. Proximity to the place of work seemed to be always the deciding factor.

Isabelle was a tall, attractive girl and seemed quite sophisticated for her age. I heard Dad refer to her as a 'femme fatale', which sent me running to consult my dictionary. You could spot from a million miles away that she was a Protestant and equally could sense she was a girl who had grown up with ponies and horses.

She had attended boarding school and arrived at our house with all sorts of cases and tennis racquets as if she had just stepped off the school bus. I spotted the necessary badminton racquet among her paraphernalia and instantly knew she would fit into the parish activities. All that was missing was the school uniform and the jolly hockey sticks.

Isabelle was a quieter, more aloof girl than Annie, but she fit into the house in spite of this. She always seemed to be on a diet. Some times she only had a mashed banana for dinner. She went home most weekends and when she arrived back she always brought fruit and vegetables from the farm for Mam.

She was a great one for going out. She loved dances and had a particular liking for hunt balls. Hunt balls were a peculiar thing. They were predominantly frequented by country people and, from Isabelle's descriptions, seemed boisterous affairs with loads of rough dancing, games and country stuff. I think girls generally attended them to hunt for husbands. She always returned home late from one of these and looked like death in the morning.

One such morning, she didn't come down at all for breakfast. Mam left her in her room. If she was sick, she was sick. 'She'll feel better if she sleeps it off,' Mam said.

Eventually about eleven o'clock, Isabelle appeared with a scarf around her mouth and still in her dressing gown. She went out into the scullery and had a quiet word with Mam. I couldn't make out what was said, but it was very hush-hush.

When Isabelle came out of the scullery, she breezed straight up the stairs. Mam came into the kitchen with a mischievous smile on her face. 'I want you to go down to the yard and tell Kevin that Isabelle is sick and won't be in work today.'

I was out of there with a flash; I wanted to get back and find out what had happened. It couldn't have taken more than minutes. Mam was still smiling to herself.

'What's happened?'

'Shush, she'll hear you.'

Mam called me over close to the fire. 'She was at a hunt ball in Tinahealy last night. When she got home, she wasn't feeling well. She went into the toilet. She took out her false teeth in case she got sick and put them on the cistern.'

'Isabelle has false teeth,' I said almost out loud. 'Wow that's a surprise.'

Mam continued. 'When she finished her doings, she reached for the handle to flush the toilet, knocked her teeth into the bowl and they were flushed away. She has no spare set and can't face work today. She's trying to get a dentist's appointment at short notice.'

Isabelle kept out of everyone's way for a few days and managed to make it look like nothing had happened when she reappeared. That's the kind of girl she was.

She kept going to hunt balls to meet a boy she liked. I did my best to help her in this department. One day while she was having dinner, I stuck a sign on her coat which read, 'Kiss me please'. She wore this for the rest of the day and was only aware of it when someone in the bank told her. She wasn't pleased and more or less guessed it was me. I avoided her for a while.

At one stage when Isabelle stayed with us, Algy moved in as well.

Sitting down at the table with them each evening for tea, I was struck even at my age at the marked difference between the two girls.

Isabelle's dieting meant she ate little while Algy consumed everything that came her way without putting on a pound; hence the nickname Twiggy. Equally, like Connie, Algy seemed capable of getting by on a cup of tea and a cigarette. Algy was all miniskirts and mod gear, while Isabelle was costumes, cardigans and ball gowns. I expect their paths never crossed socially.

They both left our house forever within weeks of each other. Isabelle finally hunted down and married the man of her dreams, while Algy emigrated with two friends to London in search of hers.

26

'Dancing on the beach in a hippie hat'

On warm spring mornings, our house was at its quietest. Dad and whoever was staying with us at the time had eaten their breakfasts and were about their business. If I was off school, it was a truly serene time for me. I pretended to do school work while listening to my few records on my treasured record player. Scattering a few books and copies about the room usually convinced Mam I was hard at work. As long as I looked like I was working, she tolerated the music.

One such morning, I heard a soft knock on the front door and an accompanying jaunty 'Yoohoo.'

'Come in, Kitty,' my mother shouted.

Kitty was already on her way into the house. I caught a glimpse of her as she walked through the hall and breezed past the open front room door. She said, 'Howaya, Richard' as she sailed through.

Kitty was a larger-than-life and a hugely enthusiastic and compassionate woman, who always seemed to be living the moment. She was our next-door neighbour 'but one', as my Mam used to say. She had six children, all at school. I reckoned it was bedlam in their house each morning, compared with the relative tranquility in ours. When she finally got them out of the house and on their way up the quay, she occasionally popped in to our house for a cup of tea and a cuffer with my mother. She brought her own pot of tea, sometimes she brought biscuits.

It was the promise of biscuits that made me follow her into the scullery, but I quickly noticed it was just tea today.

Kitty said to me, 'Aren't you the lucky one, not having school this week.'

I had to agree with her. I was indeed lucky. Being a Protestants attending the Christian Brothers School definitely had its advantages. This week was a Retreat Week in the school, with its accompanying sermons, devotions and Stations of the Cross. It was of course all a complete mystery to me. I was happy to keep it that way.

My mother called the week's goings on 'devartions', but not when Kitty was present. This free week off gave me the chance to catch up with my studies and homework, although I must confess that most of the time I spent reading or listening to music. I expected also to find the time to cycle around Arklow countryside. It was always a carefree week for me. The Brothers hadn't yet thought of giving me extra work to do in lieu of this free time.

During the Retreat Week, a recruiting officer attended the school. He was there to identify individuals who might become Brothers or priests. There were quite a few likely candidates. These chaps weren't difficult to spot in our school as it seemed to me that they thought they were already priests. I expect every school had them. They dressed in black and were always nice and reasonable to everyone. They invariably took the pledge promising not to drink alcohol even when they were allowed to. Similarly they sported the Fainne, which declared them to be fans of the Irish language. In school they had a sort of diplomatic immunity from violence similar to that enjoyed by us Protestants.

About the town, everybody felt easy with them. Church-going women held them in high regard. They were non-threatening to the local girls. 'Isn't he lovely', local Mammies often gushed when they passed by. If you're holy and nice to everyone, what can go wrong? Success through sanctity was the name of the game they played. Invariably they started off as altar boys and it was their destiny to become priests. Inevitably they were feted in the Brothers school and spoken to as equals. 'He's going to be one of us soon – one of our gang' seemed to be the attitude.

These retreats weren't devoid of humour though. About a month after the retreat, each year I received several offers from various religious orders thanking me for my interest in becoming a man of the cloth, and suggesting that I discuss it with my parish priest in the first instance.

The first time this happened Mam was upset. 'What are they putting your name down for?' she asked.

'For a joke,' I explained.

The next time it happened, she had mellowed a little, and saw the funny side of it. 'I'm not the only Proddy getting these letters,' I said by way of consolation.

Kitty said, 'My gang went off complaining how boring the week was going to be.'

I didn't know in detail what went on during these retreats but if it was anything like the monotony of the hourly prayers I endured, it surely was a dreadful experience. It must have been as tedious as the sermon in our church service, but stretching out for an entire week. To me it was likely to be a festival of novenas, rosaries, saints and angels, with the mysteries of miracles, penances and indulgences thrown in for good measure.

One lighter moment was when the unfortunate visiting clerics came to answer questions about sex. The hard cases in the school had spent a great deal of time thinking up the most outlandish question to ask. While they weren't always answered, and after an outbreak of sex queries, the Brothers retaliated by giving extra sermons and talks on impure thoughts. So in spite of the moments of levity, it was far from being all fun and games.

Occasionally the baiting of visiting clerics was of such irreverence and outrage that the consequences spilled over into the next term. One year after the Easter holidays, when I went back to school, there was an official notice on the board admonishing all the students because of their treatment of a certain Father Quilter. Apparently someone bounced a ping-pong ball against the blackboard during one of his lectures. I referred to the notice as the Quilter Memorandum, after the George Segal spy film, but no one seemed to get it.

Over a cup of tea and Mikado biscuits that Mam found, Kitty said, 'And what are you up to today Richard?'

'Well, I'm working on my English essay.' This was partly true. 'Then I might ride out to Brittas Bay.'

'You should have gone yesterday,' she said, 'and you might have seen all the commotion.'

'I was going to, but the rain was just too heavy.'

Sunday had been a dreadful day, raining and an impossible wind. Everyone stayed at home, skipping church. It was a day for reading and listening to music for the entire family. Both my parents did a lot of snoring in front of the television set.

My mother said, 'I'm glad he didn't get to go out yesterday. Those Sinn Feiners are just stirring up trouble.'

Before I could say anything, Kitty said, 'Well Sally, they're only trying to get access to the beaches for ordinary people like myself and yourself. It's only right that everyone should be able to get onto our own beaches.'

The situation at Brittas Bay was a complicated one. Local farmers who owned land alongside the seafront were fencing off access to the beaches, and charging people to cross their land to get to the sea. Sinn Fein was using the situation to get publicity in the lead-up to the local and county elections. They staged a series of well-publicised demonstrations and protests to force the council and government into taking some sort of action. It was a winner as everyone wanted free access to the beaches.

This raised a lot of bad feelings with the local farmers who could see their easy earnings disappearing overnight. The situation was further complicated because one of the farmers was a foreigner. This of course was mentioned subtly by the Sinn Fein protesters.

Each weekend, there were demonstrations at Brittas Bay involving heavy contingents of Gardai. Outsiders from Dublin also came and were keen to keep the conflict in the news.

National political figures got in on the act and it was agreed that sooner or later things would get out of hand and somebody might get hurt. It was difficult to argue against Sinn Fein's stand on the issue, but everyone wanted to avoid violence.

Mam changed the subject. 'Have you not got that homework to finish?'

For once I was happy to take her suggestion on face value, if only to get away from the awkward conversation. I went back to what I'd been doing in the front room.

Our front room was the least-used room in the house. It was very cold in the winter when it got the full blast of the weather from the river and the sea. It had a small fireplace that we only occasionally lit, usually at Christmas or other special occasions. In the spring, however, the sun hit the room early in the morning, and warmed and brightened it. Mam called it the front room. Other households called theirs the parlour or the sitting room. Mam didn't like any of these names, so the front room it was

The subject of the essay I was working on was 'The Harvest', which was another blindingly inspirational topic from Brother Campion. You needed a good opening for his essays. I thought I had a good one: 'The Harvest does not only mean the reaping of wheat and corn, but also the gathering in of fish and fowl and the salvation of men.'

Old Brother Campion would read no further than that almost biblical reference. I needed to put some good stuff in to support the opening line, but I was dead sure he'd be on my side from then on.

Boredom set in as soon as I wrote these lines. I was easily distracted. Looking out the window I could see it was a warm and windy day, perfect for cycling. The road was deserted, the early-morning rush to the various schools and work places had petered out, leaving the morning to the postman, retired men with dogs, and me. I tried to turn my attention once more to the essay but couldn't muster any inspiration.

I had reached the stage in life where I needed music on all the time, especially when doing my homework. I put on a Rolling Stones LP. While *It's All Over Now* was playing, a horse and cart passed by our window. The rig made several trips past our house each day, carrying sand from the beach for building work. It was early and the horse was spritely and enthusiastic and keeping perfect time with the jaunty beat and tempo of the familiar song:

My baby used to stay out all night long.

Clip clop clip. Clip clop clip. Clip clop clip. Clip clop clip.

Coming back from the beach with its heavy load, the horse grudgingly plodded to a slower soundtrack.

My mind wandered to the photograph on the wall opposite of Mam and Dad taken before they were married; when they were walking out. It was an intriguing picture. I'd often wondered how they had met. In spite of their being the same religion, they had little in common. Mam was a great dancer before she married. Dad couldn't put one foot in front of the other; couldn't dance a step. She often told the story that she went to dances so often that she got 'run down', and her health suffered. She never elaborated. Maybe she met Dad when she was ill.

Dad told me stories of how he had cycled to Wicklow, Bray and Dublin on the weekend to meet girls. It struck me that it might have taken him the entire weekend to get there and back; he wasn't the most athletic of men. The other funny thing was that in spite of all this cycling and dancing, he married someone who lived a hundred yards from his home. Mam and Dad told me a lot about their past but their courtship remained a mystery.

I decided to cycle to Brittas Bay that day after lunch. My journey took me across Arklow bridge and out the Dublin Road. A mile or so down the road, there was a small shop owned by Jim Cuffe and his wife, Maud. They were Church of Ireland as well and were friends of Mam and Dad. I turned right after their shop, down Lovers' Lane and eventually joined the coast road out towards Brittas Bay.

Brittas Bay was my favourite place: it had an almost mystical attraction for me. In summer when the sun was out, it reminded me of photographs I'd seen of California, or Spanish holiday resorts. On the road, I passed many small farmhouses with muddy, cowshit yards in front. The vegetation was also pure Irish countryside: may bushes, rag weeds and bulrushes.

In Brittas Bay, however, the buildings and vegetation changed dramatically. The gardens all seemed to have Mediterranean plants that you didn't see anywhere else. Adobe-style houses surrounded with white walls topped with terracotta tiles were the norm. My favourite house was built on stilts and set among the sand dunes with a big glass wall facing the sea. Often there were brightly coloured open-topped cars parked underneath. Other houses were part hidden among the dunes, peeping out, giving a hint of their attraction.

The people who owned the houses all seemed very modern. I'd met some of them through Dad. The mams usually had cars of their own. They all were obviously very rich and used these second houses on weekends and during the summer holidays.

The houses all had fridges, which was a bit of a novelty in itself, but the fact that the fridges were full of Coke, Pepsi and other soft drinks convinced me that they were indeed well-off. When Dad was working in their houses and I was with him, they were always offering us something to drink.

I pulled over at the bend in the road where you got the best view of the bay. I got off the bike and walked to the edge of the cliff. I always stopped here. To my right was the holiday home of Dr Roberts. Dad did a lot of work for him over the years. Dr Roberts had bought Granny's house from Mam a few years ago. The doctor held on to this Brittas Bay house as well, using the Arklow house as his main summer home and renting out the Brittas house.

I could see for miles up the coast. The beach was fairly deserted. In the distance, I could see a few people with kids. Quite close were two nuns who seemed to have swimming costumes and towels with them. It was unusual to see nuns swimming at Brittas. Nuns had their own beach and changing hut on Clogga strand on the other side of Arklow. The wind blew their habits in front of them, reminding me of a painting I'd seen somewhere.

The bay stretched in a huge semicircle out towards Wicklow. Bordering the beach for as far as you could see was a band of large dunes. The bright houses set among them looked like cake decorations. These dunes were quite a walk from the water's edge, and gave way to a corrugated expanse of sand that reached the sea without serious incline. Occasionally there might be an intrusion of beach tar and the jetsam from passing ships.

Along the road, there wasn't much activity either, whereas in summer it was normally packed with cars. The houses themselves were used constantly over the summer when the schools shut. From the beginning of June until early September, they had that lived-in look. You noticed the bikes lying on the drives, the swimsuits and towels hanging out to dry, the lawn sprinklers hissing as you passed by.

To me it was like tomorrow's world, and as much a fantasy to me as what I had seen in movies. Brittas Bay had its own café, with a really good jukebox. For an outsider, it felt a bit intimidating walking in; it was usually filled with close-knit groups of teenagers, all dressed in beachwear or holiday clothes. As the Beachboys memorably put it, it was 'T-shirts, cut-offs and thongs' all summer long. Brittas seemed to be for teenagers. Arklow in comparison seemed to be full of old people. If Brittas Bay had been a town in America, it surely would have had a big roadway sign declaring, 'Come to Brittas Bay and you will see the sun.'

Somehow I always associated Brittas Bay with Radio Caroline. I was proud of the fact that it was an Irishman called Ronan O Rahilligh who started Radio Caroline, and delighted that he always used the Gaeilge version of his name, knowing full well that it was difficult for the English to pronounce. I was even more impressed when I discovered that he had named the radio station after Caroline Kennedy, the daughter of JFK.

Radio Caroline broadcast from a ship moored near the Isle of Man to circumvent the strict UK broadcasting regulations of the time, and there were rumours that he had plans for a television station broadcasting from an airplane flying up and down the Irish Sea. Apparently he also planned to project movies onto clouds with lasers. I completely believed it all. It was bliss to be young in the Sixties.

When you listened to the DJs on Radio Caroline, you heard American accents and you came away with the impression that you were listening to a broadcast from California. They were like big brothers talking to you. The popular songs that year all were American: *Let's Go to San Francisco*, *Massachusetts* and *California Dreaming*. The nearest thing I had to all that was Brittas Bay.

I spent all my time listening to Radio Caroline: keeping up with the new releases, the power plays, and the competitions. It was total entertainment. One of these competitions required you to name a mystery tune. It ran for weeks with the prize money was going up gradually each day until it stood at about £10,000. Mam recognised it as a Laurel and Hardy tune that was always played in their films. She couldn't quite remember the name but we entered the competition, calling it the *Cuckoo's Waltz*. By the time we eventually got around to entering it, the prize fund had reached £40,000. This was a fantastic amount of money. 'You could buy a row of houses – or maybe even a town itself – for £40,000,' said Dad.

I suspect Mam at the time wouldn't have even have known what to do with that amount of money. Well, we didn't get the name right – it turned out to be *The Cuckoo Song* – but we were so close that the DJ mentioned our entry. I pressured Mam into trying to remember the correct name but to no avail. Our chance at riches passed. We lost the moment.

Around Easter in the same year, Radio Caroline started advertising a barbecue on Brittas Bay in August. They constantly talked on air about a discotheque, live bands, food and drink, with lots of 'happenings'. I was familiar with the word 'happening' from *NME* reports on festivals in England and America. I knew it was bound to be a groovy affair.

I could hardly believe my luck. A whole weekend of music and hippie stuff just a short bicycle ride from our house. I guessed that plenty of people from England and the Isle of Man would show up too, because Brittas Bay was only thirty miles from Dublin and the Ferries.

The advertising went on for weeks, increasing my expectation to a hysterical level. A lot of groups and solo singers were going to be on the bill for the live show. I hoped the Fortunes might turn up; after all it was the Fortunes who sang the Radio Caroline signature tune. It seemed logical and appropriate.

During my visits to the bay. I didn't see any sign of where they were going to hold this great event. I looked at likely places along the beach. I knew it wasn't going to be free, so they needed a fenced area. Sometimes I had my doubts that The Radio Caroline Brittas Bay BBQ Happening would ever take place.

During these scouting expeditions, I noticed the debris left after the Sinn Fein protests; posters and banners lying around like they'd been washed up by the tide. Some were hidden in ditches, probably to be used on the next demonstration. They said in no uncertain terms what the campaign was all about. 'We shall not be charged', 'Free Right of Way to our Beaches', 'No Way No Pay', 'Land Owners – The New English' and 'Remember 1916 – What they died for'. It was heady stuff. As a secondary school student, to me this was a wonderful. The sight of oppressed citizens standing up for their rights against injustice and the dreadful police obviously attracted me. Sure, hadn't I followed the student riots in Paris like a madman, buying every magazine and paper I could find? Maybe Bob Dylan might turn up some weekend and lead the singing of that protest song he was so famous for. I became an immediate fan of the protest generation. I could go from a Protestant to a committed protester with ease.

Words like protesting and demonstrations found their way into the local vocabulary. The protests were the hot news in the *Wicklow People*. The feeling was that Sinn Fein was going to win this one and would be very, very popular people indeed among the younger protesters and music lovers in the locality.

In the months leading up to the barbecue, posters appeared around the town and the radio coverage became very persistent. If the amount of airplay given to the event translated directly into people planning to come, it was going to be a very big event indeed.

On the appointed day, I headed off in the afternoon towards Brittas Bay, and to what I was beginning to think was my destiny as a teenager. Mam must have had some inkling about was happening, and warned me to be back home before it got dark. She mumbled something about drug addicts, and Dad, usually silent on such matters, backed her up. 'You heard your Mam,' he said ominously as I set off.

I made my way to my usual stopping point and surveyed the activity. Brittas Bay had undergone a transformation. A high fence partitioned off an area of the beach, inside which I could make out several rows of toilets. They'd erected a small stage with a makeshift roof and shelter. Round about were numerous stalls selling food; other stalls seemed to sell hippie stuff, beads, hats and – worryingly – hula hoops.

The enclosure was beginning to fill up as people arrived in buses, taxis and cars with much shouting and screaming. The scenes reminded me of a crowded playground, with everybody running around laughing their heads off. From the distance, I could hear music, faintly, almost drowned out by the waves crashing on to the beach. Occasionally the crowd swayed back and forth in unison. I guessed they were listening to Radio Caroline being broadcast over loudspeakers.

There didn't seem to be much activity on the stage, but the audience was more or less facing towards a solitary man standing at a microphone. Occasionally groups of spectators rushed toward the sand dunes with bottles in their hands, laughing hysterically. I could see other small groups making their own music among the dunes, with a small film crew going from group to group recording this historic event.

I watched the spectacle with interest for about an hour, until hunger, boredom, or the evening chill helped me decide to return home. On the way, I passed a steady stream of sports cars and minibuses full of ecstatically happy people heading in the direction of the event. 'Good luck to them,' I thought.

The next day, if you went by the local radio reporting, the Brittas Bay barbecue had been a non-event, but on Radio Caroline, it was hailed as great success. I overheard Dad saying that some locals called the Gardai because revellers were spotted cavorting naked in the sea and among the dunes. By all accounts, the Gardai just watched and laughed.

27

'Hot town, summer in the city'

They said it would bring the best of times, but that remained debatable. When it was announced that a huge factory was to be built near the town, some said we had everything before us. It would be situated on the banks of the River Avoca, a mile or two above the town, between Glenart Castle and Shelton Abbey, where it would would produce artificial fertilizers on a huge scale and offer great employment opportunities. Words such as phosphates, nitrates and ammonia entered our vocabulary although we didn't really understand them or their uses. It all seemed so modern and new. The future was in our hands, we were told, and we were delighted.

The fertilizer factory or 'Fert' as it was known locally became a major topic of interest in the town and a lively topic at our dinner table and in the evenings around our fireplace. In many ways, we got more than we had bargained for.

While it was being built, the factory brought in hundreds of construction workers. They descended on a small country town that was, in reality, incapable of looking after them. Arklow had a few hotels and guesthouses which were busy through the summer months, but something on this scale was unknown.

Yet Arklow tried to cope and cash in on the situation like any other town might. Some people let out their houses and others took in lodgers. Some of the workers went to live in nearby towns of Gorey and Rathdrum.

The influx of so many unattached men had a big effect on the life of the town. In the evenings, these men went looking for entertainment, and in a town that had an over-abundance of pubs on both sides of the main street; that's where they found it. Local bars put on live music each night and the town began to take on an air of Las Vegas. Bright lights, loud music, crowds laughing up and down the streets: you name it, Arklow had it.

Local women also seized on the opportunity. Some made lots of money from lodgers, but many got in deeper. The construction workers seemed to have money to burn, which they did. The spending on non-stop enjoyment and drinking attracted some women. There was hushed talk of married women leaving their husbands and setting up house with these newcomers, who predominantly came from Dublin, Northern Ireland and England.

In our house, when the grown-ups talked about these goings-on, they began using a simple sort of code, seemingly oblivious to the fact that the conversation then attracted my attention even more because they weren't speaking normally. As the evening wore on, they often forgot that I was still there, discreetly positioned between the sofa and the fire with an open book on my knees. They dropped their strange code and began talking more openly about what was happening in the town.

Sitting there quietly in the flickering light of the turf fire, with Radio Luxembourg on low in the background, you'd hear them talking about what I'd accept were adult topics like the Iron Curtain, John Glenn in space, the Eichmann trial and poor misunderstood Marilyn Monroe. They had opinions about these things and were always ready to laugh off the affect it had on them with some sort of joke.

'Since the Fert came to the town, there's more French letters in the river than brown trout,' I once heard Dad say to Uncle Billy. That one took awhile to register.

Even as a twelve year old, I spotted changes in the town. Every day boats were docking across from our house loaded with machines and equipment for the factory. The size and scale of some of the things that went through the town caused wonderment. The local Wicklow People photographed and published everything big or odd-looking.

For weeks, it was huge wooden beams. They were similar to giant hurleys but about a hundred feet long and destined to be used in the construction of great warehouses. You could spend a day watching them being unloaded from the boat onto specially constructed lorries and trailers and then carried at a snail's pace through the narrow streets of Arklow out to the Fert.

The work attracted strange and colourful characters. I remember a German who seemed to have a collection of leather jackets. In the winter he wore a full-length black leather coat. He was completely bald, which made him all the more distinctive. He was responsible for training local men as plant operators. Several of the men who finally got jobs shaved their heads and bought leather jackets in a sort of strange hero worship copycat gesture.

Those who got jobs in the Fert earned big money. Many, who were previously destined to a passable job, earning passable money in the pottery and the like, were now able to earn top dollar. 'Money from America,' they called it in reference to the easy money that numerous families received from husbands or brothers who had gone to America to work. It changed the town more than anything else had done for years.

One Sunday afternoon when it was absolutely teeming down, we were around the fire, reading or dozing or listening to the radio. It seemed to have been raining all week. Every jacket in the house smelled of damp. The porch was full of wet shoes and Wellington boots. We had just finished our dinner and were snuggling down for a lazy afternoon. We'd got through listening to *Two Way Family Favourites* with a Bumper Bundle request for *This Land Is Mine*, the theme music from the film *Exodus*. I had enjoyed *Round the Horne* and *The Navy Lark*, before eventually really perking up to concentrate on *Top of the Pops*.

It was right in the middle of this programme, right in the middle of *Like a Rolling Stone*, that Dad broke the usual silence almost like a bolt of lightning out of a blue sky.

'C'mon, I've had enough of this,' he said. 'I'll go brain dead if I don't get some fresh air.'

Now Dad had never been a person you might describe as a fresh air fanatic. So this surprised me. 'C'mon,' he said again. 'Get that dog of yours and we'll go for a walk.'

Mam was surprised but having the house to herself for a hour or two on a Sunday evening was too good a treat to pass up. I was so surprised that I went along with it.

'Where will we go?'

'Right,' he said, 'we'll go up toward Shelton Abbey, up the lane by Harry Annseley's shop.'

I had been out that way recently. Men from the Fert were laying a pipe parallel to the lane and up through the marshes towards the new factory.

Pal ran to the door when I whistled. He'd been sheltering in the shed and looked as surprised as a dog could look at all this activity. Dad pulled on his Civil Defence boots and jacket, the only dry things he had left. I searched around for something dryish to wear.

Dad opened the small drawer on the hall stand and pulled out a plastic Mac, one that Mam had bought for herself the last time we were shopping in Dublin. It was in its own sachet and cost about a half crown. The plastic was flimsy: just strong enough for one or two wears. It had popper fasteners down the front and pocket slits that you put your hand through to the jacket underneath. 'Put that on you,' he said 'and that southwester will do on your head.'

We headed out through the front door and the porch. It looked like we were about to brave the elements up along the river to the bridge. A more sheltered walk up the harbour road towards Lower Main Street didn't seem to occur to Dad. I caught a glimpse of myself as I passed the hall mirror. I looked like something off a cod liver oil advertisement. It was dark; the weather was outrageous so it was unlikely we'd meet anyone that I'd be embarrassed to meet. Dad looked a little like one of the Three Stooges, but that was okay by me.

When we got out through the front door, I whistled Pal again. On a night like this, we didn't let him into the house. He'd have to make his way to the front through Heaney's garden.

'We'll be fine for shelter when we get across the bridge,' Dad said optimistically. This was undoubtedly true, but by the time we crossed the bridge, we'd be drenched to our skins, that's if we hadn't already been blown off the bridge into the river.

So we set off on the couple of hundred yards to the bridge. The rain was relentless but we kept going. The north side opposite was lit up by several ships that were laid up because of the storms. The river swell was pushing them up against their moorings. In spite of this and maybe because of all the lights and bright colours, the scene across on the other side looked peaceful and tranquil.

The heavy swell and high tide was evident all the way up to the bridge. Occasionally behind us in the far distance we noticed the sea exploding over the pier head; a sure sign of a big unusual storm. Along the river bank, the water was lapping up over the edge throwing stones and debris onto the road. As we passed street lights, we saw sheets of rain blowing this way and that; by the time we got to the bridge, we hadn't met a sinner or passed a car.

Crossing the bridge, I had to hold onto the rails. The wind was blowing from the sea up the river. Our jackets were all pointing in one direction.

We eventually reached Annseley's hardware shop. Owned and run by Harry and his mother, the shop was like Aladdin's cave. It had all sorts of lights, lamps, pots and pans. It was a great place for wedding presents or presents for your Mam at Christmas. Harry was a Proddy like us and lived with his mother. Mam often called him 'very eligible'. He was a leading light in the badminton club, a bell ringer and a member of the Marlborough dramatic arts. Harry was a definite all-rounder.

We turned left at the shop. Our way was barred by a gate but to my great surprise Dad climbed over it without hesitation and jumped down on the other side. I followed suit. Dad had just recovered from cracked ribs and was taking a bit of a chance jumping from such a height, but he got away with it. I mentioned his ribs. He said,' No they're fine. I got the all-clear during the week from the doctor.'

'Maybe that's why he dragged me out here tonight,' I was thinking. 'A sort of celebration.'

As we entered the rhododendron-lined track towards the Abbey, it got quite dark. The lights from the town gave some light through the occasional gaps in the hedging. Pal was really enjoying himself now, running way ahead of us and then running back towards us looking for attention. As he ran back, sometimes I'd start running towards him and he'd stop and bark with glee. He liked that game.

As we rounded the corner about halfway to the Abbey, the lights from the Fert suddenly came into view. It was lit up like Cape Canaveral with strong floodlights high on the sides of buildings. Occasionally someone walked in front of a light and projected eerie shadows on the steam and mist.

Dad was quite interested in the factory and the area around it. When he was younger, he had played out here, like I played on the Brow. He mentioned some of the changes he noticed. He whistled in amazement when we came across an area about the size of four football pitches that was completely covered by a white chemical. It looked like a snowy winter wonderland. Ominously, there were a few dead trees sticking out of the white like skeletons. 'Look at the state of this,' he said. 'Isn't this a desperate sight?'

I had to admit however that there was a certain beauty in what lay before me, 'a terrible beauty' even.

When you got up close to it, however, you saw that it wasn't all white. The areas around the spillage pipes were stained a light coffee colour and smelled of what I later learned was ammonia. So however nice it looked from afar, up close you saw it for what it was: a complete mess.

We couldn't go any further. The way ahead was blocked by the factory fence. Pal was sitting back looking at us almost quizzically. We turned on our heels and headed back the way we came.

Dad didn't say much on the way home: perhaps it was the rain which had actually become worse. The journey home seemed shorter, but doesn't it always? When we arrived home, we were soaked to the skin. Dad told Mam where we had been and what we had seen.

Mam was pretty matter of fact about the effects of the Fert. 'Some evenings when the wind is blowing down the river and out to sea, it often carries a terrible smell of rotten eggs from the Fert,' she said. She also reminded us that long before the Fert was built, we were plagued most evenings with smoke from the burning dump on the other side of the river. To Mam this new situation was no worse than the old.

28

'The folks on the hill'

Our relations from Howth visited us two or three times a year. As we didn't have a telephone, these visits were often arranged by Auntie Rose or Uncle Jack phoning one of the pubs in Arklow and to see if Dad was there or, failing that, to try and discover which pub Dad was currently patronising. Occasionally, Dad took the initiative and phoned them from a pub to arrange a visit, but that usually took weeks of coaxing from Mam. I don't think Dad was confident in the use of the telephone. It was all rather hit and miss.

I must admit to regularly nudging Mam and Dad to arrange their visit to us so we could reciprocate. I was getting to an age where the attraction of a visit to Howth was that it allowed me to spend some time alone in Dublin.

We never owned a car, but our Howth relatives always seemed to have plenty of them available. On the arranged day, Uncle Jack and Auntie Rose arrived with sometimes two or three cars full of cousins, their wives and children. It was like having our own personal Seabreeze trip arriving at the house.

Mam would be prepared for the onslaught, having laid in plenty of cooked ham, tomatoes and sliced bread. Ham sandwiches always went down well after a few pints, and you could be sure there would be quite a few with this lot.

Jack and Rose were a little older than Mam and Dad, but they got on well together. Dad was always seemed genuinely happy when they appeared. Standing outside our house while they piled out of the cars, you could feel the friendship and happiness.

After the 'Hellos' the 'How are you keepings', the handshakes and the hugging, the inevitable happened. One of the men mentioned, 'We'll pop up to the pub, just for a quick one, mind you.' There followed furtive looks to see how the women were taking it. Several times behind the woman's backs, they raised their cupped hands to their mouths making drinking gestures. I knew Mam and Auntie Rose would never think of going with them and my cousins, who were mostly more than ten years older than me and at the marrying stage, generally seemed to choose girls who didn't drink either. There really was no stopping them in fact. They had a way of making it just the normal accepted, expected behaviour.

Very soon, they were shouting, 'Are you ready Ned?'

'Where's your coat?'

'God, you don't need to shave.'

'We'll just nip up to John Joe's pub, it's close.'

'Leave your slippers on. They're grand,' all done with the type of laughing you associated with children who were getting their own way with parents who were too tired too argue.

Among all this male bravado, the women were saying things like 'Oh I'd love a cup of tea and a biscuit' and 'Oh I need to use the toilet.' Mam inevitably warned Dad, 'Don't be all day in that filthy pub. Dinner will be ready at six, so I want to see you all before that.'

Mam, without realising, gave them consent to do what they wanted to do anyway. Within minutes the men were walking up the South Quay to their chosen destination.

I was usually left behind with the women, to be interrogated about school and everything else. Although all the young wives were teetotal, they smoked very heavily indeed: Mam and Auntie Rose, who did not, tolerated those who did. It was the way things were. Nobody thought of the health implications of their habit. It was just non-stop smoking. Frequently they asked me to run up to the nearest shop and get more cigarettes.

As the room filled with more and more smoke, someone eventually opened the window to let it escape, or perhaps to let fresh air in, I never determined which. Gradually the ashtrays filled up, the filters and lipstick adding colour, like embers in a fire.

Although we only saw each other on a handful of occasions every year, they all seemed to be much closer as a family after each visit. Dad and Jack liked each other. You could see that in their behaviour.

I occasionally stayed over in Uncle Jack's house in Howth. A week in that hilly town was always welcome, especially in summer. Uncle Jack, to be quite truthful, always seemed to be a grumpy and stern old man. He gave the impression of ruling his family with an iron fist. My stay in Howth didn't change that opinion completely, but I did notice other sides to him, and how his family, especially his daughters together with Auntie Rose could manage and manipulate the man without his realising.

It was a surprise to me that Uncle Jack had several pastimes and hobbies. Hobbies were something Dad never had time for. I knew that Uncle Jack reared budgies and canaries: several times when we went to Howth on a day trip, Dad bought me a budgie or a canary as a pet. But we were never that successful as a family in keeping these birds alive. 'It's all your cats – they're terrified of them,' Mam reasoned.

What I didn't realise was all the time and effort Uncle Jack put into his birds. The aviary he built at he bottom of his garden was so big you could walk around in it. Most evenings during a visit, I accompanied him to help water and feed the birds, and clean up their mess as well. The birds often landed on Uncle Jack's hat which he seemed to wear morning noon and night. Occasionally one landed on his hand and allowed Uncle Jack to stroke it. He was very gentle and always used a special soothing tone of voice with his birds.

It was on one of these occasions, as he stroked a beautiful blue budgie, that I realised Uncle Jack looked quite like a budgie himself. He had a peculiar veined nose, reminiscent of something you might see in a butcher's offal tray, which also looked sort of like the budgies' beak The way he pursed his lips when talking quietly to the birds gave a great impression of a budgie.

I wasn't the only one to notice it. When I mentioned it to Dad, he said with a smile, 'Sure everyone in the family thinks the same as you. They say it's quite common for people to eventually take on the appearance of their pets,' he mused. 'I'm waiting for the feathers to appear.'

Often in the evenings, as I spent time in the aviary with Uncle Jack,

I noticed Auntie Rose looking at us both with a smile. I think she was proud of the success Uncle Jack had with his birds: the house was full of cups and medals he won in bird shows. It was also a comfort to her that this fairly old man, when he retired, had some interests in life outside the usual family pursuits of drinking and smoking.

My stays in Howth were quiet and, to be honest, fairly boring. We visited all the relatives: the married sons and daughters of Jack and Rose. Some lived in Howth itself; others lived closer to the city centre in Sutton and Raheny. Some were getting on well and owned their own houses and cars. Others lived in flats, which was something I had absolutely no experience of. It seemed very odd indeed to live in a couple of rooms in a house that wasn't yours and have no access to a garden.

Most evenings Jack went either to the Royal Hotel or the Abbey Tavern. Sometimes I followed him down and listened outside to the groups playing inside. That summer, a group called the Dubliners seemed to be very popular with the locals in Howth.

Uncle Jack over the years had completed a lot of building and decorating work for the Royal Hotel, and when his sons took over the business, Jack kept well in with he owner as a patron. Auntie Rose said, 'It wasn't worth it working for the Royal Hotel because whatever he earned, he spent most of it in the bar to get the next job.'

Once after we visited Howth, Uncle Jack arranged for Helen and Geraldine to come down to Arklow for a holiday. Dad asked Betty and Algy Sherwood to come over to our house each evening and take them out. They had all the Arklow hotspots to choose from: The Centre, the Ormonde Ballroom and Tracy's Café.

Dad felt it was his duty to be as strict as Uncle Jack was with Helen and Geraldine. When they went off to the dance, he gave them all sorts of rules, all sorts of 'dos' and 'don'ts' to ensure that they were safe. He got Algy and Betty to promise to walk them home: he insisted on no boys.

This was going to be difficult. Helen and Geraldine were both quite pretty: 'They didn't get it from their father's side,' Mam laughed. Both had the added attraction of being from out of town. When boys found out that they were from Dublin, it was even better. They were like exotic birds to the local lads.

Going out with Algy and Betty immediately brought them into contact with every boy they knew: that is to say every boy in the Fishery if not the whole of Arklow. Keeping them safe from boys proved nigh on impossible. However they didn't appear to get into any kind of trouble for the week they stayed with us. Dad walked the floor from the very minute they left the house until they came back, laughing and tittering, in the small hours of the morning.

Helen and Geraldine were a little older than Algy and Betty. They both smoked like troopers and seemed to spend most of their time dressing up and putting make-up on to go up the street, to go to dances or to go to the cinema. They were no different from Algy and Betty in that respect. They all were keen to become what their mothers were not.

However, in spite of coming from Dublin, the big city bright lights, they didn't seem to know much about pop music. They didn't know what it was all about. They hadn't a clue what was in the charts, whereas I was hungry for any information about new releases, new recordings and new groups. They were outside looking in, but they didn't know it.

Helen and Geraldine were Catholics of course, like Jack and Rose. On Sunday, Dad insisted that they went to Mass. Algy called over to walk them up to the chapel. They all headed off much the same way as we went off to St Saviour's each Sunday. I couldn't actually swear that they ever went to Mass, but the way they talked it seemed likely that they were diverted and probably ended up seeing the Sunday morning sights of Arklow instead. Everyone I knew had the same attitude to church-going and religion. We felt the same about trudging up the street and then suffering the brain-banging boredom of the church service, whether Protestant or Catholic.

Sometimes, inadvertently to be sure, the church gave us a good laugh. A story I heard from students in the CBS reassured me that the Catholic religion was as comical as the one I was lumbered with.

Just outside the railings of the Catholic church stood a life-sized statue of Father Murphy. This priest – a hero in one of the numerous struggles for our independence – was depicted leaning on a walking stick with the other arm raised as if pointing the way. 'The way to the NET factory for people looking for jobs,' was the interpretation of local wags. But there was better to come.

Surrounding the statue was a chest-high railing of gold-tipped spears. It was only some years after the statue's erection that parishioners noticed that at certain times of the day, with the sun behind it, it looked like Father Murphy was holding something a little more personal than a walking stick.

In the true Irish spirit of providing an Irish solution to an Irish problem, the good and the great of the parish one dark night lopped off the offending piece. It was never mentioned again, and another national hero's reputation was saved.

29

'In the heat of a hot summer night'

Inasmuch as TV had become our latest obsession, subtly and covertly changing our attitudes to most things in our lives, it was however a gift that only gave for a few hours each night. RTE, the national television service, bombarded us with programmes that told us who we were but rarely told us where we were going. We had occasional undependable access to BBC and ITV broadcasts; but only when the wind was blowing in the right direction, it seemed. Initially I found sitting at home watching TV stifling, as probably most of my own age did.

We awaited movies like *King Rat*, *In the Heat of the Night* and *The Graduate* with anticipation and not a little impatience. The time lag in the mid-Sixties from the publicised premiers in London to the movies' subsequent release in Dublin before they finally made their way to the cinemas in Arklow was always unbearable.

Unlike Mam, who abandoned the movie experience with the arrival of the TV set, I found movies – especially new movies directed by the angry young men of the English film world – provided me with so much of what now I needed as a stimulus.

I went to the pictures most Friday nights with John and his friends, in spite of my experiences in the Sunday matinees. The cinemas were bleak and dirty but there was a certain beauty in the projector light shining through the billows of cigarette smoke and the respectful silence of the audience.

The first film I remember seeing was *The Lavender Hill Mob*, the little old lady in it reminding me of several of the little old ladies that Dad worked for.

Another was *Birdman of Alcatraz* – not the most exciting film I'd ever seen but we were all interested in the story of how the Burt Lancaster character tamed those birds. We knew of course that it was a film and you couldn't believe everything you saw, but it was based on a true story, so we accepted that the main idea of the film was true. I was impressed how close he got to the birds, similar to Uncle Jack's experiences, but the general feeling was that if you were in prison for life, you could just about do anything. You had all that time to concentrate on things. It reminded me a little of the stories Dad told me about his three years in hospital, but I didn't mention that.

A series of teenage films came to the Ormonde Cinema that seemed to signal the growing difference between the older and younger people in the town. *Rock Around the Clock* and *Let's Twist Again* seemed to start it all. A lot was written in the papers about these films, but I picked up just as much or more from listening to Mam, Dad and Uncle Billy talking about them incessantly around the dinner table. There was a lot of trouble during the showing of these films in England and in Dublin. By the time the first one reached Arklow, it had achieved such notoriety that the local council debated whether it should be shown in our cinemas. The parish priest mentioned it from the pulpit, trusting that all god-fearing Catholics gave the films a miss. Such free publicity almost guaranteed what happened next.

True to form, the majority of Protestants I knew were oblivious to the whole phenomenon. Algy and Betty weren't in the dark though. They knew exactly what was going to happen.

The film went ahead and every teenager in town queued up to see it. Before it started, the cinema manager spoke to the audience from the stage. He implored the audience not to behave like those English and Dublin gurriers that had made the newspapers. He asked them to show calm and restraint. 'Ladies and gents, please show a little decorum,' he said without conviction, and was screamed and booed off the stage.

From that moment on, it was Sunday matinee all over again, except for the fact that these were grown-up teenagers. They screamed through the advertisements, screamed through the trailers and screamed through the support bill of a travelogue about Spain and the Pathe News.

When the feature film came on and the crowd heard the first bars of the twist music, the whole hall erupted. Everyone jumped to their feet and began jiving and twisting the night away. Inevitably, damage was done to the seats as in Dublin and England. Flick knives were popular among the older boys like my cousin John, and they used them. The poor innocent seats never had a chance.

More seats were broken when people jumped up on the backs of them to copy part of the routine that was happening on the big screen. The whole scene was one of bedlam and mayhem. After about half an hour of trying to bring about some order and get everyone seated, the manager switched off the projector and turned on the house lights. The show was cancelled for the night.

Dad was called up to the cinema the next day to help repair the damaged seats and doors. 'It was as if a bomb had gone off in the hall,' he said. The cinema closed for a week for repairs. This was a great blow to the town as there weren't a great many alternatives to the cinema for entertainment. People just didn't know what to do with themselves.

The cinema opened up later that week, but *Rock Around the Clock* was no longer on the programme. Arklow did not get the chance to see the film until it appeared on the circuit again.

The whole episode seemed to change Arklow. It was as if the young people of the town stepped over a line; somehow the spell of innocence was broken.

The cinema was all-important to young people in the town. It was a place you could go with friend or alone if you wished. I think I took after Mam in liking movies. I remember the many great films I saw, but other things stuck with me as well. There was a scene in *Young Cassidy*, a movie about the Irish playwright, where some women were protesting that 'There were no prostitutes in Ireland.' I was about to let that pass, not really knowing the facts of the situation, when the greatest, dirtiest laugh rang out from a member of the audience. It was definitely Algy's laugh. On hearing her guffaw, the rest of the audience joined in and it was ages before everyone calmed down. The ushers were running ragged about the place.

Another time, they were reshowing the *Bridge Over the River Kwai*. I'd seen it some years earlier but went to see it again. I'm glad I did. During the beach scene with William Holden and the nurse, he and said to her, 'All I need is love.' The nurse then replies, 'All you really need is love' – the exact same words as the Beatles song.

I couldn't believe it. I wondered if the Beatles got their inspiration from this film. You could just visualise John Lennon sitting in a cinema somewhere in Liverpool with his round glasses and chewing his bubblegum in that lazy fashion... Picture the scene: it's raining outside and he's watching the movie, bereft of inspiration for his next song when he hears, 'All you really need is love.' So he writes it down, perhaps on a cigarette pack, and heads off to somewhere quiet to complete the lyrics. Fantastic.

On the way down from the cinema one Friday night with John, we bumped into drinkers who were beginning to spill out of the pubs. They were mostly loud groups of men and women. I didn't know any of them but John seemed to know them all, the girls in particular.

Outside the Golf Bar, there was one particularly loud bunch of three girls and four men. John knew the girls and when they spoke to him, it was obvious that they were the worse for drink. The girls were wearing very short skirts, tall boots and short leather jackets, all the rage at the time.

'Hello Sherry!' one said loudly to John. Sherry, short for Sherwood, was John's nickname. That would have embarrassed the hell out of me, but John laughed it off and replied, 'Hello Mary, how's it hanging?'

'Cheeky fecker,' she replied as quick as you like.

Another girl said in a proud laughing way, 'Look at us, we're out on the town with the Tholstrup boys.'

'They know how to treat a girl.'

John replied, 'Ah they're all right but you can't beat the real thing. Isn't that right Mary?'

We all moved off and one of them shouted after us, 'I haven't seen Algy for a while. When you see her, tell her to call up and see us.'

The Tholstrup boys, sailors from Germany, Holland or Sweden, crewed the Tholstrup company boats that called regularly to Arklow to deliver ammonia or heavy fuel oil for the Fert. They were a regular sight around the town, often seen shopping and all dolled up in their uniforms.

The Tholstrup boats moored directly opposite our house. They all had girls' names: the Lise, Anna and Margarethe Tholstrup. They were lovely boats with a red-orange hull and gleaming white cabins and wheelhouse.

All this new traffic rejuvenated Arklow port. Prior to the NET starting, the whole river and dock area were run down, but suddenly it was a hive of activity.

The boats attracted a lot of attention when they docked. Local grocers supplied them with provisions. There were rumours that the boats supplied local pubs and shops with illegal bonded spirits and beers. John once let it slip that the great supply of German and Dutch dirty books in the town was thanks to the Tholstrup boats, but I'd yet to experience this.

As I reached home I noticed the three girls we met earlier making their way slowly down the north quay. At the moment they were at O'Toole's office. Occasionally they emerged from the shadows cast on this orange–mooned August night.

One of them was trying to climb up on the old Second World War mine that had been converted into a huge collection box for maritime charities. The girls were quite loud and seemed to be throwing anything they could lay their hands on into the river as if to delay their progress down to the ships. Occasionally I heard the clip-clop of their high heels as they ran to catch up with each other. A lot of laughing ensued, but the sailors hardly said anything and behaved a little like onlookers. Perhaps they weren't used to the behaviour of tipsy Arklow girls. They continued to shout and swear and seemed to be having running conversation on every topic under the sun, to the exclusion of the men. The sailors, it seemed, just wanted to get back to their boat.

As the girls got closer, I heard bits and pieces of their conversation, carried across the river on the night breeze. One said quite clearly, 'I love youse Swedes.'

Another one laughed. 'Ah Mary, you only love their money and their easy ways.'

'I don't think you should be calling anyone here easy. God but I hope they have something more interesting to drink tonight than that Oranjeboom piss.'

'Boom boom!' they all suddenly started shouting together. 'Boom boom!' they continued, until it tailed off in the night breeze. Then one said, 'Oh I suspect we'll get something different all right,' and they all laughed their crazy drunken laugh.

The laughing and shouting died away as they got nearer their destination. The boat was all lit up, and there seemed to be a lot of activity on board. It was possible they were still unloading. All this late night work was beginning to annoy the residents along our side of the river.

The men went on board the ship first, walking confidently up the gangplank. The girls seemed to take off their boots before following them. Unsteadily they all tottered up the gangplank in quick succession, footwear in hand. Once on board, they all headed towards the stern where they reappeared momentarily to enter a cabin.

Behind me, the windows in our house were open, as were those of the neighbours. A long hot summer's day had become a pleasantly warm night. I leaned over the wall and stopped to take it all in. On a night like this, you just didn't want to go inside; if you did the night was effectively over.

Across the river and in the direction of the swimming pool, I could just see and hear the commotion from the carnival that had arrived in for the Bank Holiday weekend. The colourful lights were arranged high in the air, like a necklace in the dark.

The Supremes' hit *Baby Love* faded in and out on the breeze, enticing many a listener to fill in the familiar words during the silences. People were still out and about enjoying the late evening. Men with dogs and couples linking arms. Occasionally a passer-by called a whispered 'Good night'. You could fall in love with a night like this. Eventually I went inside and reluctantly went to bed .

A couple of hours later, or so it seemed, I woke up. I looked through the window. Across the river, all activity on board the boat had died away. The lights were still on though. It took me a little while to make out what had awoken me. I spotted what appeared to be two of the girls making their way back up the quay. They were walking in complete silence although every now and then one of them kicked something into the river with a laugh. The clip-clop of their heels initially breaking the silence of the stars, got fainter as they got further and further away. I fell back to sleep.

The next morning I awoke very early and by chance looked across the river. A night watchman flicked off his cabin light to welcome in the dawn. As I took in the tranquil scene, I noticed the third girl heading up the quay on her own. She was moving quickly and had her shoes in her hands. There was no clip-clop of high heels to draw anyone's attention; just a lonely, furtive figure making her way home in the pale light of the new day, anxious not to set any curtains twitching and tongues wagging.

30

'Turn, turn, turn'

One morning, Connie was in our house early, on one of her mysterious visits perhaps. She and Mam were laughing at one of Dad's latest adventures. Listening in on these conversations was very helpful. The chats filled in missing aspects of things for me. Well almost.

There was the time he was off work after having fallen on stage during *The Ghost Train*. He had to travel to Bray for x-rays to monitor the progress of his recovery. He initially dreaded these expeditions but eventually embraced them wholeheartedly. A peaceful day out on a train or bus to the Big Smoke had its attractions, it seemed.

Some time after the doctor signed him off as fit to return to work, he was diagnosed with peptic stomach ulcers. There were differing opinions in our house as to what caused these. Whatever the cause, Mam was pleased and somewhat smug that he had to forego alcohol for several weeks. The recommended diet of milk and sponge cake caused some hilarity.

Dad had to visit the hospital outside Bray occasionally for blood tests. His preparations for these trips were similar to when he was going for a drink up town: washing, shaving, best clothes, whistling and singing.

So off he went, with Mam not really knowing when he'd be back. He attracted adventures. His first words when he stepped in the door were invariably, 'You'll never guess who I met.' My Mam and I had bets on whether he'd say it.

On one such trip, while waiting for the return bus, he found himself at loose ends for several hours, and nipped into a nearby hotel to treat himself to a pint and a sandwich. It was just after midday, but the hotel bar was packed. He made his way to the counter and was just about to order when the big man to his left turned to him and, in a loud American accent, asked him his name. A little taken aback I'd imagine, Dad blurted out, rather formally, 'Edward Ruxton.'

The man shook Dad's hand and shouted, 'Barman, please give my friend Edward Ruxton a drink.' It was only then that Dad recognised his generous benefactor. It was the film star Robert Mitchum who had just finished making *A Terrible Beauty* at Armore Studios in Bray and was having some end-of-shooting celebrations. It seemed once the barman recognised that Dad was a friend of the great man, the drinks kept flowing.

Somehow, and probably regretfully, Dad had to leave the celebrations and catch that damned bus back to Arklow. When he got home, he told us of his latest escapade. We were suitably impressed the first time we heard the story, and of course we heard it many, many times, as probably most of the town did, with the amount of drink involved increasing on each telling.

The following Christmas, Dad got it into his head to send his friend, Robert Mitchum, a Christmas card. After much deliberation, he addressed it to him at DRM Productions Inc, Hollywood, California. 'I noticed the address on some luggage I saw in the hotel,' he explained. Tapping his forehead, he added, 'Good memory.'

Dad hoped for a return card from the star, but after weeks of expectations, he accepted that his friend hadn't written him a reply. 'Perhaps it got lost, or maybe it just wasn't passed onto him,' he occasionally muttered to himself. 'The post can be a cruel thing.'

As if to confirm this notion, one morning there was a knock on the door. I raced to open it. It was Denis the postman. 'Mam,' I shouted but she was already behind me.

'I've got a registered letter here for Mr Ronald Tyrrell,' Denis quickly said in his best official voice. Mam was a little taken aback but soon realised it was a letter for Uncle Ronnie. 'He's not here at the moment,' she said sort of defensively. 'I think he's in Japan or China or somewhere like that.'

'Well he's got to sign for it; I can only give it to Mr Ronald Tyrrell.'

Mam was getting a little tired of the Ronald crack. She took the letter abruptly from Denis and examined it for what seemed a very long time indeed.

'Denis,' she said quietly to the postman, 'the letter's for Ronnie. You remember Ronnie who lived across from your house for years in Tinahask?'

Connie, who was there as usual, rolled her eyes. The stress of the situation was getting to her. She lit up a cigarette.

Still being officious, Denis replied, 'It's for Mr Ronald Tyrrell. So he's not present at this address then?'

'No,' Mam replied, and said wearily, 'Japan, Denis, Japan.'

'Have you any idea when he'll be home next?'

'I'm not sure. It might be anytime,' Mam replied. 'We're not expecting him soon, I'm afraid. The shipping agent will have a better idea.'

Finally, she asked the question that was on my mind. 'Is it important do you think?'

Denis took a sly look at the envelope. He whistled and held up the letter for us to see. Printed on it, in big blue letters, the words Littlewoods Pools jumped out

On Radio Luxembourg, advertisements for Horace Bachelor's system to win millions interrupted the music every fifteen minutes or so. To get his help in winning the pools, you contacted him at his address in Keynsham spelled K-E-Y-N-S-H-A-M. We all laughed when we heard it and imitated his posh voice. Winning millions seemed to be so simple.

'Oh,' Mam said, 'Do you think he's won the pools?'

Denis replied, 'Well I don't deliver these every day of the week, but it does look important. If it's undelivered we'll have to return it to Littlewoods.'

Eventually Denis went off with the letter, whistling *Who Wants to be a Millionaire*.

Mam was very excited. 'God, Ronnie might be a millionaire,' she said, but quickly added, 'Of course he'll drink himself into an early grave. We'll have to contact him some way.'

Dad was enlisted to go across the Bridge to O'Toole's Shipping Office to try and locate Ronnie. I think Dad was quite pleased to be involved; perhaps it made him feel rich and important.

They finally got word to Ronnie, who turned out to be a lot closer to home than Japan: he was actually on a ship tied up in Parkeston in England. When he was eventually contacted, the inevitable happened: he gave up his job and travelled to Liverpool to collect his fortune.

We heard nothing from him until one day, weeks later, he turned up with his suitcase at our front door. It transpired that when he eventually made it to Liverpool to claim his prize, probably making a lot of drinking friends on the way, it turned out to be a mere hundred and nine pounds. A lot of people apparently won the week Ronnie got lucky.

While he recovered from the embarrassment, Ronnie stayed with us for ages and seemed reluctant to go back to sea. After several months, Mam noticed that our collection of records had disappeared from its place in the cabinet. After much speculation and recriminations, we found out that Ronnie had sold or swapped them in the pub for drink. Mam shouted and cried a lot. Dad stayed out of it. I think he had some pity for Ronnie being out of work. Everyone seemed to forget it was Ronnie that had bought and brought most of the records into the house anyway.

Inevitably Mam told Ronnie to pack his bags and he went to live with Auntie Connie. Connie had little room or money to put him up for long. Within weeks, he was back at sea. The episode with the records was soon forgotten. Six months later, Ronnie was again at our front door with his suitcase and presents for us all. He was definitely back on his feet.

In early January, Uncle Ronnie came back to Arklow and this time stayed with us for a long time, longer than I could recall. I remember him saying that he had come from Archangel. To me, the name Archangel conjured up all sorts of exotic and mysterious images. 'Archangel was the last place god created,' Uncle Ronnie declared, "and he was in a bad humour when he did it.' So much for exotic images.

After Archangel, Ronnie seemed to lose interest in travelling. He didn't go to the shipping agent for ages. Usually if you wanted a job, you declared yourself available and they rang where Dad worked or sent a messenger boy to our front door to say that they had a job. Ronnie then packed his bags, got the money for his ticket either from O'Toole's or from Mam, and was on his way for yet another twelve or eighteen months.

We should have noticed that he was getting a bit fed up of being absent from home. Each time he came home, he discovered that one of his friends had married, or had a child, and was living in a good house, while the only thing that he had achieved was few more thousand miles on the ocean blue and another tattoo. I suspect Ronnie just wanted to settle down and get married.

There was talk of him getting a job on one of the local fishing boats. To push him in that direction, Mam bought him a set of oil-skins.

He didn't immediately get the fishing job, but as September crept into October, and the herring season began, Ronnie one day in late October announced that he'd signed up with one of the local fishermen. In spite of being quite young, Ronnie was a very experienced sailor, and had an lot more experience than most of those he'd be working with. He picked up the fishing skills pretty fast and soon began earning a steady wage.

Fishing in those days was very good. Ronnie, like all other fishermen, was paid on a share basis. The owner of the boat got extra shares for the boat, the fuel, the food provided, and the upkeep of the nets and so on. The remainder was divided among all the workers on the boat. When the fishing was good, the money built up. This of course was all paid out in cash with no deductions ever mentioned. No-one seemed to be bothered about paying income tax.

As this new fishing job began to pay off, Ronnie settled into a more normal way of life. He went drinking only on a Saturday night. The fishing week began early on Monday morning and finished on Saturday morning. That only gave him Saturday afternoon, Saturday night and Sunday for socialising. His drinking habits became more regulated.

After a few months, we found out that Ronnie was seeing a woman called Mary and that he was walking out with her. Mary was a Catholic from an old Arklow family. I feared the religion thing was going to cause problems again. However I think Mam felt that Ronnie was big enough and ugly enough to decide what he wanted to do himself, so nothing much was said at the outset of the romance. Maybe Mam felt that on past performances the romance might fizzle out.

But it didn't, and while tidying up Ronnie's room, Mam found some books that indicated Ronnie was about to change his religion. It's fair to say that since Billy tried to marry a Catholic girl, our family had changed its attitude somewhat. However, as in Ronnie's case, a Protestant family could tolerate having one of its members marry a Catholic as long as they didn't change their religion. So if Ronnie was thinking of changing his religion, or 'turning' as she called it, it came as a big blow to Mam.

She moped around the house all day, waiting for Ronnie to come home. She got the books from his room and threw them into the bin outside the back door. Then she had second thoughts about this and retrieved them.

I watched Mam working herself up into a state. 'Not under my roof,' she muttered. I resigned myself to saying goodbye to another of my uncles. She planned to tackle Ronnie on her own. She didn't ask me to go get Connie for support. I suppose she may have not known where Connie stood on the matter.

Ronnie arrived home and they had a brief but loud row. And there it ended. Although Ronnie found himself in her bad books, I think Mam had begun to reconsider her position, seeing as I was attending a Catholic school and happy to have the chance, and Dad was earning a living working for nuns. I don't think irony was uppermost in her vocabulary but this smacked of it.

Innocently and unwittingly, Ronnie had made a stand to do what he thought right for himself and with it challenged convention. He made it feasible for others in the family to contemplate the same action.

I'd learned that religion only matters until that time arrives when it doesn't matter. People that were affected lived in a peculiar non-religion, accepted by neither side but living happily married lives with children. In the end, Ronnie was no different from countless other couples in southern Ireland. However, I think everyone agreed there was no such thing as a former Protestant or Catholic.

31

'Take me from this road'

Over the years, it had become obvious that our religious caretakers were capable of meting out any punishment they deemed necessary to achieve their educational endeavours. Few questions were ever raised and, short of the necessity for medical help which hardly ever happened, they knew they could probably get away with any violence. They had an immunity that was all protective. Inevitably toward the end of my time at the Brothers, things started to change. More and more lay teachers began to fill vacancies due to falling vocations in the orders. By the time I left, we even had a female teacher whose employment caused much excitement and curiosity among her fellow lay teachers and the student body alike.

Lay teachers had no such religious protection. They lived in the community outside the protection of the school walls. Any action of theirs could potentially be challenged in a pub or on the street, with subsequent repercussions. They however became our true educators, and their casual insights into the real world were invaluable to students trying to make sense of it all.

Eventually we reached a stage where we could talk freely with them. They knew who we were and they had time to listen and gave us time to answer. And yet they were there to be challenged. We continually baited our English teacher over grammar anomalies like in the Rolling Stones song, *I Can't Get No Satisfaction*, which seemed to have annoyed most of the adult population in England. Loftier religious and ethical questions were debated. Nevertheless, we always seemed to get the answers we expected.

After a violent maths or Gaeilge morning with the Brothers, afternoons with lay teachers were quiet and dreamy. The sun creeping through the windows in speckles and the sound of the venetian blind being pushed sideways in the gentle breeze were what I expected education to be like. I read and I studied. Occasionally I pretended to learn my Latin verbs or, when translating Ovid, hoped to stumble across 'fecit' which always had the effect of disturbing the tranquility of the lesson. There was always Latin roots to be learned. Often I spent time filling in the O's in whatever text book was in front of me. Sometimes I dozed.

We were introduced to the literature of the famine. Joyce and Beckett were discussed. We were duly appalled when we heard stories of the Berlin Wall, but soon were equally horrified to learn that we had our own walls of separation on this little island. One of my favourite teachers, called Mr Hickey, explained the history that led to the Crusades and the obscenity that was the Children's Crusade. He somehow made a valid connection between these and Dr Noel Browne's doomed Mother and Child Scheme. Under his breath he muttered, 'Religion began when the first scoundrel met the first fool.'

We were introduced to events and items happening in other parts of the world. One teacher, probably after reading Time magazine, told of a play that opened in New York called US, and drew our attention to the alternate meaning of the title. This knowledge stayed with me and I remember being secretly smug at understanding what the teacher was trying to get across.

They continually dropped into the discussion items that had little or nothing to with the curriculum but seemed to dominate our lives. In fact, some of these items had little or nothing to do with anything but remained a tremendous and powerful experience. One such was the tale of Samuel Becket's sixteen sucking stones. I remember the hilarity as the process was revealed in his novel *Molloy*, and the conundrum realised with my newfound knowledge of permutations and combinations. The teacher broke down laughing several times while reading it. I think two or three facets of maturity collided during this lesson, but I'm not entirely sure what they were.

In a time when the Brothers' aim in life was to get everyone into a job with a good pension, lay teachers were grinningly optimistic about life. They seemed to be in a state of dedication without faith, not continually filling our heads with hopeful life goals.

It was delightful to learn from individuals who bypassed the spiritual challenge of an Order. Their ultimate aim was not to colour us Irish and definitely not to scourge us for Jesus.

Despite these almost halcyon times, there were always spoilers ready to pounce, if the occasion rose. As often happened when bad news arrived, it invariably came from the religious direction. For a couple of years, I had successfully avoided any contact with St Saviour's. Mr Poyntz apparently had accepted that I had gone native, as it were. I was a prodigal son and perhaps Mr Poyntz was biding his time.

However, nothing remains static. Mr Poyntz decided to retire and was replaced by a much younger minister. Mr Vanston was married, had a son and was somewhat more progressive that his predecessor. He put himself about in the community. In social occasions, he would have a small sherry, but he was an unrelenting true Christian. It was inevitable that his concerned eyes would spot our precarious situation.

There were six of us at this stage, all Protestants in a Catholic school, ostensibly members of his flock and attending school but receiving no religious instruction. It was probably illegal, and possibly kept him awake at night

So in true and topical ecumenical spirit, Mr Vanston agreed with the Brother Superior that we should be saved. We were not amused. They signed us up for religious instruction two days a week. The classes took place in St Saviour's vestry room, at the same time as our Catholic fellow students were having their RE in school. Our Catholic counterparts gloated. We were all in the same boat now.

To say there was general discontent about this development among the six is a monumental understatement, but such was the regime in the school that for reasons of self-preservation, we decided to comply. Six reluctant sinners trooped down to St Saviour's for a few weeks.

Of course these sessions with Mr Vanston were mind-numbingly boring. Where Mr Poyntz's discourses in primary school were biblical stories and we learned by rote, Mr Vanston's sessions were elevated and exalted as befitted our ages. He was an academic and intellectual, but we were too low-flying and not really ready for what he was trying to achieve. As a group, we quickly lost interest, the classes were universally dreaded, sessions were missed, people came late or not at all.

If Mr Vanston and the Superior had contrived to have these lessons in the school building, they would surely have been rigorously attended. Unfortunately the journey from the school to the church, only a couple of hundred yards in all, offered escape options.

So each day that we had lessons, we left school *en masse*, most of us on bicycles. Those without a bicycle were given a lift. We were a true band of brothers. The journey down resembled the slow bicycle races I experienced at the Carysfort summer sports. We dawdled. We stopped. We performed wheelies. Nobody wanted to be in the lead.

As we approached the imposing railings of St Saviour's, someone often had a change of heart, and for whatever reason sped past the group. The rest had a decision to make; to go in or follow the breakaway reprobate.

I was in my final years at the CBS and knew that you could get away with nearly anything while you prepared for the final examinations. I was also the oldest of the group. When we got to St Saviour's, it was often me who decided not to partake. I cycled to the front of the throng and sped down the small hill that took me rapidly onto the main street. Often I heard shouting and swearing as I sped away. Looking behind, I hoped eternally that at least someone had gone into the church for this dreaded experience.

I was always exhilarated by my escape. The similarity with other escapes was profound and sweet. That frantic run from the church grounds to the River Walk with my cousins was a dear memory. They had managed, in the intervening years, to split with all parish activities, but I, by a simple twist of fate, had been drawn inexorably back again.

32

'Nuclear seemed unclear'

Ever since the Cuban Missile Crisis, Mam and Dad had frequently talked about nuclear and atomic bombs, although I'm not quite sure if anyone knew the difference. Usually it was something they read in the *News of the World* which prompted these strange conversations. It seemed to be the bible of all knowledge and opinion for adults.

'Of course it won't be a real war... the next war I mean,' Dad said.

As usual this statement came completely out of the blue and not really directed at either Mam or me. After what seemed an eternity, he concluded, 'The next war will be a Cold War.' He was still hidden behind the Sunday newspaper at this stage, puffing away.

After another lengthy silence Mam said, 'God I hate the cold.'

The Cold War was mystifying to me as well. I expected it might be fought in Siberia, Alaska, Sweden and inside the Arctic Circle. Maybe the intense cold neutralised the effects of the atomic bombs. Who was to know?

The yearly reference to the Domesday Clock also triggered worrying discussion. It seemed to happen every New Year's Day when some bespectacled and bald boffin informed us that we were four or five minutes from nuclear annihilation. The dreaded midnight was always closer than the year before.

As the family lethargically recovered from the rigours of the festive season, we were able to look forward to another year and face another uncertain time while others very far away indeed decided our fate. Sitting silently on the sofa, watching the Domesday Clock on the TV, how we wished we could move that minute hand backwards towards the half-hour mark. It would give us some welcome breathing space in the race to oblivion.

Over the years, the general paranoia about the coming nuclear holocaust grew and grew. The Irish government periodically issued pamphlets telling us all what to do when the bombs began to fall. They had a style all their own, with badly drawn cartoons and often a black-and-white photograph of an improbable-looking husband reading the details to a worried-looking wife and children. I often felt it would have been more in keeping with our existence if they had used a parish priest to inform the family.

The information was vague and comical. What it seemed to boil down to was you needed to fill up the bath as soon as possible. Many people I knew didn't have baths in their houses, so presumably it was goodbye and sayonara to them.

The second instruction was slightly worrying. Everyone in the house had to get down under the stairs. Underneath the stairs seemed to be an important, almost magical place when the bombs dropped. It was deemed so important that I wondered why the government didn't just build great air-raid shelters in the shape of stairs so whole communities could shelter there.

In our house, this stairs thing was a problem. Only one person at a push would be able to fit under them.

Whether it was related or not I don't know, but about the time of this great worry, Dad got it into his head to build a small cupboard under our stairs. 'At least the dog will be safe,' I thought.

Teachers were tasked with talking about it in schools, and of course terrifying the kids out of their tiny minds. Children in Ireland had a lot to worry about, what with purgatory, the dreadful mortal sins lurking everywhere; and now we had the nuclear nightmare.

To add to this general concern about war and bombs, Dad came home from work one day and announced that he'd joined the Civil Defence. To my mind the Civil Defence was like the Life Boys for grown-ups. It seemed to be made up of failed firemen and Saint John Ambulance first-aiders. They wore a uniform that was faintly reminiscent of Mussolini's Black Shirts. It was a bunch of strange people who I thought of as akin to the Keystone Cops. It was embarrassing, but that was something I was quite accustomed to.

Dad had an affinity for doing the unexpected, which could be deeply annoying to a self-conscious teenager. Once he came home with a brown paper bag under his arm. Eventually Mam asked him what it was. 'It's a paint-by-numbers kit that I bought for myself,' Dad replied. 'I always wanted to take up painting and this is a cheap way of getting into it.'

Mam was not impressed. 'There's plenty of painting to be getting on with in this house,' she sniffed.

After tea, he proudly opened the box and started his new endeavour. It was a scene in a jungle with a tiger. The kit had small thimble-like pots of paints and an inadequate scrawny brush. Dad however was delighted and worked on it for a few nights. When it was finished, he showed it to us. It wasn't great. I could tell Dad realised this too. The painting and kit quietly disappeared, never to be spoken of again.

The Civil Defence was just another in a long line of strange things Dad took upon himself. Days after he'd signed up, he came home with his uniform and paraded around the house in it. He also got an axe with a rubber handle.

'What's the rubber hatchet for?' I said.

'It's for hacking down electrical cables,' he replied enthusiastically.

I'm not sure where it all fit in with nuclear bombs, but Dad seemed to like the idea. He continued with the Civil Defence and prepared and awaited the impending disaster. At least we were in the know: all we needed to do was fill up the bath, get under the stairs and wait a thousand years for the radiation to disappear.

As if to amplify all this worry about atomic bombs, it was announced in school that an educational exhibition was coming to Dublin. It was called 'Atoms in Action' and was being held in the Royal Dublin Society showground. It was funded by the American government and toured the world attempting to explain the pros and cons of nuclear and atomic energy, and hopefully to allay fears. Its aim was to explain the impact of the Nuclear Age on day-to-day living, to those poorer countries who could not afford this magic stuff. I suspect in fact it had the opposite effect.

So a school excursion was arranged for all of our class to go and see it. I put my name down immediately; you dared not miss a thing like that.

The exhibition itself was interesting. It showed us the peaceful applications of this new energy; practical uses of nuclear fission which, as it happened, was part of our exam curriculum. We were all too aware of the military uses, so it was interesting to see what else it might do besides blowing us all up.

I remember it showed in some detail that engineers could excavate large amounts of earth for, say, a canal with a series of nuclear explosions. 'What about the fallout?' was the question nagging me. Even with my meagre knowledge of the process, I knew it might be another millennium before it would be safe to use this canal or whatever other genius project they'd come up with.

I never did ask the question; it seemed wrong to challenge the obvious enthusiasm of the clean-cut and suited young Americans promoting an age of atomic trains and boats and planes and a spaceship for every house.

That same year I bought *Sgt Pepper's Lonely Hearts Club Band*. I remember seeing it in the flesh for the first time in the local bicycle-cum-record shop. In this shop, it was best to order a copy. However, if your order was a popular record, you were certain the owner's son listened to it a few times before you got it. You hoped that at least he didn't scratch it before you did.

After my momentous purchase, I walked down the main street, with the album cover distinctly visible under my arm, displaying my good taste to the world at large. It was perhaps my most exciting day ever.

My record player was one of those old box affairs: all red and silver. It cost me (really my mother) seven shillings and three pence a week on the never-never. A record player was like an electrical heart beating in a teenager's chest, your own private jukebox. It was mono as, of course, was my copy of *Sgt Pepper*.

Even at this stage I recognised that the last few years had been a bit of a musical journey for me. Music had got better and better, had grown with me, kept pace with my interests and introduced me to new possibilities and adventures. I did not know if this hold over my life would last, but it sure seemed so.

Music gave you something to argue or talk about with friends. It separated you from some and brought you closer to others. Some you left behind and abandoned to showband and celidh music. Others were ahead of you and introduced you to West Coast acid rock or electric folk.

One such character was Des Heaney who lived next door. I thought he was the coolest guy in the neighbourhood. Des lived with his mam and brother to the right of our house; beside the shipyard. He worked as a ship's cook and often dropped by with something he had made to see if I liked it.

Des dressed like a hippie and had a great record collection, but it wasn't just that; he was just cool. He walked and talked cool. Occasionally he was dressed a little like Geronimo with a white T-shirt, a red waistcoat, blue jeans and a bandana around his head. I think he wore the bandana because his hair was thinning. His clothes made him stand out around the town. I was proud that he gave me a couple of psychedelic T-shirts which had the same effect for me. They became my pride and joy.

When he spoke he used 'man' and 'cool' a lot. He never used 'fab' or 'groovy'. He'd say things like, 'The future belongs to you and me and don't forget it, man.'

When I spotted him going past the house, I always dashed out to see if I might catch him and have a word. When he spotted me he always said, 'Hey man, where are you off to now?'

'I'm going up to Ma Gallagher's to get the *NME*,' I said. hoping to keep the conversation going.

'Great,' he said, 'can I have a look at it after you're finished with it?'
'Sure,' I replied.

This in fact gave me bit of a problem. I collected the *NMEs* every week for future reference, and was never too sure of getting it back from him. It was a small price to pay.

Des was away from home a lot. When he returned, he brought great records with him, usually the kind that you either could not get easily in Ireland or those records that you were unwilling to spend money on. Over the years, he introduced me to groups like Jefferson Airplane, Moby Grape, Big Brother and Iron Butterfly.

It was well-known that he smoked marijuana. He offered it to me as well but my problem was I never mastered the requisite skills of the smoking experience. Everywhere he sailed, he got the drug easily and came home with a supply. Arklow was quite a busy port with all the foreign ships coming and drugs like marijuana became quite common, so sometimes it was readily available.

When Des's stash ran out, and when he couldn't get it or couldn't afford it in Arklow, he had to look for alternatives. One wheeze was buying packets of birdseed. His mam had a canary and maybe that's where he got the idea. He sifted through the packet and found the hemp seeds. He ground them and sprinkled the powder on the tobacco; an Arklow solution to an Arklow problem. Why he didn't just sow some of the seeds as soon as he came home was beyond me.

On my trip to see 'Atoms in Action', I had my first brush with the drug culture, such as it was. While we waited to catch the train home, someone suggested we visit the Dandelion Market which was near the top of Grafton Street and across from Stephens Green.

Parked on the road were well-dressed guys and girls lounging in sports cars. I immediately thought 'medical students.' At the entrance, there were numerous hippie-type guys hanging around who were obviously eyeing up the visitors going past. One of them looked to me like a cross between Jimi Hendrix and Des Heaney. I probably stared at him a little too long because he walked over to me and said in a slow American drawl, 'You dudes up from the sticks, man?'

'Yes,' I blurted, 'Arklow', trying to be as cool as I possibly could.

'Oh, I'm sorry about that, but hey – c'est la vie.' Then he said very quietly, 'Hey man, do you wanna buy some grass?'

My mind raced. I was flattered he'd picked me out to make the offer, and I thought of poor Des Heaney trying to grind those infernal bird seeds. It seemed too good an opportunity to miss. 'How much does it cost?' I asked.

'How much you got?'

'Three pounds,' I ventured, which was true. Dad had given me that sum for emergencies.

'That's the exact price for you,' he said.

I thought that was quite decent of him. We made the transaction and while I pocketed the plastic bag of drugs, he seemed to disappear into the passing crowd.

When I got home I popped next door to Des to bring him the good news and the gift. He opened the package and said, 'What have you bought?'

'Grass,' I said, and told him the story.

He laughed. 'It is grass indeed,' he said, 'the grass you get when you mow a lawn!'

33

'Closing books and long last looks'

My last couple of weeks in the Brother were full of exams, some in the afternoon, others in the morning, and such was the schedule that for days I went without any exams at all. After the routine of attending lessons, this generous gift of time seemed like practice for freedom.

During my five years in the Brothers, Arklow's main street had changed. The explosion of singing pubs bore testament to the money the NET factory put in people's pockets. Sandwich boards placed inconveniently on the foot path displayed prominently the musical delights that were available to patrons. As if to confirm this recent growth in economic and financial well-being, we were treated to a refurbished bank and Post Office. Beside Powers' souvenir shop, the Boyle brothers opened a shop which offered an alternative and perhaps cheaper opportunity to purchase those necessary religious objects.

The man who had sold fish from a wooden box on a dilapidated pram was replaced with a man in a spotless apron and sporting a hygienic hat. He sold his wares from a white van containing white plastic trays, in which his fish were generously garnished with ice. The white weighing scales were the final arbiter of his price.

Nearby there was a new delicatessen with a range of foreign and hitherto unknown delights. Dotted about the street were several new cafes where you could get the desirable espresso and the life-saving latte.

There were a great many more cars about, both in the street and in new housing estates. Foreign models were familiar sights. Our teacher Mr Hickey drove a Renault 4, often saving late-running students with an accommodating lift to the school grounds. I thought his car was the height of cool. I yearned for a Renault 4. On Saturdays the newly arrived AA man, dressed in his immaculate khaki uniform, handed out enrolment leaflets to potential customers while children and adults alike marvelled at his bright yellow three-wheeled motorcycle.

Almost as an acknowledgement that the town had so many young boys, a fun fair on the main street had opened with an assortment of fruit machines and electronic games. Despite many attempts, the Brother Superior failed to stop students frequenting the establishment, and it became a favoured staging post for us on the way back to school after lunch.

The Ormonde cinema was now embellished with a Hollywood-styled advertising sign splashing all of the nightly showings. Two Beatles films had come and gone without any commotion, as had the very numerous Elvis movies. This week, the impressive sign screamed *The Great Escape* and *From Here To Eternity* at the scowling chapel facing it.

On the way, the town was buzzing with students on the cusp of that freedom associated with summer holidays. Gone were the uniforms, replaced by newly acquired hippie beads and coloured sunglasses in anticipation of weather to come.

It was Friday and all week I had seen teachers and Brothers walk out of the school full of '*Slan slan*' and 'See you in September.' Rucksacks and cases were everywhere waiting expectantly for that lift or taxi to the train station. It was known that some Brothers were not returning to Arklow CBS after the break; pastures new and other flocks to terrorise in the name of education and godliness.

That last afternoon was hell, but looking out the window waiting for the exam to start, it seemed reassuringly that life outside was continuing according to the summer plan. Groups of people were cycling past the school on their way to the beach or out in the country. Others were walking along with purpose, tennis rackets and beach bags in hand. Three young women sauntered by, two wearing floppy straw hats and the other sporting what looked like a tea cosy.

Inside the school building, the noises of distant doors banging and keys jangling attracted unwanted attention. I heard running water, occasional muffled conversations, and steps hurrying down the stairs. A unanswered phone rang somewhere. It was all very unsettling. I saw no one. I panicked that I might be left here alone, worried that I might be locked up for the entire summer to be discovered in September, a desiccated cadaver trying to claw its way out of a locked classroom. This surely was to be my solstice, my longest day.

The examinations had delivered some entertainment. One chap smuggled a large geometry theorems book into the exam hall, and looked totally perplexed when it fell out of its hiding place onto the floor in full view of the invigilator. Nervous giggles had a brief moment. It reminded me of those plans we all had to possibly cheat during the Primary Certificate examination. At eleven years of age, we had discarded these improbable strategies.

On that last day in the Brothers, my exam subject was Drawing. Only a few of us were taking the examination, so it was going to be a tranquil event. We trooped in and sat in a circle under a flickering fluorescent light. The still life object we were required to draw was a large display of boxes, books and cartons. It was a mound of jumbled objects. I'm not sure anyone knew just where to start with it all.

Eventually the invigilator went through the exams procedures and after awhile left us alone in the room. He came back occasionally and the afternoon droned on. As each of us finished, we handed in our masterpiece and shuffled out seemingly making as much noise as possible. I was one of the last few and used all the time available. My piece looked like a cubist interpretation of a pyramid. In fact it looked remarkably like the huge pyramid mausoleum which lay in a graveyard outside our town.

And then it was all over. The invigilator walked into the room with a few seconds to go. I was looking directly at him as he said, seemingly to some non-existent throng, 'Stop writing please and finish. Bring your papers to the top of the class please, ensuring that your examination number is on the workbook and each additional workbook you may have used.' I handed over my stuff and walked out of the classroom.

Making my way to the exit for the last time, I stared across the unkempt and unmown lawn. It would remain like this until September.

I noticed a bunch of kids walking up the road with adults in tow. The spectacle had a distinct familiarity. It was of course Carysfort school making their way *en masse* to the end-of-term sports day. Walking in front, leading the throng was Miss Marshall, helped on each side by a couple of teachers or perhaps parent volunteers herding the assembly towards their destination.

Excited and buoyant, a trio of boys ran to the middle of the road unnoticed by these chaperones. Shoulder to shoulder they marched military style, Life Boys style, whistling a tune that sounded like something I should know. With a practised eyes-left and almost staring directly at me in some kind of homage, they saluted. Hup two three four. Hup two three four. One pretended to play a flute, another banged an imaginary drum.

Heads erect, shoulders squared, whistling that tune, they marched the length of the CBS building, perfectly in step, before being reined in by a youngish looking teacher. They slowly took up position with the rest of the school, doubling up with laughter as they dropped back to normal gait, and continued their slow walk to their destination over the brow of the hill.

A group of well-dressed people carrying flowers walked purposefully behind them. Helpers for the sports day or mourners going to a funeral: I couldn't tell which.

I dawdled down the stairs, expecting to meet a teacher or Brother one last time, but saw no one. Suddenly a crash and a shuffle of heavy feet behind me attested to another soul's presence. A gangly bespectacled young man in his mid-thirties appeared through a door. He wore the ankle-length black robes of a Christian Brother, but seemed almost too young, too fresh-faced to be part of the crew. A new face. His priestly half-smile however was all too familiar. He appeared lonely and I wondered how he would cope growing into his life of celibacy. I was beginning to hear echoes of my recent past.

Carrying an unseasonal black umbrella in one hand, with a hurried sleight of hand he transferred a large bunch of keys to somewhere in his tunic. I had seen those keys before. They were the perpetual property, the virtual badge of office of the Brother Superior.

'I bid you anon,' he declared and pointed the umbrella in the direction of the main door. Shuffling along ahead of me, he kept repeating to himself, '*Ultima multos, ultima multos.*' When he did catch my eye, he conveniently translated, as if it was his habit, his duty, '*Ultima multos*: the last day for many; the last day for many.'

'And so it may seem to you,' I thought, 'but for me it's the first day of freedom, of everything that comes next, of life!'

Afterthoughts

The thing for me about culture and especially pop music is the lyrics and melodies remind you of people and places, the highs and lows, things you've done and things you wish you'd done (or not done), because they're basically the soundtrack to your life. This is the playlist that accompanied me through these memories.

1. 'Once upon a time in the Fishery' – the opening to all good fables and fairy tales, this one took on another dynamic in the hands of Quentin Tarantino in his movie *Once Upon a Time in... Hollywood*.
2. 'The school around the corner' – everyone of a certain age in Ireland will have watched this TV show.
3. 'Where have all the good times gone?' – a line from a song of the same title by The Kinks.
4. 'He fell through the door' – who in Ireland hasn't heard this phrase used to describe a state of inebriation, or indeed something more innocent?
5. 'Kids are the greatest fun' – a line from a song by Love, an obscure US band led by a guy who went by the moniker Arthurly.
6. '*O mio babbino caro*' – the title of an aria in Puccini's opera *Gianni Schicchi*, which translates as 'Oh my dear father'.
7. 'In a pew losing my religion' – a line from the REM song of the same title off their album *Out of Time*.
8. 'Everybody needs good neighbours' – yes, a line from that Aussie TV show.
9. 'Bells were ringing out for Christmas Time' – a line from *Fairy-*

tale of New York by the Pogues – Ireland's Christmas national anthem.

10. 'It's hard to bear' – nope, can't remember where this is from.

11. 'Riddle of the Sand Dunes' – a paraphrase of the famous book by Erskine Childers.

12. 'A world where I could go' – an idea from a Keane song.

13. 'Lord don't stop the carnival' – from an Alan Price Set song of the same name.

14. 'No more working for a week or two' – sentiments from Cliff Richard's *Summer Holiday* theme tune.

15. 'Too much sun will burn' – a line from *Paper Sun* by Traffic.

16. 'It's a rich man's game' – a paraphrase of Abba in *Money, Money, Money*.

17. 'Who shaves the barber?' – Bertrand Russell is to blame for this one.

18. 'Pretty soon you're going to get older' – a line from the David Bowie song *Ch-ch-changes*.

19. 'Keep still and draw another breath' – from a line in *London's Calling* by The Clash.

20. 'One mad dog and his master watched' – from Roy Harper's song *When an Old Cricketer Leaves the Crease*.

21. 'I wish today could be tomorrow' – a line from *Days* by The Kinks.

22. 'We gotta get out of this place' – yes, that Animals' song popular during the Vietnam War.

23. 'Life was Medium Cool' – this refers to *Medium Cool*, a 1969 cult movie about TV's increasing effects on society.

24. 'Fed up? Turn the Beatles up instead' – no idea where this came from other than my own sentiments then, and now.

25. 'East Coast girls are hip' – opening line of the Beachboys classic *California Girls*.

26. 'Dancing on the beach in a hippie hat' – inspired by Jeff Beck's *Hi Ho Silver Lining*.

27. 'Hot town, summer in the city' – from the Lovin Spoonful song of the same title.

28. 'The folks on the hill' – abbreviated line from Peggy Lee's *The Folks Who Live on the Hill*.
29. 'In the heat of a hot summer night' – a line from *Hot Summer Nights* by Night.
30. 'Turn, turn turn' – written as *Turn! Turn! Turn!* by Pete Seeger and immortalised by The Byrds.
31. 'Take me from this road' – inspired by *Take Me as I Am* by Bob Dylan.
32. 'Nuclear seemed unclear' – a play on words.
33. 'Closing books and long last looks' – a line from the theme song of *To Sir With Love*, sung by Lulu.

Lightning Source UK Ltd.
Milton Keynes UK
UKHW041924211122
412606UK00001B/106

9 781906 852603